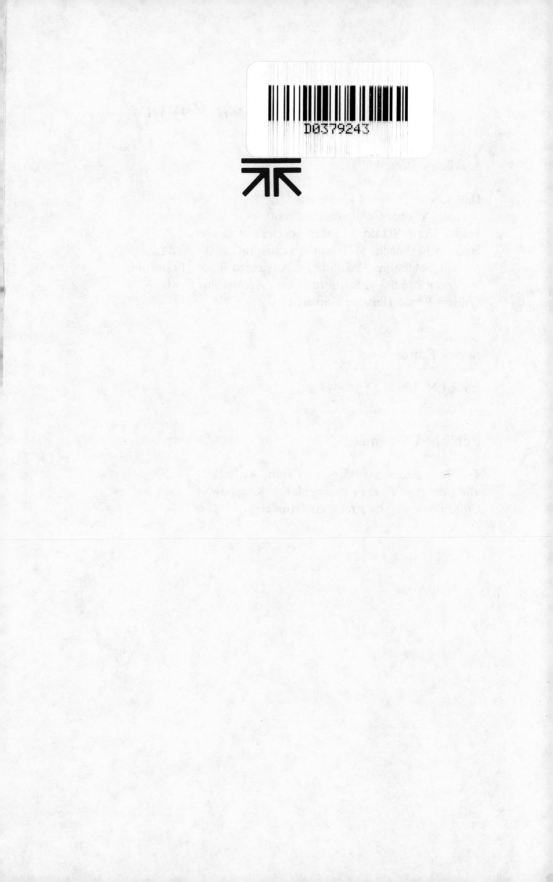

Masters of Modern Physics

Advisory Board

Series Editor

Published Volumes

CITIZEN SCIENTIST

FRANK VON HIPPEL

A TOUCHSTONE BOOK
Published by Simon & Schuster

New York   London   Toronto   Sydney   Tokyo   Singapore

Touchstone
Simon & Schuster Building
Rockefeller Center
1230 Avenue of the Americas
New York, New York 10020

First Touchstone Edition 1991
Published by arrangement with The American Institute of Physics

TOUCHSTONE and colophon are registered trademarks
of Simon & Schuster Inc.

Manufactured in the United States of America

10 9 8 7 6 5 4 3 2 1 Pbk.

ISBN 0-671-74331-7 Pbk.

This book is volume three of the *Masters of Modern Physics* series

To my father, who stood up to the Nazis
and brought up his children with the motto,
"We shall not be intimidated."

Contents

AUTOMOBILE ENERGY EFFICIENCY

NUCLEAR REACTOR ACCIDENTS

FINAL THOUGHTS

CONTENTS

About the Series

Masters of Modern Physics introduces the work and thought of some of the most celebrated physicists of our day. These collected essays offer a panoramic tour of the way science works, how it affects our lives, and what it means to those who practice it. Authors report from the horizons of modern research, provide engaging sketches of friends and colleagues, and reflect on the social, economic, and political consequences of the scientific and technical enterprise.

Authors have been selected for their contributions to science and for their keen ability to communicate to the general reader—often with wit, frequently in fine literary style. All have been honored by their peers and most have been prominent in shaping debates in science, technology, and public policy. Some have achieved distinction in social and cultural spheres outside the laboratory.

Many essays are drawn from popular and scientific magazines, newspapers, and journals. Still others—written for the series or drawn from notes for other occasions—appear for the first time. Authors have provided introductions and, where appropriate, annotations. Once selected for inclusion, the essays are carefully edited and updated so that each volume emerges as a finely shaped work.

Masters of Modern Physics is edited by Robert N. Ubell and overseen by an advisory panel of distinguished physicists. Sponsored by the American Institute of Physics, a consortium of major physics societies, the series serves as an authoritative survey of the people and ideas that have shaped twentieth-century science and society.

Preface

When Joel Primack and I began to write about the role of scientists as citizens in 1970, the scientific community was giving its input to public policy almost exclusively through a huge federal science advisory establishment. Senior scientists were being invited to Washington to provide confidential advice through the panels of the President's Science Advisory Committee and more than a thousand other advisory panels organized by the various government agencies and under the auspices of the National Academy of Science's National Research Council. These arrangements were largely patterned on the advisory system that had helped the U.S. organize the successful nuclear, radar, and other secret military programs of World War II.

By 1970, however, the great faith that the American public had sustained in the wisdom of its government since World War II was finally crumbling. Indeed it was the eloquence of the student protests at Stanford University against the Vietnam War that moved Joel, then a graduate student in physics, to join in organizing the Stanford Workshops on Social and Political Issues, and me, then an assistant professor of physics, to join with Joel and other students in a year-long workshop on "Scientists in Washington."

The years 1967–1970 had also been years of special ferment in the physics community because, in 1967, President Johnson had given into political pressure and decided, against the advice of his own and all previous presidential science advisors, to deploy a U.S. antiballistic missile (ABM) system. As a result of this decision, a few high-level science advisors (notably Hans Bethe, Richard Garwin, and Jerome Wiesner) had gone to the public with their arguments that such a system would be a waste of effort because it could be relatively easily neutralized. We younger physicists wondered how the federal government could have possibly rejected such seemingly compelling arguments. We also wondered why most of the high-level science advisors we knew continued to commute to Washington to give their advice, even though it was apparently being ignored, and why the physicists in the elite "Jason" group were continuing to do secret summer studies for the Pentagon despite a rising tide of opposition to the Vietnam War.

The science advisors who came to talk to the student workshop did not provide satisfying answers to these questions, so Joel and I decided to do some library research.

After reading a number of advisory reports that had become public in one way or another and comparing them to what their government recipients had said about them while they were still secret, it became apparent to us that scientists were being invited to Washington not only for their advice but also to give political decisions the appearance of objectivity.

We concluded that this "legitimizing" role of science advisors was undermining the democratic policy-making process because it was allowing government officials to reject citizen concerns as "uninformed." We therefore decided that some scientists at least should begin to give the benefit of their expertise to the public *directly*. Since consumer advocate Ralph Nader had been recruiting young lawyers to the practice of "public-interest law," we termed the activity that we were advocating "public-interest science."

In fact, as Joel and I discovered as a result of our researches, quite a few scientists were already practicing public-interest science:

· The Federation of Atomic Scientists* had been founded in 1946 to try to teach the American public that "There is no secret and there is no defense."
· Biologist Rachel Carson, by publishing *Silent Spring* in 1962, had unwittingly launched the scientist-dominated Environmental Defense Fund—along with much of the rest of the environmental movement.
· Harvard biochemist Matthew Meselson had been waging a lonely but remarkably successful campaign against the Defense Department's chemical and biological weapons program.
· Physicist William Shurcliff was leading the successful fight against the Department of Transportation's program to develop a supersonic transport that would have blasted those under its routes with powerful sonic booms.

* Later renamed the Federation of *American* Scientists.

· And the physicists fighting against the Johnson-Nixon ABM deployment proposals were laying the basis for the 1972 Treaty Limiting Antiballistic Missile Systems.

There was therefore ample evidence that, given favorable conditions, a small number of scientists—even one—could have an impact on public policy. Joel and I tried to identify the ingredients in such successes and wrote up our findings in a number of articles and in a book, *Advice and Dissent: Scientists in the Political Arena* (1974).

In 1973, having taken this look before I leapt, I decided to change my own career from elementary-particle to public-policy physics. This transition was facilitated by a year-long fellowship in Washington at the National Academy of Sciences (NAS).

I used much of my year with the NAS trying to understand the technical aspects of the debate over nuclear-reactor safety that was raging at the time and, when the Academy was unwilling to sponsor a study on the subject, persuaded the American Physical Society (APS) to do so. In that era of activism, even the usually staid APS was willing to sally forth into the public-policy arena—as it has done from time to time ever since.

In 1974 I moved on to a research appointment in Princeton University's Center for Energy and Environmental Studies. There I did the research which is the basis for the articles in this book on nuclear-reactor safety, automobile fuel economy, and the consequences of "limited nuclear war." In addition, Harold Feiveson, Ted Taylor, Robert Williams, and I worked together for a few years making the technical and economic case against the Department of Energy's program to commercialize a liquid-sodium-cooled plutonium breeder reactor.

In each of these involvements with a major public-policy debate, I was amazed to find that the government's policy was built on thin air:

· The Nuclear Regulatory Commission and its predecessor, the Atomic Energy Commission, had simply decided that a major release of radioactivity to the environment from a nuclear-reactor accident was "incredible" and had made no plans for mitigating the consequences if such a release should nevertheless occur.
· In 1979, in the midst of the second oil crisis, Congress simply assumed that there were no significant additional fuel savings to be achieved from improved automobile energy efficiency and therefore turned its attention instead to the creation of the ill-fated Synthetic Fuels Corporation.
· The Air Force, while designing "limited" nuclear attacks on Soviet

military targets, to be implemented in case "deterrence" should fail, was deliberately ignoring the implications of the fact that tens of millions of Soviet citizens would inevitably be killed by such an attack. And the plutonium-breeder reactor program was premised on the *assumption* that U.S. consumption of electric energy would continue to almost double each decade for many decades into the future.

For someone who had been brought up in the world of elementary-particle physics, where an unfounded claim could end one's career, the discovery that there was no real analytical basis for key public policies was nothing short of mind boggling. Once again, I felt driven to tell my fellow physicists of the enormous service that they could do the country by providing some of the missing peer review—this time in an article in the American Institute of Physics' magazine, *Physics Today* (1981).

However, physicists did not respond in droves. Public-interest science has continued to be an activity indulged in by a relatively small number of university scientists and the small but growing number of scientists who were being employed by public-interest groups such as the Natural Resources Defense Council and the Union of Concerned Scientists.

One reason for this very limited involvement in public-interest science activities is that many scientists are pretty much totally absorbed by their science. A second reason is that most scientists have never learned how the democratic policy-making process works and how they could usefully contribute. However, there is still another reason that I became aware of as a result of a personal experience in 1972. At the time, I was working at one of the Atomic Energy Commission's (AEC) national laboratories and Joel and I had just published our first article on "The Politics of Technology" in the 25th anniversary issue of the *Journal of Applied Spectroscopy.*

In that article, we discussed a number of cases in which science-advisory panels had been used to legitimize policies that they had warned against. Unfortunately for me, two of the cases we cited concerned the AEC, and someone drew that fact to the attention of a high-level AEC official whose division provided the lab with half its funding. That official expressed his displeasure, and I was asked by the lab management to stop writing such articles. I doubt that I would have been fired for failing to comply with this request but I never found out because, shortly thereaf-ter, I left to take up the fellowship at the NAS.

This experience, and subsequent stories of retaliation against other scientists who had taken public positions that their employers did not appreciate, sensitized me to the fact that, although the Bill of Rights guarantees U.S. citizens freedom of speech, it does not guarantee that they will keep their jobs if they exercise this right.

Later, I helped to convince the American Association for the Advancement of Science to set up a Committee on Scientific Freedom and Responsibility. Rosemary Chalk, the Committee's first staff director, and I organized workshops and wrote papers on ways in which professional societies could strengthen the protections of the free speech of their members. But the national tide of activism was receding and most of our suggestions were not acted upon.

In the early 1980s, I was caught up by the nuclear-weapons "freeze" movement and tried then and later to help provide an analytical basis for some of the initiatives that this movement called for. This is how I happened to begin working on the technical basis for a halt in the production of fissile material for nuclear weapons.

During that same period, I was recruited by Jeremy Stone, president of the Federation of American Scientists (FAS), to be chairman of that organization. This led, in 1983, to my meeting Evgeny Velikhov, chairman of the new Committee of Soviet Scientists for Peace and Against the Nuclear Threat. My resulting relationships with Velikhov and to Roald Sagdeev, his successor as chairman of the Committee, resulted in my spending several years on joint U.S.-Soviet research and demonstration projects relating to the verification of various possible arms-control agreements. These collaborations also led to the establishment of a new international journal, *Science and Global Security: The Technical Basis for Arms Control and Environmental Policy Initiatives*.

In rereading this selection of the articles and chapters that have emerged from my past 20 years of involvement in "public-policy physics," I am struck by how slowly the policy process really moves when one deals with such huge issues as nuclear disarmament, our energy future, and the freedom of speech of scientists. None of the policy issues discussed in this book has yet been dealt with in a definitive manner. Making these articles available again in an updated form may therefore be useful to those interested in becoming involved in the fray.

ADVICE AND DISSENT

Scientists as Citizens

WITH JOEL PRIMACK

Although scientists as technical experts make important contributions to the federal policy-making process for technology, that process remains basically political. At present, the primary recipient of technical advice on matters of public policy is the executive branch of the federal government. To the extent that this arrangement results in an informed executive branch dealing with a relatively uninformed Congress and public, a corresponding shift in power occurs. Indeed, it is not unheard of for the executive branch to abuse its near monopoly of politically relevant technical information and expertise. We cite below several case studies exemplifying the sorts of abuses that occur: politicization of advisory committees; and suppression and misrepresentation of information, and analyses.

This leads us to the question of whether individual scientists can contribute significantly to a restoration of a balance of power between the public, Congress, and the executive branch of the government. We find, again on the basis of case studies, that a few scientists can be surprisingly effective in influencing federal policies for technology if they are sufficiently persistent and skillful and if various other circumstances are favorable. These success stories and the present high level of concern about the adverse side effects of technology among scientists and the public suggest that the time is propitious for a much more serious commitment within the scientific community to "public-interest science."

This essay is divided into two main sections. The first deals with devices by which the executive branch exploits its scientific advisers for political advantage while concealing much of the information provided;

the second discusses ways in which scientists can help bring into being counterbalancing political forces by providing the public and Congress with the information they need.

For brevity we refer to scientists advising officials in the executive branch of the government as "insiders" and scientists taking issues to the public and Congress as "outsiders." Of course, the same scientist can, and sometimes does, find himself in both roles at different times.

Abuses of the Executive Advisory System

Many thousands of scientists serve part-time on committees advising officials in the executive branch. It appears, however, that, if substantial political and bureaucratic interests are at stake, the dangers these insiders point out are often ignored. This is not surprising; it is one reason why our government was designed with checks and balances. These checks and balances are undermined, however, when executive spokesmen can use the authority of inside advisers to mislead the public and Congress about the technical facts or uncertainties that must be taken into account in the policy-making process.

Thus, for example, when William Magruder, director of the supersonic transport (SST) development project, appeared before a congressional committee to allay fears about the SST sonic boom, airport noise, and stratospheric pollution, he summarized the administration's views on these issues as follows:[1]

> According to existing data and available evidence there is no evidence of likelihood that SST operations will cause significant adverse effects on our atmosphere or our environment. That is the considered opinion of the scientific authorities who have counseled the government on these matters over the past five years.

Compare the above with the following quotations from the report of a panel of President Nixon's SST *ad hoc* review committee[2,3] which included in its distinguished membership the president's science adviser. Regarding the effect of the SST on the upper atmosphere, the panel noted that a fleet of SST's "will introduce large quantities of water vapor into the stratosphere," and concluded that much more research was needed before serious deleterious effects could be excluded. With regard to the impact of the SST sonic boom on the human environment, the panel concluded

. . . all available information indicates that the effects of the sonic boom are such as to be considered intolerable by a very high percentage of people affected.

Finally, as to the impact of the SST engine noise, they stated

. . . over large areas surrounding SST airports . . . a very high percentage of the exposed population would find the noise intolerable and the apparent cause of a wide variety of adverse effects.

In its adverse statements on the SST's environmental impact, the *ad hoc* committee report echoed many other reports available to the Nixon administration.[4] Thus Magruder's statement is extremely misleading. Similar misrepresentations of scientific advice have been made by spokesmen for the federal executive branch in virtually all the other cases that we have studied.[5]

Perhaps the most frequent means by which the public is misled is through the incomplete statement. Typically, an executive-branch spokesman tells Congress that agency A, after consulting the greatest authorities, has decided to do X. The spokesman neglects to mention, however, that the experts have given mostly reasons why X might be a dangerous policy. The public cannot check what the experts actually said, because the reports are kept secret. Of course, Congress can ask several well-known scientists to appear before it and offer their views on the matters at issue in congressional hearings, but this is no substitute for requiring an executive-branch agency to make available for public review and criticism the detailed technical basis for its decisions.*

Examples of Abuses

There is a whole spectrum of devices by which the federal executive's advisory establishment has been used to mislead Congress and the public. Perhaps a few additional examples will indicate the possibilities:

· In the final throes of the SST debate, an advisory committee report was released which stated that, with noise suppressors, the SST airport

* The federal government has become much more open, except in military-related areas, since this was written. The most important developments relate to amendments that strengthened the Freedom of Information Act in the wake of the Watergate scandal and court actions enforcing the National Environmental Policy Act of 1969, which requires Environmental Impact Statements on federal actions which could have a significant impact on the environment. The Advisory Committee Act of 1972, which mandated a significant opening up of federal advisory committee meetings, has had a much smaller impact.

noise could be reduced to tolerable levels.[6,7] No report was issued on what these changes could do to the SST performance, however. Every indication is that the noise suppressors, whose weight was of the same order of magnitude as the total payload of the aircraft, would seriously threaten the already questionable economic viability of the aircraft.[7] Thus, government officials can selectively make public advisory committee reports that present only some of the positive terms in a cost-benefit calculation.

· A report on sonic boom effects by an advisory panel organized by the National Academy of Sciences-National Research Council,[8] was so written that, when it was released, it stimulated a *New York Times* headline,[9] "Sonic Boom Damage Called 'Very Small.' " In fact, simple calculations based on extensive government test results led to the estimate that, with 400 SST's flying supersonically over the United States, the sonic boom damage each year would be of the order of a billion dollars.[10] What the advisory committee had meant to say was that the probability is small that a single sonic boom would damage a particular building, and therefore that experiments on sonic boom damage should be carried out in a laboratory with a sonic boom simulator. When a clarifying statement was eventually issued, after a petition from Academy members, it appeared only in the Academy newsletter and received no press coverage.

Thus advisory committee reports may be so written that they are seriously misleading, at least to the press. Political and institutional pressures may prevent the issuance of a proper clarification, or the press may ignore it.

· In 1966 a report by an independent laboratory under contract to the Department of Health, Education, and Welfare indicated that 2,4,5-T (2,4,5-trichlorophenoxyacetic acid), a popular weed and brush killer, causes birth defects. This report was repeatedly sent back for "further study" for three-and-a-half years[11] until it finally became public, as an indirect result of a Ralph Nader investigation.[12] In the meantime, enormous quantities of this chemical were used in the defoliation of about one-eighth of the area of South Vietnam.[12,13]

It may give an idea of the amount of bureaucratic foot-dragging involved in this case to note that, when one of the chemical manufacturers suggested that an impurity, not 2,4,5-T itself, might have caused the birth defects, the experiments that had taken three-and-a-half years to complete were repeated in about six weeks. Both 2,4,5-T and the contaminant were found to produce birth defects.[11] When these results became public, the use of 2,4,5-T in Vietnam was banned, its domestic use was partially restricted, and further restrictions were debated.[11]

The studies relating to the question of whether pesticides cause birth defects were undertaken partly in response to the public furor caused by Rachel Carson's *Silent Spring*.[14] Nevertheless, even while the public was being assured that the government had undertaken to protect it from such possible dangers, the government was concealing relevant new information. Thus, when the government has exclusive access to certain information about a public health hazard, it can simply ignore it.

· In October 1969, Secretary of Health, Education, and Welfare Finch was forced by law to ban foods containing cyclamates because cyclamates had been shown to cause cancer in animals. At the same time, he decided to overrule protests from the Food and Drug Administration (FDA) and allow manufacturers of these products to continue to sell them as nonprescription drugs for the treatment of diabetes and obesity.[15,16] After announcing his decision, he called together an advisory committee which reported back that, indeed, Secretary Finch was right in overruling the FDA medical people. The committee concluded:[15]

. . . the medical benefits in these instances [treatment of diabetes and obesity] outweigh the possibility of harm.

After the publication of a Nader study report on the background of Finch's decision,[17] its legality was examined in a rather devastating congressional investigation. The advisory committee was then called together again, and, although it had received essentially no new evidence, it issued a new report on the safety and effectiveness of cyclamates. This time the committee contradicated its earlier statement by saying:[16]

The literature provided to the group does *not* contain acceptable evidence that cyclamates have been demonstrated to be efficacious in the treatment and control of diabetes or obesity. [Italics ours]

Cyclamates were thereupon totally banned. In this example, it appears that an advisory committee became so political that it adapted its advice to the political needs of the official whom it was advising.

Correcting the Record

It is natural to ask whether insiders cannot do something to curb these abuses. In fact, advisers have tried to set the record straight in a number of cases:

Richard Garwin, a member of the President's Science Advisory Committee, was chairman of a committee of scientists reviewing the SST project for President Nixon at the beginning of his presidency. Although his committee's report was kept secret its existence was not, and Garwin was invited to testify at congressional hearings.[4] In his testimony he expressed his personal criticisms of the SST, documenting them from publicly available sources.

Garwin explained his actions in the following words:[18]

I'm not a full-time member of the administration, and I feel like a lawyer who has many clients. The fact that he deals with one doesn't prevent him from dealing with another so long as he doesn't use the information he obtains from the first in dealing with the second. Since there are so few people familiar with these programs, it is important for me to give to Congress, as well as the administration, the benefit of my experience.

Kenneth Pitzer was chairman of a President's Science Advisory Committee panel charged with looking into the safety of underground testing of large nuclear weapons in November 1968. The panel concluded that there was a significant danger of earthquakes and resulting tidal waves being triggered by bomb testing in the Aleutians. They also commented:[19]

. . . the panel believes that the public should not be asked to accept risks resulting from purely internal government decisions if, without endangering national security, the information can be made public and decisions can be reached after public discussions.

The report expressing the panel's concerns was kept secret. Pitzer, however, helped make these concerns public.[20]

Sidney Drell and Marvin Goldberger served on a committee advising John Foster, director of Defense Research and Engineering, on the effectiveness of the Safeguard antiballistic-missile (ABM) system. When Foster misrepresented their committee's report as supporting the administration's position, they spoke up to set the record straight.[21] Goldberger expressed their opinion of Safeguard rather pungently. He said

... I assert that the original Safeguard deployment and the proposed expanded deployment is spherically senseless. It makes no
sense no matter how you look at it.

Unfortunately, these examples appear to be the exceptions. It seems
that advisers usually watch in silence when they know that the public is
being misled. The authors of the National Academy of Sciences sonic
boom study mentioned above, and also academy officials, actually
resisted the issuing of a clarifying statement.

Two main reasons are given for this silence: First, most advisers have
very little faith in the effectiveness of speaking out, and they fear that by
going public they would lose their inside influence. And second, there is
also the argument that, since the president is elected by all the people, he
has the ultimate responsibility for making national policy. In its extreme
form, this "elected dictatorship" theory of government leaves the adviser
with only the responsibility to see that the president and the officials in his
administration are well informed.

The loss of effectiveness argument emphasizes the serious dilemma in
which a frustrated inside adviser may be placed as a result of the
executive branch's insistence upon loyalty and confidentially. However,
insiders should beware of exaggerating their supposed effectiveness, and
of confusing prestige with influence.

The elected dictatorship argument obviously denies the whole system
of checks and balances by which our democracy has been safeguarded. It
also ignores the fact that the ultimate responsibility in a democracy
resides with the individual citizen, and that denying him the information
he needs to defend his own health and welfare effectively deprives him of
the rights of citizenship. The writers of our constitution understood this
very well. James Madison said:[22]

Knowledge will forever govern ignorance. And a people who mean
to be their own governors must arm themselves with the power
knowledge gives. A popular government without popular information or the means of acquiring it is but the prologue to a farce or
tragedy, or perhaps both.

It is obvious that the responsibilities of government science advisers
should be discussed widely, both within the scientific community and in
the larger political community. Lack of such discussion leaves scientists
unprepared when they become advisers and find themselves confronted
with difficult and unfamiliar decisions—often in an atmosphere of great

pressure. Science advising, no less than scientific research, needs a code of ethics. And this code should take into account the fact that we live in a democracy in which the ultimate responsibility resides not with the president, or even with the government as a whole, but with the individual citizen.

Before going on, let us try to rectify the misunderstandings that may have resulted from the discussion so far. We do not wish by our criticisms of the abuses of the executive science advisory system to diminish or obscure the many important and legitimate functions inside advisers perform.[23] Their roles as independent critics and connoisseurs of technical policies and people are essential throughout the executive branch. The executive advising system also provides a tremendously important path by which information and ideas can flow rapidly through the government, and between governmental and independent scientists, by-passing the slow bureaucratic filter. Indeed, in our opinion it has been a serious weakness of the most recent administrations that they have failed to exploit adequately these potential strengths of the advisory system.

Public-Interest Science

The executive branch of our government has not been acting in an unbiased manner in making available to citizens the technical information they need. Scientists must therefore make their expertise directly available to the public and Congress.

The idea that the public, as well as the government and industry, should have scientific advisers is an old one—as is the idea that the interests of the public should have lawyers to defend them. It was not until the 1960s, however, that public understanding of the insensitivity of governmental and industrial bureaucracies led to a substantial commitment in the legal profession to public-interest law. It appears to us that the scientific community may now have reached a similar point. The growing public awareness of the dangerous consequences of leaving the exploitation of technology under the effective control of special industrial and governmental interests has led to a readiness within the scientific community to undertake a serious commitment to what we will term "public-interest science."

There is an important difference between the practice of public-interest law and public-interest science, however. In a legal dispute, once both parties have obtained a lawyer, they can hope to obtain a fair and equal hearing in front of a trained judge who gives their arguments his or her undivided attention, whereas in a public debate over an application of technology tremendous inequalities exist. The contending sides must speak to a distracted public through news media to which executive officials have comparatively easy and routine access. Moreover, an executive official speaks with the authority of office, while an independent scientist is usually an unknown quantity to the public.

In view of these inequalities, it is interesting to find out whether the public-interest activities of independent scientists can activate political and legal restraints on irresponsible actions of the executive branch. In working on this question, we have thus far examined the effectiveness of outsiders in informing the public about the negative aspects of the SST, the decision to deploy the Sentinal and Safeguard antiballistic-missile systems, the program of crop destruction and defoliation in South Vietnam, and the regulation of pesticides. We have also studied the effectiveness of a local group of scientists, the Colorado Committee for Environmental Information, in bringing to public attention in 1968 through 1970 the dangerous practices of two federal agencies in Colorado.

Examples

In all these instances, outsiders have had a surprisingly large impact, considering their small numbers, in bringing to public attention an aspect of the issue that concerned them. Consider a few examples:

· Serious public opposition to the SST developed only after a few scientists, notably William Shurcliff, made dramatically clear in press releases and advertisements that the sonic booms created by a fleet of SST's flying supersonically overland would be intolerable.[4]
· The residents of the Denver area did not realize that they might have a problem until scientists of the Colorado Committee for Environmental Information (CCEI) issued a public statement describing the possible consequences of an airplane crashing into the huge stockpiles of nerve gas stored near the end of Denver's busy airport. After trying in vain to reassure the public, and then to transport the nerve gas across the country to dump it in the ocean, the Army finally agreed to destroy it.[24]
· The U.S. program of defoliation and crop destruction in South Vietnam came to an end when a group of scientists sponsored by the American Association for the Advancement of Science (AAAS) brought back photographs and a detailed report of the devastation that had resulted.[25]

· The deployment of an ABM system to defend the major cities of the United States became a public issue only after scientists in the Chicago area and elsewhere raised what most experts considered a negligible danger—the possibility of the accidental denotation of an ABM (antiballistic missile) warhead in the metropolitan area it was supposed to be defending.[26]

Of course, we could equally easily compile a list of cases in which public protests by scientists have had little effect on federal policy. Most technical issues cannot be taken directly to the public because there is little public resonance with the ideas involved. That does not decrease the importance of the issues that *can* be taken to the public, however.

The effectiveness of outsiders in influencing government policy seems to depend on many factors. For one, where outsiders have been influential, the dangers they pointed out usually threatened huge numbers of people. Their effectiveness seems also to have depended upon how important the policy being criticized was to the government. Consider the obsolete nerve gas, for example; leaving it at such a dangerous location was simple negligence that could be, in principle at least, rectified by spending a little money when it became clear that reassuring statements would no longer suffice. On the ABM, SST, and pesticide regulation issues, however, the critics attacked policies that governed the allocation of billions of dollars. In these cases, the battles were rough and prolonged and required the active involvement of large numbers of citizens in addition to scientists.

The effectiveness of outsiders also often depends upon the timeliness of an issue. Thus, after Shurcliff and a few others had been denouncing the SST for years, the new environmental movement came to see it as a symbol of all that is destructive to the environment. Similarly, the ABM became a popular issue in part because the public had become concerned about the insatiable appetites of the military-industrial complex. And, after a few biologists and ecologists had been protesting for years about defoliation and crop destruction in South Vietnam, they were finally heard when the public had become disgusted with the United States' entire Indochina policy.

Our case studies give substantial encouragement that some issues can be taken to the public by scientists with partial success at least. It is not easy, however. Enormous persistence and skill are required, as well as a good and timely case, to be heard above the din that accompanies everyday living in this country.

Credibility

It is also necessary for the scientist to establish credibility—that is, that he or she is not a "crackpot." Credibility has sometimes come from the quotation of government reports that contradict the official line. It has come from preparing a compelling and well-documented case from the open literature, as Rachel Carson did in her criticism of pesticide regulation.[14] It has come from a study sponsored by a scientific organization: for example, the AAAS study of the effects of defoliation in Vietnam.[25]

Yet another technique for handling the credibility problem was applied quite effectively by the CCEI.[24] In two of the debates in which it became involved, the CCEI publicly challenged the responsible government agency to establish the basis for its assertions. The Colorado group accompanied the challenge with a specific list of technical questions, the answers to which would make possible an independent determination of public safety.

The scientist's public credibility must, of course, be earned. Specialists who use their professional authority to lend support to a political position without presenting the technical arguments cast doubt on both their political position and on scientific authority. The standards of accuracy to which scientists adhere in public statements should be no lower than those they strive to attain in their scientific work. It is also necessary for scientists to maintain a sense of perspective; it is all too easy to exaggerate the significance of a subject on which a critic happens to be an expert. Obviously, the proper ethics for outsider science advising deserves discussion within the scientific community no less than the ethics of insiders.

During and after each of the major technological debates discussed above there have been charges that scientists who participated as outsiders were politically biased and scientifically irresponsible.[27] However, while there have certainly been a few instances that substantiate such charges, the vast majority of independent scientists who have argued technological issues before the public have been honest and accurate. A scientist's reputation is his or her most precious possession, and scientists who misrepresent the truth or make unsound technical judgments call down upon themselves the censure of their colleagues. In any event, technical arguments presented in public can be rebutted in public, in the usual self-correcting manner of scientific discourse. Indeed, it is unfortunate that the statements of executive-branch officials are not subject to similar restraints. Apparently, the standing of these officials depends more on their loyalty than on the accuracy of their public statements.

As we have mentioned, the route of taking issues to the public is very important but also quite limited; many issues cannot be so treated. Other routes are available, however. Sometimes recourse to the courts is possible. Developments in the law, particularly the National Environmental Policy Act of 1969, make this approach increasingly effective. Using the law requires more than public-interest lawyers, however. It requires public-interest scientists as well. The collaboration of scientists and lawyers in the Environmental Defense Fund is one notable example; another was the collaboration between the MIT-based Union of Concerned Scientists and a number of the leading environmental organizations in a legal challenge to the Atomic Energy Commission to establish an adequate basis for evaluating the safety systems of nuclear reactors.[28]*

Organization and Funding

There is still relatively little funding for public-interest science. Almost all who are involved do it as an unremunerative sideline. Perhaps this is good. As governmental regulatory agencies have repeatedly demonstrated, responsibility cannot be successfully delegated—it can only be shared. Large numbers of part-time outsiders are required to keep the system honest.

More than part-time people are required, however. The coordination of the efforts of part-time people and the lobbying to see that the issues they raise get a fair hearing rapidly become a full-time job. This is a function pioneered by Jeremy Stone, president of the Federation of American Scientists.[29]† A number of academics seem also to have become nearly full-time public-interest scientists. Universities have the advantage of having undergraduate and graduate students who are willing to commit great amounts of energy and idealism to a project,[30] although, as Ralph

---

* The UCS challenge helped persuade Congress in 1973 to remove the responsibility for regulating civilian nuclear activities from the Atomic Energy Commission (AEC) and create the independent Nuclear Regulatory Commission (NRC). However, the vigilance of the NRC has continued to be a subject of great controversy. The reorganization also broadened the development mission of the AEC and renamed it the Energy Research and Development Administration (ERDA), which (in 1977) became the Department of Energy (DOE). The dominant mission of ERDA and the DOE continued, however, to be the development and production of nuclear weaponry.

† Although the ecological niche for full-time public-interest science remains relatively small, there are today on the order of 100 scientists based in public-interest groups and foundation-supported public-policy research groups.

Nader has shown, such students will go where the action is even if it is not at a university.

Foundations have shown an interest in funding public-interest science projects. Responsibility for some funding should be closer to the scientific community itself, however. Scientific societies could do some of it.* Another possibility would be for universities and other research contractors to devote part of their overhead on research contracts to a fund for public-interest science, controlled by the scientists at the institution. This is in effect how law firms and medical doctors support their *pro bono* activities.

One need only look at the student-funded Public Interest Research Groups in many states[31] to see how varied the possible sources of support for public interest science are. The more diverse the sources of support, the more securely established public interest science will become as one of the responsibilities of the scientific community.

---

* In 1973, the American Physical Society (APS) and the American Association for the Advancement of Science (AAAS) created Congressional Science Fellowships which give scientists an opportunity to work for a year on a congressional staff. As of 1986, 15 science and engineering societies and the Congressional Office of Science and Technology, State Department and Agency for International Development had developed similar programs—which are coordinated through a central office at the AAAS. Many of the graduates of these fellowships have stayed on with Congress or elsewhere in Washington. In 1974, the American Physical Society also sponsored (with federal funding) its first summer studies on the technical aspects of important public-policy issues: the APS Study Group on Light-Water-Reactor Safety and the APS Study Group on the Technical Aspects of the More Efficient Utilization of Energy.

Peer Review of Public Policy

Scientists learn early that no statement should be accepted without question. Indeed at the core of the scientist's approach to both experimental data and theoretical structures is an insistence on asking questions, looking for patterns and checking for consistency. In this context, incorrect data, bad analysis, and overblown claims are subject to immediate challenge to prevent them from being perpetuated and making the already difficult work of understanding natural phenomena even more difficult.

The skeptical attitude of the individual scientist is reinforced at the community level by various informal and formal mechanisms of "peer review." These mechanisms are used to give feedback to individual researchers, to ensure that limited research funds are being used effectively, and to impose quality control on the research results that are published in professional journals.

While independent peer review helps to maintain the health and integrity of science, its relative weakness in the political arena is one of the reasons why public policy making is too often based more on prejudice than on understanding. Our society is simply too shortsighted to encourage its technical experts to put public policy analysis to the test of peer review. This means, however, that there is a great opportunity for the individual scientist who abhors that vacuum to fill it and thereby make a major contribution to the clarification of the national policy agenda.

Today, thanks to movement towards a more open process for making public policy, the federal government publishes a great number of analyses of its policy alternatives—perhaps most notably the Environmental Impact Statements required by the National Environmental Policy Act of 1969.

These documents offer a starting point for outside peer review. However, although they often include lots of graphs, tables of numbers and references to the technical literature, they do not often seriously consider policy alternatives. The reports are written more like encyclopedias, dutifully discussing each relevant subject but often with a thoroughness inversely proportional to the importance of that subject to the policy choices being discussed. This is understandable in view of the fact that these policy analyses are generally written and published by agencies that have already decided what the final policy should be. It sometimes seems as if the principal purpose of such reports is to serve as monumental evidence that a "comprehensive" analysis has indeed been done.

Curiously enough, even scientists who would put the work of a colleague under a microscope before accepting it, tend to find even primitive indications of credibility, such as the size and cost of reports, persuasive in the case of public policy analysis. Perhaps this is because outside scientists are aware of the enormous resources of expertise that are available to organizations such as the Department of Energy or General Motors but do not see how these resources are actually used. Under these circumstances it is easy to assume that even if a large technical organization doesn't know what it is doing, its mistakes must at least be a type too subtle for a nonexpert to detect. Like the adults in Hans Christian Andersen's fairy tale, we tend to assume that the problem is with our own eyes rather than with the emperor's apparel.

In large part because the greater scientific community has averted its eyes instead of observing that the emperor is indeed naked, it is virtually standard practice on the part of large technical organizations today to do "answer analysis"—that is produce analyses in support of preselected positions—even during their internal decision-making process. Whereas in science, an answer analyst is fairly firmly encouraged to find another way to make a living, in policy analysis it is too often the other way around. Thus Robert Simpson of the *Wall Street Journal* (July 30, 1980) quoted one formerly high-level analyst as receiving the following advice before he was fired:

> Bill, in general, people who do well in this company wait until they hear their superiors express their view and then contribute something in support of that view.

Not surprisingly analyses produced under such circumstances often contain errors so egregious that even a scientific child could point them out.

Using three cases histories, I will illustrate why outside peer review of public policy analysis is critically needed, that it is feasible, and that it can have an important impact. The case histories also relate to issues which still are of major public concern and therefore of interest in their own right: the safety of today's commercial, nuclear power plants; the necessity of plutonium-breeder reactors; the consequences of "limited" nuclear war.

The APS Reactor Safety Study

A great public debate has raged around reactor safety, ever since the nation's utilities began to build commercial nuclear power plants in large numbers. In 1974, therefore, the American Physical Society (APS) sponsored a Study Group on Light Water Reactor Safety. Coincidentally, the Atomic Energy Commission (AEC) released its own 2,000-page-long draft *Reactor Safety Study* (also known as "WASH-1400" or the "Rasmussen report" after its spokesman, Professor Norman Rasmussen of MIT's Nuclear Engineering Department).[1] This report was made most memorable by the comparison it drew in one of its summary figures between the risk to life from reactor accidents and from meteorites (see Figure 1).*

If nuclear power plants had indeed been proven to be as safe as this figure suggests, then it would appear that there was little for the APS group to concern itself about. Before accepting this result, however, the group decided to try to understand how the *Reactor Safety Study* had obtained its result. In effect the group decided to do—to the extent that it could—a peer review.

It was difficult to check many of the calculations in the *Reactor Safety Study* in the short time available in a summer study because the authors of WASH-1400 had used computers so heavily. It did prove possible, however, to do "back-of-the-envelope" checks of the radiation "population-doses" calculated in the *Reactor Safety Study* for specific hypothetical releases of radioactivity to the atmosphere. (The population radiation dose is simply a sum of individual radiation doses and is a useful measure of the long-term impact of a reactor accident because it gives a

---

* Since the publication of the *Reactor Safety Study*, a radical upward revision of estimates of the risks from large meteorites has resulted from the hypothesis that the extinction of the dinosaurs and many other species of animals and plants approximately 65 million years ago was caused by an asteroid impact. Note that extrapolation of the "meteor" curve on Figure 1 to a frequency of 10^{-8} (once per 100 million years) would predict 100,000 fatalities while the asteroid extinction hypothesis would suggest the death of most if not all of the human race.

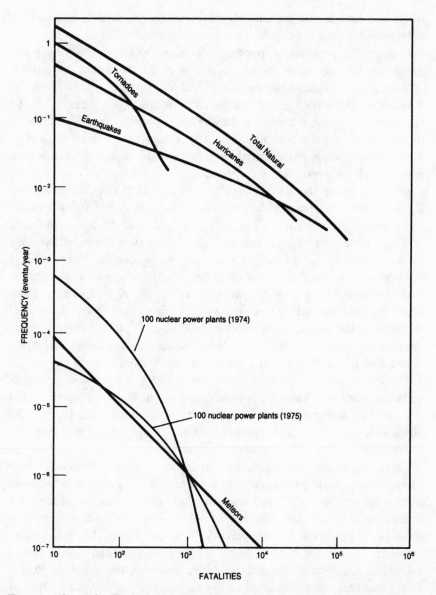

FIG. 1. *The risks from reactor accidents, as put into perspective in the Executive Summary of the AEC/NRC Reactor Safety Study. An APS review concluded that the probabilities estimated for large releases of radioactivity from reactor accidents were uncertain by orders of magnitude. Also, the numbers of fatalities estimated for given releases were under-represented by two to three orders of magnitude because of the omission of long-term cancer deaths.*

rough measure of the increase in the incidence of cancers and genetic defects which might result.[2])

Because the population doses calculated in the *Reactor Safety Study* for given releases of airborne radioactivity to the atmosphere were obtained by averaging wind directions and atmospheric stability classes, it appeared to the APS group that the calculations would probably not be very sensitive to the details of either the atmospheric dispersion model or the population distributions assumed. The APS group therefore used in its own back-of-the-envelope calculations a uniform population distribution and a simplified atmospheric dispersion.

When the group checked the results of its simplified calculations against the results of the *Reactor Safety Study* computer calculations it found some major discrepancies. Ultimately, the AEC calculations were found to be in error: It had been assumed that the population radiation dose from a reactor accident would stop growing within one day after a release of radioactivity. This was a bad error because the whole-body population dose downwind from a reactor accident is dominated by external radiation from 30-year half-life cesium-137 that is deposited on downwind surfaces by the radioactive plume. It would be impractical to reduce the population-dose greatly using long-term evacuation and decontamination because of the large areas of contamination involved.[3]

The authors of the *Reactor Safety Study* (RSS) were initially exceedingly reluctant to acknowledge their error, but ultimately they corrected it in the final *Reactor Safety Study* report, issued in October 1975 by the Nuclear Regulatory Commission (which had in the meantime taken over the AEC's regulatory functions).[1]

Curiously enough, however, the figure presented in the report's Executive Summary comparing the risks from reactor accidents to other risks had hardly changed at all. The reason is that the fatalities shown there for reactor accidents are only the early fatalities—those occurring within 60 days. In the final *Reactor Safety Study* there were several hundred cancer fatalities (which, of course, show up after more than two months) calculated for each of the early fatalities shown in the summary figure. There was almost no indication of the existence of these cancer fatalities in the Executive Summary, however; the leadership of the RSS had rejected even the suggestion that the adjective "early" be added before the word "fatalities" on the horizontal axis of Figure 1 so that readers would be alerted to the fact that not all fatalities from reactor accidents are shown there.

It took four years and another bout of peer review before the Nuclear Regulatory Commission acknowledged the misleading character of the

Executive Summary or accepted another, truly fundamental criticism of the Draft *Reactor Safety Study* made by the APS study group and by many other groups and individuals. This criticism was that the calculations of accident probabilities made in the *Reactor Safety Study* were so uncertain as to be virtually meaningless.

A critical role in sustaining the review process during this period was played by Morris Udall, who chaired a House of Representatives subcommittee that oversees the Nuclear Regulatory Commission. Udall's subcommittee held a hearing on the final *Reactor Safety Study* in June 1976 and issued a very critical report on it in January 1977.[4] In response to this pressure, the Nuclear Regulatory Commission (NRC) decided in 1977 to sponsor its own outside group to review the *Reactor Safety Study*.

The work of the NRC's new Risk Assessment Review Group (which included three veterans of the APS group) was made more difficult by the fact that various members had already previously taken public stands for or against the Reactor Safety Study. After more than a year of work, however, the group did piece together a report to the NRC out of agreements on many narrow issues.[5] I believe that this convergence was only possible because of the basic respect for truth that scientists absorb along with their discipline.

In any event, the statement issued on January 19, 1979 by the NRC in response to the report of the Risk Assessment Review Group was quite forthright:

> The Commission withdraws any explicit or implicit past endorsement of the Executive Summary. . . .
> The Commission agrees that the peer review process followed in publishing WASH-1400 was inadequate and that proper peer review is fundamental for making sound technical decisions. . . .
> The Commission does not regard as reliable the Reactor Safety Study's numerical estimate of the overall risk of reactor accident. . . .

To my knowledge, this is the first time that the peer-review process had worked effectively enough in the public policy arena to force a federal agency to reverse its position so completely and publicly.

The Plutonium Breeder Reactor

The federal government's program to commercialize plutonium breeder reactors has been controversial since the early 1970s, principally because the associated fuel-cycle technology is virtually indistinguishable from that required to secure plutonium for the production of nuclear weapons. In the mid-1970s, however, breeder advocates were arguing that fission was the only energy source that could be relied on to satisfy the world's growing energy appetite and that an immediate commitment to plutonium breeders was necessary if the world was to avoid a nuclear fuel-supply crisis shortly after the turn of the century.

The argument, as laid out in 1974 in the Atomic Energy Commission's *Proposed Environmental Statement on the Liquid Metal Fast Breeder Reactor* [LMFBR] *Program* went approximately as follows: U.S. consumption of electric energy was expected to continue to grow at almost its historical rate and most new generating capacity was expected to be nuclear with the result that nuclear power plants were projected to be generating by the year 2020 *ten times* as much electrical energy as all U.S. electrical power plants did in 1980 (see Figure 2).[6] U.S. supplies of high-grade uranium ore were believed to be sufficient to fuel only the light-water reactors to be built by about the year 2000. It was felt therefore that the continued growth of U.S. nuclear generating capacity could only be assured in the years after 2000 if much more uranium-efficient reactors such as plutonium breeders were introduced.*

In 1976 a group of three physicists and a policy analyst at Princeton published a critique of such projections. The group argued that electricity consumption growth rates in the future would be much slower than in the past and that therefore a commitment to the breeder could be postponed for decades at least.[7] A comprehensive critique of the AEC's cost-benefit analysis justification for the breeder program had been published two years earlier by another physicist, Thomas Cochran, who by 1976 was working full-time on the staff of a Washington-based public-interest group, the Natural Resources Defense Council.[8]

The issue was brought to a head in early 1977, as the result of the election of President Jimmy Carter. During his campaign, Carter had expressed concern about the implications for nuclear weapons proliferation of the proposed "plutonium economy." One of his first actions after the election was to order a review of the direction and pace of the U.S. breeder-reactor development program. The review was organized by the Energy Research and Development Administration (ERDA), which had in 1975 taken over all the AEC's functions, other than the regulation of

* Light-water reactors release efficiently only the energy of U-235, which makes up only 0.7 percent on natural uranium. A plutonium breeder reactor would release efficiently the energy in U-238, which comprises the remainder of uranium, by transmuting it into chain-reacting plutonium-239 through neutron capture.

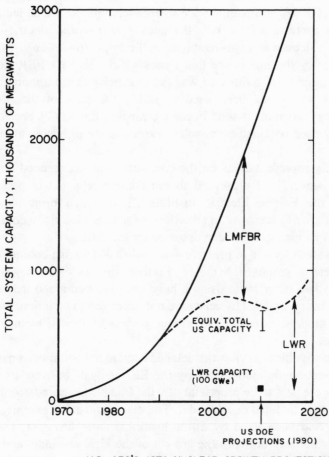

US AEC'S 1974 NUCLEAR GROWTH PROJECTION
(80 PERCENT AVERAGE CAPACITY FACTOR ASSUMED)

FIG. 2. *Justification for the liquid metal fast breeder reactor (LMFBR) program. Extrapolating U.S. nuclear electricity-generating capacity as shown, in 1974, the AEC argued that breeder reactors would be necessary to satisfy the demand. The extrapolation was based on extravagant assumptions about electricity generation and use. For comparison, we show the 1990 projections of the AEC's successor agency, the U.S. Department of Energy (U.S.DoE) for U.S. light water reactor (LWR) capacity in 2010 and the equivalent capacity that would be required to produce the kilowatt-hours projected by the DoE to be generated by all power plants that year. (We use the same assumption used by the AEC in making its projection, that the power plants would operate at an average of 80 percent of capacity.)*

commercial nuclear power activities. To give its breeder review greater credibility, ERDA set up an outside steering committee, which included, along with representatives from the nuclear-energy and electric-utility industries, Cochran and two members of the Princeton group.

Not surprisingly, one of the first issues which this "LMFBR Review Steering Committee" addressed was the electricity consumption growth projections which had been used to justify the pace of the breeder development program. It soon became clear that the AEC's projections had simply been obtained by mindless extrapolation of historical growth rates.

The utility representatives on the committee quickly stepped into the breach, however, and presented to the committee a newly published study by the Edison Electric Institute (EEI) which projected in a "moderate growth scenario" a growth rate for U.S. electricity consumption almost as high as had been assumed by the AEC.[9]

The EEI study looked impressive—more than 400 double-column pages with numerous graphs and tables. Furthermore its electricity-growth projections had been made using a huge and well-pedigreed macroeconomic computer model. Physicists are not supposed to be intimidated by computer models, however, so a peer review of the EEI study was undertaken.

It was impossible to review the detailed economic assumptions made in the macro-economic model used by the EEI analysts because its inner workings were held to be proprietary by the Cambridge-based economics consulting firm that had developed it. The many adjustable parameters in the model had been fixed by fitting historical data, however, and the historic relationship between the growth of the U.S. economy and U.S. electricity consumption has a remarkably simple pattern.[10] As Figure 3 shows, while U.S. electricity consumption per unit of the gross national product (GNP) rose by a factor of four between 1930 and 1970, economies of scale and large increases in the thermal efficiency of power plants lowered the average price of electricity by a factor of four during the same period, with the result that the share of the GNP going to the purchase of electricity was no more in 1970 than in 1930.

The EEI model projected another doubling in the electricity intensity of the U.S. economy per unit of GNP between 1975 and 2000. This would be consistent with historical trends but it would lead to serious stresses in the economy unless electricity prices continued their historic rate of decline. At a constant price of electricity, for example, a doubling of the kilowatt-hours consumed per dollar of GNP would also double the share of the GNP going to the purchase of electricity. This would imply an

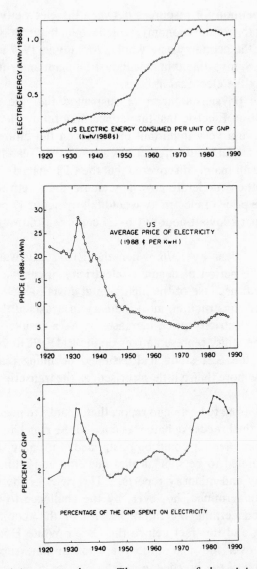

FIG. 3. *Electricity use and cost. The amount of electricity used per dollar of U.S. GNP (in constant, 1988 dollars) increased by about a factor of four between 1940 and 1970 (top); during the same period (center) the average price of electricity (again, in constant dollars) dropped by about a factor of four. As a result, the share of GNP going to the purchase of electricity did not change very much (bottom). Since 1970, however, the price of electricity has increased by about 50 percent, and demand has grown at about the same rate as the GNP; as a result, the projected growth of nuclear capacity has dropped far below that projected by the AEC in Figure 2.*

intensified competition for resources between the electricity-supply sec-
tor and other sectors of the economy, which would in turn have significant
implications for the economy as a whole. Already in 1975 more than 20
percent of all U.S. investment in new industrial plant and equipment was
accounted for by the electrical utilities.[11]

The Princeton physicists therefore suspected that the assumptions
made by the Edison Electric Institute concerning future electricity price
trends would have a very important influence on the future, which the
macroeconomic model would project. As a result they searched for these
assumptions and ultimately discovered that the EEI analysts had assumed
in constructing their moderate growth scenario that, between 1975 and
2000 the average price of electricity would fall by about 40 percent, from
about 2.7 cents per kilowatt-hour to 1.6–1.7 cents per kilowatt-hour (1975
dollars).

It was already clear by 1976, when the EEI study was published,
however, that the period of declining electricity prices was over. (See
Figure 3). Indeed, because of the high capital costs of new nuclear and
coal plants under construction, most industry forecasts at the time were
projecting large electricity price increases.[12] As a result, when it was
pointed out to the utility representatives on the LMFBR Review Steering
Committee that the EEI study had assumed declining real electricity
prices, they were more than a little surprised, as the transcript of the April
4, 1977 meeting shows.

It would be pleasing to be able to report that, thanks to peer review, the
Gordian knot of the breeder debate was cut and the panel agreed that the
deployment of the breeder could be postponed. In reality, the Steering
Committee continued to be split on that question and ultimately issued
separate majority and minority reports.[13] The case for the breeder had
been seriously undermined, however, by the challenge to the conventional wisdom concerning the future growth of the required nuclear-
energy capacity, and this fact helped the Carter White House to resist
great pressures over the next three years to continue subsidizing the
commercialization of the breeder reactor.

Since early 1977 when the Steering Committee produced its report, the
utility industry's average annual growth projections for the period of
1975–2000 have been dropping steadily: from 5.3–5.8 percent in the EEI's
"moderate-growth" scenario to 4.6 percent in late 1977, 3.5 percent in
1980 and 2.4 percent in 1989.[14] This corresponds to a reduction of
projected electricity consumption in the year 2000 by more than 50
percent.

Industry projections of U.S. nuclear capacity dropped still more rapidly during the same period—to about 100 gigawatts in the year 2000 and zero growth projected for the foreseeable future thereafter,[15] while estimates of U.S. uranium resources have increased.[16] As a result, it became clear that U.S. resources of high-grade uranium ore will last well beyond any reasonable planning horizon. Furthermore, the economics of the breeder now look quite unfavorable,[17] so that even in the absence of concerns about the proliferation of nuclear weapons, there is no reason to pursue commercialization of this technology.*

Consequences of "Limited" Nuclear War

One of the areas in which it is particularly difficult to perform open peer review is defense policy. Occasionally, however, some internal debate bursts into the public arena, and outsiders can participate. This occurred in 1974 after James Schlesinger, then secretary of defense, argued in a secret hearing before the Senate Foreign Relations Committee that the U.S. should be prepared to fight a "limited" nuclear war in which opposing nuclear-weapons delivery systems, rather than cities or industries, would be targeted. As revealed in the sanitized transcript of the hearing, he argued that, while a full-scale nuclear exchange between the U.S. and Soviet Union might be unthinkable, a limited one was not:[18]

> I am talking here about casualties of 15,000, 20,000, 25,000—a horrendous event, as we all recognize, but one far better than the alternative.

Some of the senators, Case of New Jersey in particular, were quite astonished that *any* nuclear exchange could have such small consequences. As a result, the Department of Defense was asked to provide detailed calculations of the fatalities that would result from various Soviet attacks against U.S. nuclear-weapons delivery systems. Secretary Schlesinger cooperated and six months later returned with the requested estimates. One of these drew special attention from the senators because it projected that almost a million U.S. fatalities would result from a Soviet attack against just the 1,054 U.S. Minutemen and Titan missile silos— despite the fact that these silos are in relatively isolated locations in the Western U.S.[19] Enormous swathes of lethal fallout would be laid out for many hundreds of miles downwind from the targets of such an attack.[20]

---

* The U.S. program for a commercial demonstration of a plutonium breeder reactor was cancelled by Congress in 1983.

(See Figure 5 in "Civilian Casualties from Counterforce Attacks" in this volume.)

Senator Case was still not satisfied, however. He therefore persuaded the chairman of the Senate Foreign Relations Committee to request that the Congressional Office of Technology Assessment (OTA) convene a group of experts to review the Defense Department's calculations.

The OTA assembled a panel of prestigious nuclear-weapons analysts and this panel did in fact have a number of criticisms to make of the assumptions used in the DOD's casualty calculations. In particular the panel noted that the weapon yields and height of burst chosen in the DOD scenario (a one-megaton warhead airburst over each silo) would not maximize the probability of destroying the U.S. missile silos. This put in question the purpose of the attack postulated by the DOD. The panel was also highly skeptical about the DOD assumption that, under the circumstances of a surprise attack by the Soviet Union, the U.S. population would be able to make optimum use of existing civil defense fallout shelters.[21]

Once again the Office of the Secretary of Defense cooperated and recalculated the expected fatalities for more effective attacks on U.S. strategic nuclear facilities, for less optimistic assumptions about fallout protection, and for various weather conditions. Assuming that 40 percent of the downwind population did not find refuge in fallout shelters, 16 million fatalities were estimated for the most effective attack considered (including two one-megaton weapons over each silo—one airburst and one ground burst).[22]

Peer review had therefore effectively challenged the idea that the U.S. should consider "limited" nuclear war as a rational policy option.

Other Reviews

It is important to acknowledge that peer review had more impact in the case histories that I have recounted here than is typical. The ingredients for success in each case was dedication and persistence on the part of both the reviewers and an important political actor who made certain that they were heard.

In the case of the Nuclear Regulatory Commission's Reactor Safety Study, it was Morris Udall who persisted over a period of years in pressing for a more adequate response from the NRC to the reviews sponsored by the APS and other organizations. In the case of the Energy Research and Development Administration's review of the breeder reactor, it was Jimmy Carter's White House that insisted that at least a minority of critics be added to the steering committee of utility and nuclear industry breeder supporters that ERDA had assembled. And in the case of the Defense Department's limited nuclear war casualty study it was Senator Case who arranged for congressionally sponsored peer review.

When such special conditions are not present, large technical organizations ordinarily try to ignore unwelcome reviews. This is only to be expected. Thus, after a public review of his new clothing, Hans Christian Andersen's emperor did not quickly admit his error. Upon hearing the assembled multitude, released by the child's voice, shout out together "He has nothing on at all!" "The emperor was angry and ashamed for he knew suddenly that they were right. 'But I have to go through with the procession,' he said to himself, so he drew himself up and the lords in waiting tightened their hold on his mantle and stalked on."

Perhaps the emperor could not respond otherwise if he wanted to remain in office. Perhaps large organizations also would be weakened politically if they admitted their errors. This does not mean, however, that peer review has been ineffective when, despite harsh criticism, a bad policy is not immediately withdrawn. The review process educates many audiences—including the peers and the organization which is pretending not to listen. Even an emperor cannot afford to play the fool too long. Andersen does not tell us what clothes the Emperor wore in his next procession, but probably they were a big improvement.

The Advisor's Dilemma

WITH JOEL PRIMACK

I have a feeling that a lot of them see me with a kind of horror—not just anger, but with an awe of the sort you'd have for an astronaut who stepped out of that capsule and cut his umbilical cord and just floated off into space and had become weightless, drifting in a black void, because he cut himself off from the capsule and from NASA, and the U.S. government, and the U.S. budget that supports that entire system. . . .

I think four-year-olds have fantasies like that . . . of what the world would be like when the mother went away. And the mother is the U.S. Executive Branch.[1]

—Daniel Ellsberg
describing the reactions of his
colleagues at the Rand Corporation
after he made public the
"Pentagon Papers"

The executive branch's science advisory establishment makes many essential contributions to the effectiveness of policy making. It is also obvious that administration officials have learned to use the advisory establishment to mislead the public and Congress about the technical bases of executive decisions. In any particular case the advisor must therefore decide whether he is being asked to advise or to "legitimize." But what then? If he refuses to participate in a system which is being used to mislead the public, he will also be refusing to give his government the benefit of his advice. Such is the advisor's dilemma.

One deceptively easy resolution of this dilemma would appear to be for an advisor to say to himself: "I will give the administration the best advice that I can concerning technical considerations. Then, if I find that executive spokesmen mislead the public about these considerations, I will give the public directly the benefit of my knowledge and experience."

Unfortunately, things are not quite so simple, because executive officials do not in general find such behavior acceptable. Advisors, like permanent government employees, are expected to be loyal and to abide quietly by final executive decisions, or else to "get off the team."

When an advisor decides to "go public" he is aware that he may very well at the same time be sacrificing his future access to the corridors of power and the sources of inside information. Since there are, in the first place, few advisors willing forcefully to present an unwelcome point of view to important government decision makers, an advisor can legitimately be concerned that the long-term cost to the country of his replacement by a "yes man" may outweigh any short-term benefit the public might derive from his setting the public record straight on a particular issue. When concern about loss of future effectiveness within the executive branch is combined with the considerable doubt that most advisors have about the effectiveness of speaking out, it is not surprising that it is so extraordinarily rare that advisors "go public."

There are also strong social and psychological pressures operating against "going public." The high-level government advisor has undergone typically a long process of "socialization" in Washington during his slow climb up through the hierarchy of advisory committees. His self-esteem, not to mention his position in his home organization and in the eyes of his colleagues there, may not be unrelated to his advisory activities and his association with men in power.[2]

It is becoming more and more clear, however, that to the extent that the administration can succeed in keeping unfavorable information quiet and the public confused, the public welfare can be sacrificed with impunity to bureaucratic convenience and private gain. Thus advisors who keep their information and analyses confidential in the interests of preserving their "effectiveness" may find that very effectiveness decreasing as a poorly informed and uncertain Congress and public become less and less able to call the administration to account for irresponsible actions.

There is no consensus within the scientific community as to how the advisor's dilemma should be resolved. In fact, there has been very little discussion at all within the scientific community of the issues involved. Lack of such discussion leaves scientists unprepared when they become advisors and find themselves confronted with difficult and unfamiliar decisions, often in an atmosphere of great pressure. It is no wonder that under these circumstances advisors find themselves looking for guidance to the experienced government officials whom they advise and adopting rather uncritically the code of confidentiality and team spirit to which these officials themselves adhere.

Arguments Supporting the Confidential Advisory Relationship

Let us consider a few of the arguments which, by and large, advisors adopt as their own:

1. The relationship between a scientific advisor and the government official whom he or she advises should be confidential, just as is that between lawyer and client.

This analogy compares a scientist or engineer who provides information and advice to the government—presumably with the intention of helping bring forth an optimal policy for the country as a whole—with the private lawyer hired to devise the optimal strategy in presenting a client's case. If we follow this analogy through, it would appear that the executive branch sees itself in an adversary relationship with Congress and the public. The fact that one side in the confrontation has a near-monopoly on the "lawyers" (science advisors) then becomes quite disquieting.

It is unfortunate that the ethical principles proposed for advisors by executive-branch agencies have more in common with the ethics of lawyers and physicians, which stress the protection of the client, than with the ethics of responsible public officials or public health officers, for whom the general welfare must be the primary concern. Science advisors, who are concerned with questions of the national interest, should also owe their first loyalty to the nation as a whole and to fundamental democratic principles, rather than to the personalities or policies of any particular administration. Patterning the ethics of science advisors on those of private lawyers or physicians is therefore inappropriate.

2. The president is elected by all the people and has the ultimate responsibility for making national policy. This leaves the advisor with only the responsibility of seeing that the president and the officials in his administration are well informed.

In response to the great inequality of activity and influence which has developed among the three branches of our government, the popular identification of our form of government as democratic has come to depend less on the theory of checks and balances and more on the fact that the president is elected "by all the people." We might caricature this view of our government as the "Four-Year Elected-Dictatorship Theory of Democracy." This theory was particularly popular with the Nixon administration, whose behavior gave the country a most vivid demonstration of the dangers posed by an executive branch which feels that it can be held to account only once every four years.

What the elected-dictatorship idea leaves out entirely is the role of the individual citizen in the governmental process. The ultimate responsibility under a democratic government always lies with the individual citizen, and the government advisor cannot escape his or her responsibilities as a citizen. In fact, by virtue of their greater knowledge of the subject on which they advise, government advisors take on enlarged responsibilities for the defense of the public interest in that area. The confusion of allegiance to the public interest with allegiance to the president in power indicates a basic lack of understanding of the meaning of democracy. That this misunderstanding has been shared by so many science advisors should be a matter of great concern to the scientific community.

Such concerns were raised about the long acquiescence of science advisors in presidential policies for the Indochina War. Although a number of prominent government science advisors may have had private qualms about U.S. actions in Vietnam, they confined themselves to producing a secret report, prepared during the summer of 1966 under the auspices of the "Jason" division of the Institute for Defense Analyses (IDA). The report argued against the bombing of North Vietnam, not on any moral grounds, but on the technical grounds of its ineffectiveness.[3] Their criticism of the bombing was largely ignored by the generals— although it appears to have influenced Defense Secretary McNamara, who attached its conclusions to a memorandum to President Johnson opposing the increased bombing of North Vietnam.[4] McNamara failed to convince Johnson and subsequently left the Pentagon. But a related proposal endorsed by the advisors was partially adopted: an electronically policed barrier along the northern borders of South Vietnam. The advisors claimed that such a barrier would be more effective than bombing in choking off the flow of military support to the Vietcong.[5] The result was the "McNamara Line," which ultimately grew into the military fantasy-nightmare of the "electronic battlefield."[6] But the bombing went on. One of the leaders of the Jason summer study (George Kistiakowsky, who had been President Eisenhower's science advisor) told us that he was so embittered by this experience that he subsequently resigned from all his government advisory posts. "I was a dupe," he said. "Whatever advice you give the military will be twisted."

When government officials repeatedly fail to hear or heed their science advisors and when an advisory committee begins to moderate or even alter what it would really like to say (Trojan Horse strategy), advisors should perhaps consider other approaches. Bringing serious matters into the open and to the attention of government decision makers through their morning newspapers is one tactic for breaking through their bureaucracy-created isolation. It has been established repeatedly that public exposure of important issues can result in crucial facts and perceptions coming to the fore which would have been missed in the ordinary governmental process.

3. It is quixotic for a lone scientist with no political constituency to hope to influence the public to reject the misrepresentations of administration spokesmen.

A lone scientist *can* fight the bureaucracy—and win. It is true that it is usually ineffective for an insider just to sign a petition or make a single public statement and then go back to his or her usual activities. This will probably only succeed in antagonizing those administration officials he or she has been advising. If advisors want to challenge an administration policy that they consider a threat to the public health and welfare, then their dedication in raising an opposition must be commensurate with the seriousness of the perceived threat. Great persistence and resourcefulness are usually required—and often courage, too, since scientists may oppose agencies which fund their work or work at their institutions.

Although serving as an advisor broadens one's first-hand knowledge of the considerations which enter into federal policy making for technology, it does not prepare one for the rigors of such a battle. Advisors are not encouraged to follow through on their advice and try to see that it is taken into account. Generally they are asked to prepare and submit reports rather quickly and then to forget about them unless called upon for further advice. Often, they are not expected to look seriously into the nontechnical aspects of the issue on which their advice is sought. Instead, they are expected to form an opinion based primarily on the knowledge they already have and on the briefings they receive from government officials and from full-time government experts. They are usually paid for this, they gain prestige because their advice is sought by important government officials, and they make professional contacts which may prove important in the advancement of their careers. This is quite a different situation from the harsh and lonely world in which dissenters often find themselves.

Thus, of the three rationales offered in defense of the confidential advisory relationship, two—the lawyer-client analogy and the the-president-has-the-ultimate-responsibility argument—seem upon reflection to be absurd. The third, the you-can't-fight-city-hall argument is, as we said, simply a restatement of the fact that the life of a confidential advisor can be relatively easy and secure while that of the dissenter can be arduous and uncertain. As Abraham Lincoln said, "Silence makes men cowards."

It is obvious, from the superficiality of the widely held views which we have been discussing, that the ethics of advising should be subjected to a careful examination by the scientific community as a whole. Science advising, no less than scientific research, needs a code of ethics. And this code should explicitly take into account the fact that we live in a democracy in which the ultimate responsibility resides not with the president but with the individual citizen.

Discounting Future Effectiveness

The rather old-fashioned lecture on citizenship just delivered does not by any means resolve the deeper dilemma in which science advisors often find themselves: it simply acts to blow away the smoke screen concealing it. Generalizations cannot resolve such dilemmas, for each case concerns an individual scientist's judgment of how he or she may most effectively serve the public interest. Advisors contemplating going public in order to challenge an emerging executive policy that they consider inimical to the public interest must weigh two great uncertainties: the effectiveness of such a move versus their future effectiveness as insiders.

High-level advisors find themselves in a position which has usually required years of apprenticeship. It is therefore natural, before challenging a policy, to think: "I've worked hard to gain my position of influence—for what it's worth. Let someone else take the issue to the public. That way I can keep presenting my arguments on the inside while they present theirs on the outside. (Besides, I'm the director of a large laboratory, and a lot of people will be hurt if I become unpopular with the current administration.)"

The problem, of course, is that such advisors represent a considerable segment of the leadership of science, and if they, in their positions of relative security, are unwilling even occasionally to set an example by taking the risk of going public, it is unreasonable to expect that enough

high-caliber scientists outside the advisory establishment will step forward in their stead. Also, by asking other scientists to assume the entire
burden of public-interest science, advisors may be asking them to close
doors to positions of honor and influence such as those that advisors often
enjoy.

Unfortunately, it appears characteristic of human nature to overesti-
mate what one's future effectiveness might be in comparison to what one
judges one's effectiveness to be in the issue at hand. Participants in
politics often must revise their hopes for future accomplishment down by
an order of magnitude during the battle when they realize how tough it is
to accomplish anything. This means that an advisor weighing the effectiveness of going public in a current situation is weighing this reduced
expectation against his still-high hopes of future effectiveness. This gives
rise to the common situation where advisors conserve their effectiveness
until they fade from the scene.

What Does the Advisor Do About Uncertainty?

Uncertainty arising from incomplete information is one of the major
problems facing technical experts—advisors or not—when contemplating
making an issue out of their concerns. It was not clear during the 1969–70
debate over the U.S. program to develop a supersonic transport (SST),
for example, to what extent a fleet of SSTs would increase the Earth's
cloud cover or deplete its protective layer of stratospheric ozone. Nor
was it clear during the Vietnam War how many birth defects would occur
in South Vietnam from the massive use there of 2,4,5-T as a defoliant.
And finally, it was not clear in 1970, when Jacqueline Verret, an FDA
scientist made public her concerns about the safety of cyclamates, how
many cases of cancer and birth defects would result from the public's
massive use of cyclamate-sweetened drinks and foods.

A concerned scientist might therefore well have asked: "Is this a false
alarm? Am I putting my reputation on the line over a danger which later
information will prove not to exist?"

In these circumstances the decision must hinge on the advisor's answer
to the question: Who should determine whether the benefits of the
proposed policy exceed the risks? The President's Science Advisory
Committee panel reporting on the danger of tsunamis being triggered by
nuclear weapons testing suggested that:[7]

the public should not be asked to accept risks resulting from purely
internal governmental decisions, if, without endangering national

security, the information can be made public and the decisions reached after public discussion.

(The panel's report was subsequently suppressed.) Thus, even if the dangers which concern a scientist might not materialize, members of the public should have an opportunity to express their opinions as to whether the potential risks are worth the benefits.

This does not mean that every such matter should be made the subject of a national referendum. What it does mean is that, in a democracy, citizens should have an opportunity to defend their vital interests. Not infrequently a government decision is made in secret and then, when the story gets out, the decision is reversed. What has happened is that the publicity has brought new political forces into play.

Guidelines for Advisors

While there are many cases in which advisors have failed to come forward to warn the public about real dangers, we are unaware of a single case in which an advisor has sought publicity for an unfounded concern for the public welfare. It is not surprising that a bias exists toward acquiescing to the executive branch's demands for confidentiality. It happens also that the counsels of timidity and ambition work in the same direction.

However, some advisors have not only accepted confidentiality as a necessity, they have even embraced it. Thus the technical society of operations analysts, the Operations Research Society of America (ORSA), includes in its "Guidelines for Professional Practice" the following admonitions:[8]

Scrupulously observe any ground rules about confidentiality laid down by the organization being served.

Report the study's results only to the organizational elements sponsoring the study, unless specifically authorized by them to report to a wider audience.

They further declare that[9]

an analyst called upon to testify on behalf of a client whose decision he has helped to shape by his analyses should support his client's case. . . . An analyst who wishes to disagree publicly with his client is placed in a difficult ethical position.

The perspective implicit in these guidelines seems rather narrow in comparison with that expressed in the *Code of Ethics for United States Government Service*, adopted by Congress in 1958, from which we quote the opening words:[10]

Put loyalty to the highest moral principles and to country above loyalty to persons, party, or Government department.

We submit that this higher loyalty implies a commitment on the part of government science advisors to provide their fellow citizens with the information and analyses necessary for effective participation in the political process. As a reminder of the fundamental democratic principles which are occasionally forgotten in the practical business of running the government, we offer here two simple guidelines on the limits of advising confidentiality:

1. Advisors have the obligation to bring to public attention government policies or practices that they believe may threaten the public health and welfare.

2. Advisors have the responsibility to speak out when they believe that public debate is being needlessly hampered by the misrepresentation or suppression of information.

We do not propose that our guidelines be engraved in stone. Our purpose is rather to stimulate discussion of the issues. Advisors themselves and the scientific community as a whole must define the role of science advisors in a way which emphasizes their larger responsibilities.

In order to put into perspective the unformed fears referred to Daniel Ellsberg in our opening quote, consider the following examples of advisors who lived up to our guidelines and lived to advise another day.

Warning the Public

When he was invited to testify before Congress about the U.S. supersonic transport development program, after chairing a presidential advisory panel on the same subject, Richard Garwin drew congressional attention to the degradation of the quality of life in metropolitan areas which would result from the enormous takeoff noise of the SST and to the technological setbacks which had compromised the plane's design. And, at the beginning of the public debate over the Sentinal antiballistic-missile (ABM) system, Garwin and Hans Bethe, both long-term, high-level advisors on nuclear-weapons policy, presented in a *Scientific American* article[11] the arguments which led them to believe that building an ABM system designed to defend the population of the United States was futile.[12]

Garwin and Bethe's actions in these cases stand in striking contrast to the ordinary behavior of most advisors, who remain silent—or, at most, mutter a little. Members of the Food and Nutrition Board of the National Academy of Sciences, for example, seem to have displayed a forbearance which can only be compared with that of Job while, for almost fifteen years, the Food and Drug Administration ignored their repeated expressions of concern about widespread public consumption of cyclamates.

Correcting the Record

Typically, advisors directly contradict statements by administration spokesmen only when misquoted *by name*. Thus, for example, in the ABM debate, when Panofsky's name was taken in vain by Deputy Secretary of Defense Packard, and later, when Drell and Goldberger's confidential advice was misrepresented by Director of Defense Research and Engineering John Foster, a confrontation became unavoidable. In the case of the SST, Garwin, as we have already noted, tried to set the record straight—not by directly contradicting government statements, but by laying out the actual technical basis for the decision at issue.

It is not an infrequent occurrence for confidential government reports, which contradict the statements of administration spokesmen, to be "leaked" to the media. For example, an advisory report to the Environmental Protection Agency (EPA) on the safety of 2,4,5-T entered the public domain without official approval. In this case the "leaker" was presumably concerned because the report uncritically dismissed serious concerns about possible dangers to public health. If so, the tactic was effective: as a result of criticisms of the leaked report by independent scientists, EPA administrator Ruckelshaus rejected its recommendations that 2,4,5-T be given a clean bill of health. This was an unusual case, however, in that there was a qualified group, the Committee for Environmental Information, outside government which immediately picked up and articulated the issues involved. In most cases one cannot expect a leaked report to be as influential as an advisor who draws the spotlight to the existence of a suppressed report and speaks to the broader implications of its conclusions. Even less useful than a leaked report is leaked advice without supporting documentation. For example, President Nixon's *ad hoc* SST Advisory Committee's negative views of the SST were accurately reported in the *New York Times* in March 1969,[13] but it was not until the documents themselves were released seven months later that widespread public interest was generated.

Due Process
for Dissent

WITH ROSEMARY CHALK

On August 23, 1977, Glenn Greenwald, a chemist in the Public Utilities Department of the City of North Miami Beach, Florida, was called to 800 N.E. 182nd Terrace by a resident who complained that the water coming out of the tap tasted, smelled and looked peculiar. Greenwald agreed, and his tests showed that the water contained an abnormally small amount of free chlorine.

Laboratory analysis completed the next day revealed coliform bacteria in the water sample, and Greenwald decided that action was needed. Unable to find his supervisor, he asked his department head for an immediate flushing of the water distribution system in the area. Such flushings are accomplished by opening a neighborhood's fire hydrants, usually at night, but—trusting Greenwald's judgment—the department head ordered immediate action.

Greenwald's supervisor was irate when he learned of the flushing: he doubted that the action had been necessary and he feared that the residents of the affluent neighborhood where it had taken place might become unduly alarmed. He therefore told Greenwald that he should consider resigning if he could not work through channels.

But the contamination problem had not been solved by the flushing, and—in contrast to his superiors—Greenwald continued to believe that there was a potential health hazard. He wanted to continue tests and to advise residents of the house officially not to drink their tap water until further notice. His supervisors agreed to the continued testing but refused to authorize the official notice.

On the third day after Greenwald had first visited 800 N.E. 182nd Terrace, a teen-age resident asked him why the testing was still going on. Greenwald described the contamination problem, and suggested that the family not drink the water until the problem had been cleared up. Later that same day, however, when the chemist told his supervisor and department head of this conversation, he was summarily discharged for insubordination.

Greenwald promptly took his case to the city's Civil Service Board, which three months later upheld his firing. Then he took his case to the U.S. Department of Labor, appealing under the employee protection section within the Safe Drinking Water Act of 1974. The relevant part of this legislation states that "No employer may discharge any employee or otherwise discriminate against any employee . . . because the employee has . . . participated . . . in any . . . action to carry out the purposes of this title." The Labor Department's administrative law judge who heard the case agreed that Greenwald's discharge was indeed a violation of the Safe Drinking Water Act. The judge went on to observe that "to punish or discriminate against a chemist for recommending a procedure which, at worst, would be a precautionary step, would be to demand that all subordinates at all levels remain silent if so instructed until harm has occurred or is imminent." But Greenwald's was an empty victory. Since his complaint had not been filed within a 30-day statutory limit contained in the Act, the judge had to recommend to the secretary of labor that the appeal be dismissed.

The Dilemma of the Employed Professional

Glenn Greenwald's experience in exercising his professional responsibility highlights a serious dilemma for modern scientists and engineers. Early assessments of adverse impacts of technologies on society are often made by professionals working within large organizations, but such organizations are usually eager to avoid what they describe as "premature" disclosure of concerns which may later prove to be insubstantial. Since judgments of the importance of such concerns typically involve value judgments as well as professional judgments, there is often considerable room for disagreement.

The tension between an organization's concern to control its own affairs and the public's interest in knowing of possible hazards is mirrored in a tension of loyalties within its professional employees. Scientists and engineers are expected to be loyal to their organization's management, and they are so instructed by their professional societies. In its "Guide-lines to Professional Employment for Engineers and Scientists," the Engineers Joint Council writes that:[1]

> the professional employee must be loyal to the employer's objec-tives and contribute his creativity to these goals.

But—because of their special expertise—engineers and scientists also have special responsibilities for the protection of the public. The "Engi-neer's Code" of the National Society for Professional Engineers states, for example, that:

> the engineer will have proper regard for the safety, health, and welfare of the public in the performance of his professional duties. If his engineering judgment is overruled by nontechnical authority, he will clearly point out the consequences. He will notify the proper authority of any observed conditions which endanger public safety and health. . . . He will regard his duty to the public welfare as paramount. . . .

Ordinarily these expectations do not conflict. Occasionally, however, as in Greenwald's case, an issue cannot be resolved within organizational channels, and an employee is moved by feelings of professional respon-sibility to make sure that his concerns are heard by higher levels of management or responsible outside individuals. If without authorization, an employee makes known his or her concerns to individuals outside the organization he or she is said to have "blown the whistle."

Though the public is clearly more receptive to criticism of large organizations today than formerly, such "whistle-blowing" remains an extreme and rather rare manifestation of the phenomenon of dissent. Many technical dissenters win an audience—and eventually a resolution of their concerns—within their organizations. And the vast majority of dissenters whose employers are unresponsive either do not feel strongly enough about their dissents or are too timid to blow whistles publicly. Unfortunately, most managements see dissenting employees as challeng-ing the legitimacy of management's authority, and "whistle-blowing" is taken as a challenge to the credibility of the organization as a whole. Dissent therefore provides the ingredients for a confrontation between a technical expert and his or her management—an intimidating prospect for most employees. After finding that they are unable to obtain a full hearing for their concerns without antagonizing their supervisors, most dissenters therefore decide to "swallow the whistle" rather than blow it.

Swallowing the Whistle: The Aircraft Brake Scandal

In 1972 James Olson published the results of a survey of 800 randomly selected members of the National Society of Professional Engineers. Almost half of the respondents indicated that they felt "restrained from criticizing their employer's activities or products," and more than 10 percent felt that they were "required to do things which violated their sense of right and wrong."[2]

An example of a situation in which dissenters swallowed their ethical concerns at least temporarily is provided by the following case concerning the certification in 1968 of some new aircraft brakes at the B.F. Goodrich Wheel and Brake plant in Troy, Ohio.

In 1967, this plant won a subcontract to provide brake assemblies for the Air Force's new A7D light attack aircraft. Unfortunately, the brake assembly, as initially designed, turned out to be too light. When tested in simulated landings, the brakes heated to such high temperatures that the linings burned out before the design lifetime had been reached.

The young engineer in charge of testing the brake assemblies concluded that a heavier design was required. The project management, however, had already committed itself to delivering the lightweight brakes. Repeated attempts were therefore made to find lining materials which would tolerate the high temperatures.

When it finally became clear to all involved that a lining material with the necessary characteristics would not be found, time was running out; the project management, apparently unwilling to admit its misjudgments at such a late stage, decided to paper over the problem. Orders were given that the brakes be nursed through the qualification tests and that the documentation of the tests be fudged to conceal the irregularities. The engineers in charge of preparing the qualification reports protested; but, when offered the alternative of resigning their jobs, they decided to prepare the reports.

The brakes were duly delivered and installed in the A7D. But problems developed during the aircraft flight tests: the brakes locked during two landings, causing the plane to skid to a stop. This dramatic confirmation of their concerns finally overcame the hesitations of a junior engineer and a technical writer at the B.F. Goodrich plant, and they went to the FBI.

Subsequent investigations by both the Air Force and the Congressional General Accounting Office confirmed that the brakes had indeed been improperly qualified. In the meantime, Goodrich quickly developed a new set of brakes which passed the qualification tests and the two "whistle-blowers" found other jobs.[3]

As this case shows, the dissenter is not the only one who has something at risk when dissent is ignored by management. Technical dissent is often an "early warning" signal of real problems that may escalate into serious issues for the enterprise if not dealt with early and effectively.

The suppression of professional dissent can also have another damaging effect on the organization: it can alienate employees who otherwise would care enough to do their jobs well and creatively.

Due Process for Dissent

For all these reasons, organizations and enterprises should develop due-process procedures for dealing with dissents and dissenters in a fair and responsive manner. Such procedures might, for example, include rights for dissenters to:

- Document and present concerns in writing to a qualified and balanced review group;
- Request that the review group hear others whose testimony is relevant;
- See and respond to the counterpresentations by management;
- Receive the review group's findings in writing within a reasonable length of time.

In addition to offering dissenters due-process protections, these procedures would offer some protection to the employer, by:

- Requiring that employees express their concerns in writing and in detail;
- Assuring the organization of an independent evaluation of the significance of these concerns;
- Giving the organization a basis for defense against possible later accusations that it retaliated against dissenters if, in fact, only legitimate personnel actions had been taken.

Such due-process procedures could in some cases lead to the discharge, for reasons of insufficient competence, of a professional employee who had persistently raised issues mischievously or without reasonable grounds. It should not, however, be required that concerns raised by dissenters be proved correct for their jobs to be protected. Many legitimate concerns about hazards to the public arise in areas where basic technical data are missing or uncertain. Indeed, the initial difference of opinion may arise because a dissenter's predisposition is to delay a project until hazards can be more thoroughly understood—while the employer is unwilling to change plans for less-than-proven hazards. The procedures should recognize that the dissenter may be performing an important service by drawing greater attention to a significant but previously neglected area of uncertainty, whether or not the dissenter's worst nightmares are ultimately confirmed.

Given due-process protections, dissent is less likely to develop into confrontation. In the absence of due process procedures, unfounded and exaggerated accusations proliferate and the credibility, character, and motivations of both dissenters and organizations can become as controversial as the subject of the dissent itself, with the importance of the latter often lost.

If this kind of confrontation develops, management's leverage can be used to make the dissenter's employment situation quite unpleasant. The dissenter is represented as a "difficult person"—perhaps with ulterior motives—who is trying to impose exaggerated concerns on a conscientious management. While, to his or her supporters, a dissenter may appear to be a dedicated individual acting as the conscience of an irresponsible organization, a dissenter who overreacts to an *ad hominem* attack by the organization and responds in kind, will often damage his or her professional credibility. Indeed, technical dissents are often complicated by emotional actions and reactions which tend to mask and subvert the important technical issues which are at stake. As one congressional aide summarized his experience with management's treatment of dissenters at the Nuclear Regulatory Commission, "First they drive them crazy. Then they tell us we shouldn't listen to them because they are crazy."

Thus extension of due-process protections to dissenters is important not only as a protection for human rights but also as a mechanism by which the credibility of the assertions of both sides can be tested. With due-process procedures, arguments are likely to be conducted more responsibly, and the record of the proceedings will provide a reasonable basis for outside review of the technical issues.

Who Should Protect Dissenters?

Due-process protections for dissenting professionals can be established by a number of parties: by the organization which employs the dissenter, by professional societies, or by the larger society through laws and regulations.

It is encouraging to find that a significant number of managements are moving away from their traditional dependence on discretionary procedures for protecting dissent (in which, for example, high officials announce that they have an "open door" policy) toward real due-process protections where the outcome is not kept under such tight management control.

Employees who feel that they are being retaliated against because of their dissent, however, are more likely to receive an efficient and impartial review by going to individuals or groups outside the organization's hierarchy. Depending upon the degree of independence which is required by the circumstances of the case, such a review could be undertaken by an ombudsman, a panel chosen by an arbitration procedure, or a special *ad hoc* review group established by an appropriate outside organization. The value of having an outside group review the personnel issues growing out of professional disagreements between employees and management is exemplified by a case involving the Food and Drug Administration (FDA).

A number of FDA medical professionals claimed in testimony before a Senate subcommittee that they had been improperly transferred after they had recommended against the licensing of particular drugs. In response to these accusations, FDA Commissioner, Alexander M. Schmidt, conducted an internal investigation of the allegations and concluded that they were not supported by the facts. In the meantime, however, FDAs parent agency, the Department of Health, Education and Welfare, had responded to congressional pressure by establishing an external review panel to investigate the same complaints with the assistance of a legal staff. This staff documented beyond any reasonable doubt that the transfers, although they were made under a variety of other pretexts, had in fact generally been made because the FDA management felt that the professionals were displaying an attitude of "negativism" toward the drug industry.[4] In response to these findings, a new FDA commissioner issued letters of admonition to two bureau chiefs, reassigned one employee who had been improperly transferred, and apologized by letter on behalf of the agency to 12 employees and consultants who the panel said had been treated unfairly.

Professional societies are potentially a powerful source of support for scientists and engineers who dissent for ethical reasons, and indeed many societies have promulgated guidelines for the employment of professionals. In the future, professional societies could require that employment contracts for their members include provision for the resolution of employer-employee disputes through hearing and appeal processes; such provisions already exist in employment contracts covering unionized employees. Indeed, professional societies could persuade Congress that employment guidelines for professionals should be given legal force. This was proposed in 1976 by Alan C. Nixon, former president of the American Chemical Society.[5]

The Institute of Electrical and Electronics Engineers (IEEE) has developed procedures for reviewing complaints by members about employers' retaliation for "professional responsibility" actions. In the first opinion issued under these procedures, the IEEE endorsed the action of a member who was dismissed for circulating a memorandum detailing her safety concerns after they had been ignored by her supervisors.[6] But other professional societies, with the notable exception of the American Association of University Professors, have been strikingly reluctant to defend actively the professional independence of their employed members. In the case of some societies, this may reflect a lack of confidence in their probable effectiveness. But in many cases, it probably also reflects the impact of a veto by influential high-level managers among their members who equate dissent with disloyalty. Thus a local chapter of the National Society of Professional Engineers which came to the defense of a group of dissenting engineers on the staff of the Bay Area Rapid Transit authority was subjected to heavy criticism from leadership groups in both its state and national parent organizations for its activities; some of the society elders argued that the chapter's actions impugned the professionalism of the engineer-managers who were in charge of the design and construction of the project.

In the absence of effective actions by employers and professional societies and, as the public has become more aware and concerned about the suppression of employees' concerns about hazards or illegal actions, the courts and Congress have become more involved. Two arguments have been principally used to justify such governmental intervention into the employee-management relationship which has been traditionally almost sacrosanct:

1) In some cases retaliation against dissenting employees may infringe on their rights to freedom of speech;
2) The public interest requires protection for employees who are trying to bring their organizations into compliance with federal standards.

Civil Rights in the Workplace

David W. Ewing of Harvard Business School has argued that the controversy over dissent and "whistle-blowing" within large organizations simply represents an extension into a new arena of the historical struggle over individual rights. Ewing has therefore discussed the problem of employee-employer relationships in terms of the need for a new bill of rights for employees.[7] This analysis has considerable force—especially in connection with the need to protect employees' freedom of speech. Employees generally are experts in issues which arise in connection with their employment; if they cannot speak freely to their fellow citizens about what they know best, then their freedom is very limited indeed.

Traditionally, the view that employees should have any rights, beyond that of resigning in case of a professional disagreement, received very little sympathy in the courts. The prevailing view was expressed by the oft-quoted opinion, given in 1892 by Justice Oliver Wendell Holmes, then a member of the Massachusetts Supreme Court:

> There are few employments for hire in which the servant does not agree to suspend his constitutional rights of free speech as well as idleness by the implied terms of his contract. The servant cannot complain, as he takes the employment on the terms which are offered him.

(It is perhaps ironic that Justice Holmes later came to be venerated as "the great dissenter" on the U.S. Supreme Court.)

A century later, however, the prevailing legal view of the employer-employee relationship has begun to change. Perhaps the most important sign of this change was the 1968 Pickering decision of the U.S. Supreme Court, in which the Court ordered a local board of education to reinstate a teacher who had been fired for public criticism of the high priority that the board was giving to the funding of athletics. The Court found that:

> teachers are, as a class, the members of a community most likely to have informed and definite opinions as to how funds allotted to the operation of the schools should be spent. Accordingly, it is essential that they be able to speak out freely on such questions without fear of retaliatory dismissal.

The Court acknowledged that the need to protect the teacher's freedom of speech had to be balanced against the board's responsibility to preserve the effectiveness of the school; but in this case, it argued that the teacher's public statements had not interfered with the regular operations of the school nor had they called into question his fitness to teach.

Initially this protection of the freedom of speech applied only to public employees, since the Bill of Rights protects citizens only from government actions. More recently, however, the protection has been extended somewhat, to cover the employees of organizations which have a substantial "government involvement," taken to include ownership of facilities or purchase of most of the output of a contractor's plant.

Protecting the Public

In 1972 Ralph Nader remarked on the relatively small number of corporate employees who "go public" with their concerns about potential hazards caused by their company's activities:[8]

> Corporate employees are among the first to know about industrial dumping of mercury or fluoride sludge into waterways, defectively designed automobiles, or undisclosed adverse effects of prescription drugs and pesticides. They are the first to grasp the technical capabilities to prevent existing product or pollution hazards. But they are very often the last to speak out.

Congress also noticed this anomaly and therefore started to include "employee protection sections" in federal safety and environmental laws. The sections are designed to protect from retaliation employees who bring to governmental attention hazards regulated under these laws. The protections include provision for a hearing before an Department of Labor examiner. In general, however, the Department has not been aggressive in enforcing the protections; it has even neglected to issue procedures or to notify employees of the existence of their protections. For example, Glenn Greenwald, learned too late that he was required to file his complaint within 30 days after being fired.

In areas not covered by employee protection legislation, the courts have occasionally intervened on behalf of employees who were dismissed by private organizations for attempting to uphold the law. Thus, for example, the West Virginia Supreme Court ruled in favor of a bank employee who complained of retaliation for trying to bring his employer into compliance with state consumer protection laws. The Court found that "the rule that an employer has an absolute right to discharge at will an employee must be tempered by the principle that, where the employer's motivation for the discharge is to contravene some substantial public policy principle, then the employer may be liable to the employee for damages occasioned by the discharge."[9]

In the case of federal employees, Congress concluded that "whistleblowers" need special protection. The case which was most effective in convincing Congress of this fact was that involving A. Ernest Fitzgerald, a cost analyst (civilian employee) for the Air Force.

In brief, after Fitzgerald disclosed to a congressional committee a $2 billion cost overrun on the C-5A military air transport development contract, his civil service tenure was found to have been granted by a computer error (an extremely rare discovery) and then Secretary of the Air Force, Robert C. Seamans, abolished Fitzgerald's job as part of a "retrenchment program."[10] Fitzgerald spent years in the courts and hundreds of thousands of dollars in legal expenses before he was finally reinstated.

In response to such cases, Congress included a section in the Civil Service Reform Act of 1978 barring reprisals by federal officials against employees who disclose information "concerning the existence of any activity which the employee . . . reasonably believes constitutes . . . mismanagement . . . or a substantial and specific danger to the public health or safety." However, under the Reagan administration, the Office of Special Counsel, which was set up to protect whistle-blowers, turned down 99 percent of the cases that came to it because, in the special counsel's view, "most whistle-blowers are malcontents."[11]

Even with conscientious enforcement, no amount of due-process protection will protect dissenters who have become *persona non grata* in their organizations from subtle harassment. For such circumstances, in which work situations are made demoralizing by managements who want to be rid of employees but do not retaliate against them openly, additional remedies must be sought. One possibility suggested to us is a job placement service that would give a high priority to finding positions for conscientious dissenters whose employment situations have become untenable; such services could be operated by professional societies.

Dealing With The Issues

Whatever due-process protections to dissenting professional employees are provided will have little value, however, unless they are imbedded in a process which deals effectively with the substance of the dissent. Those who would develop due-process procedures for dissenters must keep in mind the necessity for providing open and balanced reviews of the issues being raised. Too often review groups present unsubstantiated conclusions which cast doubt on the integrity of the review process and become the foci of new controversies.

Fortunately, to some extent the protection of conscientious dissent will facilitate the development of impartial reviews: if dissenters cannot be silenced, it becomes more difficult to ignore their concerns.

In summary, then, silencing dissenters as bearers of ill-tidings may seem in the short term to be the simplest way to deal with the difficult problems which they raise. But, in the longer term, enhancing the professionalism of scientists and engineers, and defending them when they follow its dictates, are vital to the welfare of our entire society.

The Importance of
Defending Andrei Sakharov

Andrei Sakharov understood many years ago the importance of dissent to international security:[1] "international confidence depends on public opinion and on open society." Sakharov understood that, unless people can speak freely to their fellow citizens and to the citizens of other nations, then the basis is laid for war. His special understanding of the destructive power of nuclear weapons gave his message special urgency:[2]

> A complete destruction of cities, industry, transport, and systems of education, a poisoning of fields, water, and air by radioactivity, a physical destruction of the larger part of mankind, poverty, barbarism, a return to savagery, and a genetic degeneracy of the survivors under the impact of radiation, a destruction of the material and information basis of civilization—this is a measure of the peril that threatens the world as a result of the estrangement of the world's two superpowers.

Sakharov must have known, when in 1968 he first spoke out publicly for openness in his manifesto, *Progress, Coexistence, and Intellectual Freedom*, that a confrontation with the traditionally authoritarian Russian government would be inevitable. His special contributions to the development of the Soviet H-bomb, however, endowed him with a special responsibility to speak out and with a special opportunity to be heard.

And Sakharov was heard again and again after 1968 to the point where in 1975 the Norwegian Parliament, in its citation for the 1975 Nobel Peace Prize Award, characterized him as "the spokesman for the conscience of mankind."

Now we read in our newspapers of other courageous citizens of the Soviet Union who have lost their livelihoods for speaking out in defense of Sakharov.[3] Courage—like cowardice—is infectious.

We citizens of the United States have little to lose by speaking out in support of Sakharov. We stand to lose a great deal, however, if we do not come effectively to his defense.

Sakharov is a truly unique figure. World opinion is aroused as perhaps never before by the embarrassed attempts of the Soviet government to silence him. Not even the thick-skinned Russian leadership can ignore the moral force of aroused world opinion. It is out of grudging respect for world opinion that they tolerated Sakharov in the past. It is understandable that, in a society in which public criticism of government policy is routinely construed as a criminal act, Sakharov's outspoken condemnation of the Soviet invasion of Afghanistan must have seemed intolerable. If there is to be any hope for an evolution of a peaceful world order, however, world public opinion must insist on the continued toleration of Sakharov. It is at times of crisis when governments are considering the use of arms that the world needs dissenters the most.

It is not a long step from the argument that science can have no integrity unless scientific work is exposed to uninhibited peer review to the argument that potentially catastrophic weaknesses will be built into the edifice of public policy unless knowledgeable observers can freely criticize its design and construction. Indeed, Sakharov started down the road of dissent by coming to the aid of those scientists who were attempting to free Soviet biological research from the authoritarianism of Lysenko.[4]

Although Sakharov's exile may be related to the cooling of relations between the U.S. and USSR, it is important to make clear to the Soviet people that our protests are individual acts of conscience, not part of any U.S. government effort to move us back into a Cold War. The Soviet government will not be impressed, however, unless a significant number of scientists take some concrete and sustained action. Indeed, we have a credibility problem because our past protests on behalf of Soviet dissidents of lesser stature were solely verbal. As a KGB general told the dissident Benjamin Levich:[5]

Scientists and intellectuals like to speak, but they do nothing concrete; they make appeals to the Soviet authorities, but later they say that the protests and appeals were not serious.

The Executive Committee of the Federation of American Scientists has, therefore, proposed one method by which individual scientists can commit themselves to the support of Andrei Sakharov. This is a pledge:

> I assert my intention of refusing to participate in official bilateral scientific exchange with the Soviet government, and its scientific representatives, either here or in the Soviet Union, until such time as Andrei Sakharov is released from internal exile.

We do not ask—nor do we desire—that all U.S. scientists sign this pledge. We do not want scientific exchange ended across the board for many reasons, not least of all that it would destroy the significance of our individual refusals. Indeed, the force of the protest will be strengthened if some scientists complain *while* engaging in scientific cooperation. But do not cooperate without communicating clearly to your Soviet contacts your feelings about the treatment of Sakharov.

In this regard, our strategy avoids the dilemmas implicit in framing the issue as one of "boycott" or "no boycott." By permitting individuals to decide themselves whether to continue cooperating, or refusing to cooperate—and by making refusals temporary and contingent on the release of Sakharov—our method puts pressure on the Soviet Union, *without* rupturing scientific communications. It differs completely from a "boycott" in not putting pressure on others to join. And it is based on the natural idea of refusing to cooperate until Andrei Sakharov gets his rights back to cooperate with us.

THE NUCLEAR ARMS RACE

The Freeze and the Counterforce Race

WITH HAROLD FEIVESON

A 1980 report to the Carter administration speculated on how the Soviet Union might respond to the deployment of U.S. weapons capable of destroying Soviet missiles in their silos:[1]

> . . . adopting a launch-on-warning posture is perhaps the least expensive but the most potentially destabilizing and dangerous response option available to Soviet leaders.

Despite this risk, by 1980 the United States was already embarked on a massive effort to threaten Soviet silos. Similarly, despite the obvious danger that the U.S. would adopt a policy of launching its missiles on warning of a Soviet attack, the Soviet Union had several years earlier initiated a massive deployment of missiles equipped with accurate multiple independently targetable reentry vehicles—"MIRVs"—capable of threatening U.S. land-based missiles (see Figure 1).

This reckless superpower competition to develop "counterforce" weapons—that is, weapons designed to destroy the nuclear weapons of the adversary—finally provoked in the early 1980s a popular movement in the United States to "freeze" the nuclear-arms race. In the words of the Nuclear Weapons Freeze Campaign's *Call to Halt the Nuclear Arms Race*,[2] this would be

> a mutual freeze on the testing, production and deployment of nuclear weapons and of missiles and new aircraft designed primarily to deliver nuclear weapons.

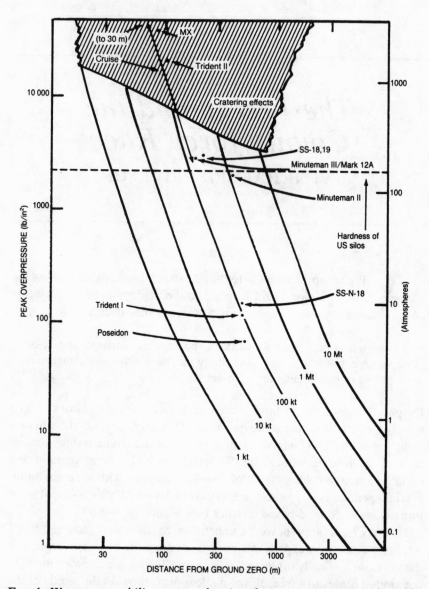

FIG. 1. *Weapon capability curves showing the overpressures produced by warheads of various yields as a function of distance from ground zero. Such curves indicate the capabilities of weapons to destroy hard targets. Cratering effects may knock out silos that are hard enough to escape destruction by overpressure;*[10] *silos in the shaded region would be covered by debris to a depth of at least 4 m. The points shown for various U.S. and Soviet warheads indicate estimated yields and median miss distances.*[13,15]

Voters in states and cities representing a third of the country's population passed resolutions similar to this.

While a freeze would catch in its net many nuclear-weapons systems, it was to counterforce systems that President Reagan referred when he rejected the idea of a bilateral freeze on the nuclear-arms race. He stated[3] that such a freeze would "only codify existing Soviet advantages," and he made clear that his administration was determined to deploy a new generation of counterforce missiles. This set the stage for a sustained national debate on U.S. policy toward counterforce weapons.

We believe that a freeze on the counterforce race then and now would be in the interests of both the U.S. and the USSR, above all because it would forestall a destabilizing enhancement of each side's first-strike capabilities.

Why Counterforce?

Because, to a considerable degree, opposition to a freeze and support for counterforce programs are two sides of the same coin, we must ask, "Why build up counterforce capabilities?" The answer appears to have many facets: the symbolic value of nuclear weapons as the "big sticks" upon which the superpowers depend as their ultimate recourse if they get into serious trouble abroad, the image held by many nuclear-weapons decision makers of a zero-sum competition between the two superpowers, and the almost inevitable progress in the areas of technology that are critical for missile accuracy.

A key factor spurring the U.S. side of the counterforce race has been an effort by the U.S. to make credible its willingness to use nuclear weapons in areas where U.S. conventional forces alone might be insufficient to deter Soviet aggression. During the 1950s, the United States promised all-out nuclear attacks against the Soviet Union, if Soviet actions threatened U.S. vital interests. However, such threats of "massive retaliation" against the Soviet population for anything other than an all-out Soviet nuclear attack on the U.S. became less and less credible as the Soviet Union built up its own nuclear arsenal.

Therefore, the U.S. shifted the focus of its nuclear threats to targets whose destruction would not quite be the equivalent of the destruction of Soviet society. The obvious targets for such threats were the Soviet military and, in particular, their nuclear weapons aimed at the U.S.

In the associated arms race, each side has tried to threaten the other and foil the threats against its own nuclear weapons. In the case of the intercontinental ballistic missiles (ICBMs), it has, until recently, been a race between the hardening of underground silos on one side and the number and accuracy of the ICBM warheads on the other. It is in this race that some have seen the Soviet Union as being ahead of the U.S., thereby weakening the ability of the U.S. to affect the decisions of the Soviet and other governments.[5]

Thus, in 1980, the Carter administration in its justification of the counterforce capabilities of the proposed MX land-based missile claimed that[1]

An asymmetry in hard-target-kill capability could lead to perceptions of Soviet advantage that could have adverse political and military implications including: (1) greater Soviet and less U.S. freedom of action in the employment of conventional forces . . .

In 1982, General Lew Allen Jr, then Chief of the Air Force, in a closed hearing before the Senate Armed Services Committee, stated that even though the developing vulnerability of U.S. ICBMs was[6]

perhaps not dangerous in that it will incite them [the Soviets] to first strike, it nevertheless gives them confidence in their nuclear forces. That confidence means that we will find the threshold of nuclear war much higher than in the past, and we will see greater Soviet confidence in their ability to be adventuresome and provocative to the United States across a broad range of areas.

General Allen is widely considered a moderate in matters of nuclear-weapons policy. Yet he argued in favor of keeping the threshold of nuclear war low!

Richard DeLauer, the Reagan administration's Undersecretary of Defense for Research and Engineering, indicated the same priorities when he worried that[7]

increases in nuclear hardness of Soviet ICBM silos and other important facilities have reduced our ability to put those targets at risk. Knowing this the Soviets feel less constrained from adventurism around the world . . .

Another purpose of the Reagan administration in pursuing increased counter-silo capabilities was to undermine the economy of the Soviet Union by forcing it to initiate costly programs of military investments in new mobile strategic systems or even active missile defense. Thus, in the

Reagan administration's first five-year defense guidance document, the Defense Department was advised to develop weapons that[8]

are difficult for the Soviets to counter, impose disproportionate costs, open up new areas of major military competition and obsolesce previous Soviet investments.

Unfortunately, when the USSR decided that its fixed land-based missiles were becoming obsolete and began to deploy mobile land-based missiles that were less vulnerable to attack by accurate warheads, the U.S. began to complain that these missiles would also be more difficult to count by "national technical means" (primarily satellites) and therefore to eliminate by agreement. And, if either side decides to deploy a defense of its ICBM silos, the result could be the abrogation of the Treaty on the Limitation of Antiballistic Missile Systems.

A final reason for the drive by both sides toward counterforce capabilities has been that it is the path of least resistance. With major laboratories working continuously on more accurate systems, as well as new warhead designs and new delivery vehicles, techniques for improvement will be found. Once new technology is available—and it is often available at relatively modest cost—the defense establishments usually find it irresistible. This is especially so for counterforce weapons, which both the U.S. and Soviet military see as more usable and appropriate to traditional military roles than "city-busting" deterrent forces.

The Chimera of Limited War

An important element in the analyses used to justify efforts to improve counterforce capabilities is the idea that it might be possible to fight a nuclear counterforce war in a carefully controlled manner. But because command and control are inevitably vulnerable to nuclear destruction, it is extremely doubtful that a nuclear war could be limited and prevented from escalating into an all-out civilization-shattering exchange.

One reason why it would be difficult to limit a strategic nuclear exchange is the vulnerability of strategic nuclear command and control systems. Such command and control systems can be "hardened" to some extent against nuclear attack, and the Reagan administration spent about $20 billion over five years for that purpose. But these systems will remain inherently more vulnerable than nuclear-weapons systems. As John Steinbruner, an expert in command and control, has pointed out[9]

. . . once the use of as many as ten or more nuclear weapons directly against the USSR is seriously contemplated, U.S. strategic commanders will likely insist on attacking the full array of Soviet military targets. Political motives for engaging in limited strategic attacks will not likely prevail against the risks of leaving a vulnerable command system exposed to counterattack from a severely provoked enemy.

Even if a nuclear exchange could be strictly limited to military targets, a strategically significant counterforce attack would probably cause tens of millions of civilian deaths. In the strategic literature, nuclear war often seems like a long-distance version of the artillery duels of World War I. The side-effects of the missile exchanges are labeled "collateral damage" and are seldom discussed. They are far from unimportant, however.

Hidden in the Defense Department's scenarios for limited strategic nuclear war, for example, are Soviet "barrage attacks" on U.S. air bases that house bombers and their refueling aircraft. In these scenarios, warheads of half-megaton size explode over and around the bases to destroy aircraft caught on the ground and aircraft that have just become airborne. The blast and heat from a single 0.5-megaton warhead exploded in the air over a B-52 base would kill the population in an area of the order of 100 square kilometers.[10] Barrage attacks on U.S. bomber bases would therefore destroy or partially destroy a number of urban areas. Such attacks would be still more damaging if, in a time of tension preceding the war, bombers were dispersed to major civilian airfields, as occurred during the 1962 Cuban missile crisis.

In the United States, ICBM bases are generally more isolated from nearby populations than are bomber and submarine bases. However, the Minuteman bases contain so many separate targets—150 to 200 silos, each of which is ordinarily assumed to be targeted by two half-megaton warheads—that the lethal radiation field from the overlapping fallout patterns would extend many hundred of miles downwind.[11]

As a result of all these effects, the Department of Defense was forced in 1975 by the Senate Foreign Relations Committee to admit[11] that a full-scale Soviet attack on U.S. ICBM, bomber and missile-submarine bases would kill 3 to 16 million Americans. More recent U.S. government estimates[12] have raised this range to 24 to 45 million. Estimates[12] of the consequences of a U.S. counterforce attack on Soviet strategic nuclear forces are of the same order of magnitude.

Dangers of Counterforce

Figure 1 shows some estimated yields and median miss distances, ordinarily termed "circular errors probable," or CEPs, of the various U.S. and Soviet counterforce warheads. These points are superimposed on a graph showing the peak overpressure felt by a silo as a function of the explosion's horizontal distance from the silo. One can see that warheads on ICBMs deployed in the 1970s—the U.S. Minuteman II and III equipped with Mark 12A warheads, and the Soviet SS-18 and SS-19—are expected to produce within their CEPs an overpressure equal to or beyond that which U.S. silos are designed to withstand. The labels at the top of the figure indicate that the successor generation of U.S. warheads—carried by the MX, Trident II and cruise missiles—are expected to be so accurate that their target would ordinarily be within the radius of cratering effects produced by a nuclear ground burst.

The principal threat to U.S. land-based missiles is the large number of accurate warheads carried by two types of large Soviet ICBMs. These Soviet missiles are designated the "SS-18" and "SS-19" by the U.S. Defense Department. The USSR has roughly 4,000 silo-lethal warheads on a total of almost 700 SS-18 and SS-19 ICBMs.[17]

Each warhead on the 1,000 U.S. Minuteman missiles is believed[13] to have a similar ability to destroy silos, but there are only 2,100 Minuteman warheads for 1,400 Soviet ICBM silos of all types, versus about four SS-18/19 warheads per U.S. silo. Therefore, given roughly equal destructive capability per warhead, a larger fraction of Soviet ICBMs might be expected to survive a U.S. first strike than *vice versa*.

The Reagan administration's initial plans[6,14] to increase the U.S. threat to Soviet missile silos included the following, as shown in Figure 2: at least 1,000 accurate high-yield warheads on a force of 100 MX missiles; thousands of silo-killing warheads on a force of new submarine-launched Trident II, or "D-5," ballistic missiles; several thousand warheads on slower but highly accurate air-, sea- and ground-launched cruise missiles; and 108 accurate Pershing II missiles, which could hit key targets in the western USSR within 10 minutes of being launched from West Germany.* The deployment of all these "hard-target killers" will make Soviet silo-based missiles at least as vulnerable as those of the U.S.

The Soviet Union has found this prospective vulnerability of its silo-based missiles disturbing. Only one-quarter of all U.S. strategic

* As of 1990, it appears that only 50 MX missiles will be deployed. The U.S.-USSR Intermediate Range Nuclear Forces Treaty requires the destruction of U.S. Pershing II and ground-launched cruise missiles.

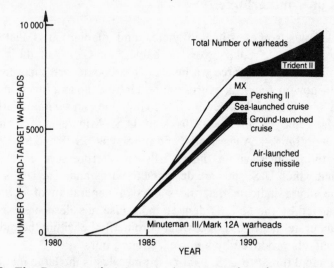

FIG. 2. *The Reagan administration's proposed nuclear-weapons "modernization" program included more than 10,000 new warheads, designed to be capable of destroying Soviet ICBM silos.*[6,14]

warheads are on ICBMs, but, in the early 1980's two-thirds of the Soviet Union's strategic warheads were based in silos. The other two legs of the Soviet "triad" were already somewhat vulnerable: The Soviet bomber force is much less capable than that of the U.S. and is not ordinarily on alert status; and the security of the small percentage of Soviet ballistic-missile submarines that are at sea at any one time has been somewhat eroded by enormous U.S. investments in large ocean sound-surveillance systems, nuclear attack submarines and antisubmarine aircraft.[1] (There is no comparable Soviet threat to U.S. ballistic-missile submarines.)

Under these circumstances, as the U.S. threat to Soviet missile silos has been growing, it is likely that the Soviet Union has been tempted to put its ICBMs on a launch-on-warning status and, would during periods of crisis, entertain ideas of preemptive attack.

An indication that the Soviet Union was at least considering launching its missiles on warning of U.S. attack appeared in an article by Soviet Defense Minister, Dmitri Ustinov in 1982:[18]

> With modern detection systems and the combat readiness of the Soviet Union's strategic nuclear forces, the United States would not be able to deal a crippling blow to the socialist countries. The aggressor will not be able to evade an all-crushing retaliatory strike.

The warning times involved in an attack could be less than 10 minutes, as Figure 3 shows. As Herbert York has pointed out, with a U.S. launch-on-warning policy, these short times mean that[19]

> the determination of whether or not doomsday has arrived will be made either by an automatic device designed for the purpose or by a preprogrammed President who, whether he knows it or not, will be carrying out orders written years before by some operations analyst.

Although the only chance—a very small one—for a successful use of counterforce weapons would be in a "preemptive" first strike, these weapons are represented by their proponents not as first-strike weapons, but as weapons that would only be used to destroy any enemy missiles held back in a first strike. This assertion is inherently implausible. If there were ever a time when a nation would be prepared to launch its nuclear weapons on warning it would be after it had struck first.

The Carter administration recognized the possibility of the Soviets being driven to a preemptive attack as one of the risks associated with the U.S. counterforce development program:[1]

> Under extreme crisis conditions Soviet leaders who had little confidence in the deterrent value of their own air-breathing, submarine and residual ICBM forces might perceive advantages in launching a first strike. In this context, such Soviet leaders might view the threat to their silo-based ICBM force as being of major concern since currently about 75 percent of Soviet strategic weapons . . . are in its fixed-silo ICBM force.

This danger was one of the fundamental rationales for the nuclear-weapons-freeze proposal.

Why Not a Bilateral Freeze?

The Reagan administration cited several objections to a bilateral freeze that went beyond its concern to protect U.S. counterforce programs. Its spokesmen argued that a freeze would be unverifiable, would lead to a loss of deterrent by eroding the ability of the U.S. to respond to a Soviet nuclear attack, and would reduce Soviet interest in negotiating arms reductions.[20] While such claims need detailed analysis, we raise here a few points of skepticism.

Although the opponents to a freeze focused on the weakest points of its

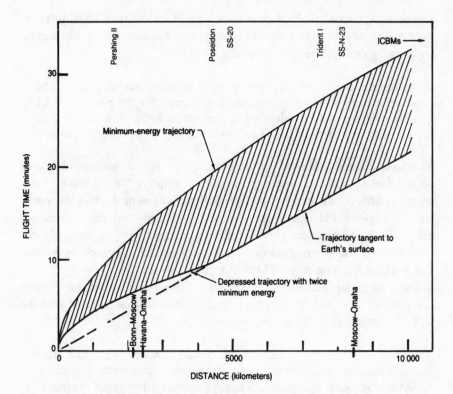

FIG. 3. *Travel times. The range of times required for warheads to follow ballistic trajectories between two points on the Earth's surface are shown here as a function of the great-circle distance between the two points. These times are upper limits on the times available for making decisions in launch-on-warning systems. The top of the band gives travel times on the "minimum-energy" trajectories, which require the minimum initial velocity for a given range. The bottom of the band gives times for circular orbits just above the Earth's surface. For short distances, the graph shows flight times along "depressed" ballistic trajectories of twice the minimum energy. Actual flight times would be 1–2 minutes longer than shown, principally because of the slower average speed of the warhead during the "boost" phase, when the average acceleration is on the order of a few times that of gravity. Also shown on the graph are a few relevant distances and the estimated full-load ranges of various U.S. and Soviet ballistic missiles.*[4.16]

verifiability, their attack should not obscure the fact that methods of verifying the most important elements of a freeze had already been worked out in considerable detail. For example, methods to verify compliance with prohibitions on flight testing and on deployment of new ballistic missiles were incorporated in the SALT II Treaty. Similarly, the United States and the Soviet Union have worked out verification procedures to monitor a nuclear test ban, including underground tests down to yields of one kiloton or so. Verification of certain other elements of a freeze, such as a ban on building cruise missiles, would be more difficult, but not impossible within acceptable limits of error, given the fact that the numbers of missiles already deployed are large. Given our vast intelligence-gathering capabilities and the comprehensive character of a freeze, it would be very difficult for the Soviet Union to conceal cheating on a scale sufficient to create a threat anywhere nearly as serious as that posed by the continuing nuclear arms race.

In addition, it was a mistake to assume that verification beyond "national technical means" would remain impractical. While the Soviet Union had not yet shown signs that it was about to convert itself into an open society, it had already agreed in the late 1970s, in negotiations on a Comprehensive Test Ban Treaty, to allow the U.S. to emplace sealed "black boxes" containing sensitive seismometers in strategic spots within the USSR. And, under the SALT I Treaty, the Soviet Union had participated constructively in the "standing consultative commission" in which each side had agreed to explain questionable activities detected by any of the multitude of telescopic "eyes" and electronic "ears" that continually monitor surface activities from outer space.

The Reagan administration claimed[20] that, in the long run, a freeze could erode U.S. deterrent capability by stopping the development of offensive nuclear systems, while allowing Soviet non-nuclear air defense and antisubmarine-warfare capabilities to develop unimpeded. In fact, under a freeze, a country's confidence in its ability to make a first strike would erode far more rapidly than its ability to deter a first strike by the other side. A first strike must be virtually perfect, with thousands of warheads coordinated in time and space to high precision. An effective deterrence force need be neither perfectly reliable nor highly accurate. For instance, the possibility that even a few bombers might get through an air defense system would represent a substantial deterrent to any rational political leader. As McGeorge Bundy, national security advisor to President Kennedy, has written,[21]

> . . . a decision that would bring even one hydrogen bomb on one city of one's own country would be recognized in advance as a catastrophic blunder; ten bombs on ten cities would be a disaster beyond history; and a hundred bombs on a hundred cities are unthinkable.

That said, it is true that freezing air-launched cruise-missile technology while allowing continued development of air-defense technology would erode the capabilities of both U.S. and Soviet bombers to deliver their weapons on target.

By contrast, the contest between antisubmarine-warfare systems and ballistic-missile submarines would be largely unaffected by a freeze. For under a freeze, as usually defined, submarines could be replaced by quieter models, equipped with the latest antisubmarine warfare counter-measures. Only the capabilities of the submarine-launched missiles would be frozen. The one capability of these missiles that is relevant to antisubmarine warfare is range, and this was already great enough in the early 1980s so that about half the equivalent megatonnage on both U.S. and Soviet submarine-launched ballistic missiles could reach the capital city of the other from home waters. Indeed, when asked about the superiority of the range of the Trident II missile over that of the Trident I, Rear Admiral William A. Williams III, director of the U.S. Navy's strategic and theater nuclear warfare division, stated in 1981 that[14]

> we are not advocating the D-5 [Trident II] because of its greater range. The C-4 [Trident I] has a very comfortable range.

Another problem with a nuclear-weapons freeze that would arise in the long run, according to the Reagan administration, is that U.S. strategic systems will begin to wear out earlier than their Soviet counterparts because they were generally deployed years earlier. In fact, most U.S. systems are not creaking with age. The Minuteman III and Poseidon missiles have all been deployed since 1970, and all Trident I missiles since 1980. Submarines are older, but as we pointed out here, they can be replaced. Only bombers—both U.S. and Soviet—would have a real problem with aging, and then only if a freeze lasted for decades. But, of course, the freeze was not proposed to last forever. It would serve best as a transition period between the arms race and genuine arms reductions.

Finally, we should emphasize once more that contrary to the impression given by Reagan administration spokesmen, significant parts of the U.S. strategic program that a freeze would have stopped, including the MX and Trident II programs, were aimed primarily at threatening Soviet nuclear missiles—not at reducing the vulnerability of our own.

The Reagan administration asserted that a freeze would weaken chances for deep reductions in strategic weapons, a goal of the then on-going "START" (Strategic Arms Reduction Talks) negotiations. It contended that only the threat of a vigorous U.S. buildup of strategic weapons would adequately motivate the Soviets to make a deal. The Reagan administration's declared passion for reductions, however, was belied by its refusal in START to offer to stop the deployment of any of the planned U.S. counterforce weapons. Only quantitative limits were proposed: Less than 1,600 ballistic missiles and bombers carrying a total of 6,000 warheads not more than 3,300 of which could be carried by ICBMs.

Within these quantitative limits, the Reagan administration proposed to pursue the technological arms race without constraint. The START Treaty will allow the United States to deploy the MX and Trident II missiles, while the older and less-threatening Poseidon, Trident I and Minuteman missiles are retired to bring the total warhead and missile count down to proposed limits. The counterforce race could, therefore, continue unconstrained under a START agreement and could indeed become more dangerous as the number of targets for a first strike are reduced faster than the number of warheads that could be directed against them. This would compound the historic mistake that the United States and Soviet Union made when they decided against seeking to include a ban on multiple independently targetable reentry vehicles in the SALT-I agreement.[22]

Role of Scientists

Scientists and engineers are not only the designers of nuclear weapons and their delivery systems, they also play key roles in developing "scenarios" for how these weapons might be used. Gerard Smith, chief U.S. negotiator in the SALT-I talks, recalls that[22]

> I sensed that civilian scientists and engineers in the office of the Secretary of Defense were more influential with Secretary [Melvin] Laird than professional military officers. These men would never have to be users of nuclear weapons. They were not members of military services with experience in fighting wars but a kind of elite which knew or gave the impression of knowing the new secrets of the nuclear-missile age.

McGeorge Bundy has also testified to the unwillingness of national leaders to challenge these "nuclear gamesmen":[21]

> Presidents and Politburos may know in their hearts that the only thing they want from strategic weapons is never to have to use them;

in their public postures they have felt it necessary to claim more. They may not themselves be persuaded by the refined calculations of the nuclear gamesmen—but they do not find it prudent to expose them for the irrelevance they are. The public in both countries has been allowed by its leaders to believe that somewhere in ever growing strength there is safety and that it still means something to be "ahead." The politics of internal decision making has not been squared with the reality of international stalemate.

Independent scientists have also, however, on occasion played a key role in challenging the rationalizations that have been proposed for continuing the arms race.

Independent scientists participated on a significant scale in critiquing the 1967–1970 proposals by the Johnson and Nixon administrations to deploy a nationwide antiballistic-missile (ABM) system. The ABM debate began with a citizens' uprising—developing first around the suburban sites originally proposed for the nuclear-armed antimissile missiles. However, the opposition continued to broaden, even after the Nixon administration shifted the ABM sites away from populated areas—in part because critical scientists used the forums created by the initial uprising to focus public and congressional attention on the ABM's implications for the arms race.[23] Thus, Hans Bethe opened his March 4, 1969 talk at a teach-in at MIT as follows:[24]

> I believe that most of the audience here is against the ABM, and I believe that I am here to tell you why.

The ABM debate in the U.S. educated both the U.S. public and the Soviet leaderships about the difficulties of missile defense, difficulties the military leadership on both sides had refused to admit. As a result, while neither political leadership was strong enough to impose unilateral abstention from an ABM race on their militaries, together they were able to prevent the nuclear-arms race from expanding into this new dimension.

Times of rising public concern about nuclear weapons create opportunities for scientists to explain to the public the even greater dangers and futility of the counterforce race. Scientists can help to define specific bilateral freeze agreements that are adequately verifiable and that can be used as a starting point for nuclear-arms reductions.

Debating Edward Teller

I n the November 1982 issue of *Reader's Digest*, Edward Teller attacked what he described as six "dangerous myths about nuclear arms." Teller stated, in the concluding paragraph of his article, that "Our first step toward stability, toward improving the prospects for peace and for the security of all people, must be the replacement of myths with knowledge." Unfortunately, however, the primary focus of Teller's article was not on raising the level of the public debate about the nuclear arms race, but on peddling his own myths.

Teller's myths about the nuclear arms race can be roughly summarized as follows:

1. *The Soviets have strategic superiority.*
2. *The U.S. nuclear deterrent has become doubtful.*
3. *The effects of nuclear war could be easily mitigated.*
4. *Soviet civil defense could be highly effective.*
5. *Defensive nuclear weapons could protect us.*
6. *You can't negotiate with the Soviets.*

Since these myths were widely believed within the Reagan administration and have been popularized by influential groups such as the Committee for the Present Danger as well as by Teller,[1] arguments put forward in support of them are well worth examining. For each of Teller's myths, the relevant passages from the *Reader's Digest* article are quoted below and it is then explained why the passages are misleading or false.

1. The Soviets have strategic superiority.

Between 1966 and 1981 the total megatonnage of the American nuclear arsenal was *reduced* to less than one half its former size. The Soviet arsenal has rapidly increased in yield and diversity during the same period and currently includes a total nuclear explosive power in excess of what the United States ever had. (Emphasis in original.)

Because several bombs can accomplish more destruction than a single bomb with the same total yield, total megatonnage is not a very useful measure of the total destructive power of a nuclear arsenal. The ordinary measure of destructiveness against large targets such as cities is "equivalent megatonnage." By this measure, the U.S. arsenal in 1981 was only about two-thirds as powerful as that of the Soviet Union.[2] The difference is unimportant, however, since both the U.S. and Soviet strategic arsenals are far into the region of "overkill" for such targets. The U.S. arsenal, for example, had in aggregate about 10 times the destructive power, which would suffice, according to conservative 1968 Department of Defense calculations, to destroy one-third of the Soviet population and three-quarters of its industrial capacity (400 equivalent megatons).[3]

The decline in the megatonnage of the U.S. strategic arsenal between 1966 and 1981 did not occur because of attrition or neglect. It was a by-product of repeated cycles of modernization. Perhaps the most important change was the replacement of most of the U.S. single-warhead ballistic missiles by missiles with accurate multiple warheads. The effective megatonnage of these missiles did not change greatly, but the number of military targets they could attack increased severalfold. The equivalent megatonnage carried by U.S. heavy bombers declined, as older bombers were retired and the typical payload of those remaining was changed from a few multi-megaton bombs to a mix of a larger number of lower yield bombs, short-range attack missiles and air-launched cruise missiles.

As of 1981, the United States had about 7,000 warheads mounted on missiles, plus a modernized bomber fleet, which by itself carried about 2,000 warheads. The average equivalent megatonnage of U.S. strategic warheads was still about seven times that of the bomb that destroyed Hiroshima.[2]

The Soviets have built the most powerful single weapons ever constructed. Militarily such weapons have very limited value, but as a blackmail threat against free-world cities, they seem to be quite effective.

In 1981, the USSR was believed to have 50 to 100 missiles carrying single warheads heavy enough to be in the 10- to 20-megaton class.[2] The United States had 52 Titan II missiles carrying comparable (9-megaton) warheads and had, in its strategic stockpile, bombs of similar yield designed to be delivered by B-52 bombers.[4] Since the United States had enough lower-yield nuclear warheads to destroy all Soviet cities many times over, these large warheads were being retired by the Reagan administration.

> The American [missile] silos are not reloadable. The Soviet silos are. This is not a breach of the treaty. American negotiators, neglecting the possibility that the Soviets might not have an equal urge to disarm, failed to insert an essential clause.

Presumably, Teller is referring here to the SALT II Treaty whose ratification by the United States he opposed. If so, his statement is false. The Treaty (Article IV, paragraph 5) explicitly states that both sides will neither "develop, test or deploy systems for rapid reload of intercontinental ballistic-missile (ICBM) launchers" nor "store ICBMs in excess of normal deployment requirements at launch sites of ICBM launchers."

The only factual basis for Teller's statement is that some Soviet missiles, like the U.S. MX missile, would be ejected from their silos before their engines were ignited ("cold launch") and the silos could therefore be reused. Former Air Force Deputy Chief of Staff for Research and Development, General Kelly Burke, has testified, however, that such reloading would take "on the order of two or three days as about a minimum time. . . . If that area has been struck by our nuclear weapons, then it might not be possible for them to get in at all."[5]

2. The U.S. nuclear deterrent has become doubtful.

> We do have sufficient power to create great damage, particularly to the Soviet industrial plant, *if* our retaliatory forces are safe from a first strike. They are not safe, however, and their deterrent effect has become doubtful. (Emphasis in original.)

Teller was presumably talking here about the "window of vulnerability," popularized by President Reagan and the Committee on the Present

Danger. According to their nightmare, the Soviet Union could, in a first strike, theoretically destroy 80 to 90 percent of U.S. missile silos by using two warheads on each silo. It is seldom noted, however, that such a first strike would be more disarming of the Soviet Union than of the United States, since on average, less than one U.S. warhead would be destroyed for each Soviet warhead expended. (There are, on average, about two warheads in each U.S. missile silo.)

Furthermore, each of the three legs of the U.S. strategic "triad" (silo-based ICBMs, submarine-based ballistic missiles, and bombers) is designed so that by itself it could destroy the Soviet Union. In 1981, more than 15 U.S. ballistic-missile submarines were always at sea (where they are generally agreed to be invulnerable). These submarines carried about 2,500 warheads, with each warhead possessing two to four times the equivalent megatonnage of the Hiroshima bomb. And the 30 percent of the U.S. bomber force, which was prepared to take off immediately on warning of missile attack, carried about 400 one-megaton bombs, plus a similar number of short-range nuclear attack missiles.[2]

In addition, the United States had dispersed around the periphery of the Soviet Union, hundreds of nuclear-armed land- and carrier-based fighter bombers. These aircraft were capable of reaching the Soviet Union with megaton-sized bombs.

A single one-megaton bomb would probably suffice to destroy Moscow. To make sure, Teller would probably insist on several bombs. In either case, it was simply absurd for him to state that the deterrent effect of the thousands of warheads which the United States could deliver on the Soviet Union, even after a Soviet first strike, had "become doubtful." They would deter anyone other than a lunatic from striking first.

3. The effects of nuclear war could be easily mitigated.

The radioactivity of fallout declines rapidly. For example, if 1,000 rems per hour (a lethal dose) were released by a bomb, seven hours later the dose would be 100 rems per hour (far below lethal). In 49 hours radiation from this fallout would be reduced to 10 rems per hour. . . .

Unwary readers could be misled by this statement into believing that it would be safe to come out of fallout shelters when the radiation level had fallen to 100 rems per hour. That is not true. Although the dose *rate* at seven hours might be only 100 rems per hour, one would still receive a lethal dose (200 to 600 rems) after several hours outside.[6] Even if one stayed in a shelter for about 49 hours, by which time, in Teller's hypothetical case, one would be receiving a dose rate of only about 10 rems per hour, the accumulated dose would still build up to a lethal level after a few days. Indeed, the dose rate of about one rem per hour after two weeks would still be high enough to limit the amount of time one could spend outdoors.

Since ordinary fallout shelters would be less than 100 percent effective in keeping out radiation and would probably provide otherwise very unhealthy conditions, their surviving occupants would have a much reduced resistance to radiation, disease, starvation and the other challenges of the hostile postwar environment.[7]

Radiation from fallout of the intensity described would be limited to the immediate vicinity of the explosion and the adjacent areas downwind. People in these areas could move to uncontaminated regions. (Decontamination is feasible if we prepare for it.)

One of the few government studies relevant to this question has estimated that an attack on the United States with a megatonnage about equal to that in the Soviet strategic arsenal in 1981 would cover about one-quarter of the area of the 48 contiguous states with fallout heavier than the example discussed by Teller.[8] If people took Teller's advice and left their shelters in an attempt to escape such fallout radiation zones, they would be exposed to the full intensity of the radiation field during the period of transit. It is unlikely that in most cases this transit period would be less than hours. For people traveling on foot, it could be days. It would seem far safer, therefore, to remain inside whatever shelter was available in the fallout zone for at least the first week.

There is nothing in the literature which supports Teller's suggestion that one would be able to decontaminate large enough areas to reduce greatly the risk to the population from fallout.

Few people realize the following facts about the effects of the Hiroshima and Nagasaki bombings. Earth-covered conventional bomb shelters practically under the air-burst atomic bombs were essentially undamaged even though blast and fire destroyed all other buildings in the area.

Note that Teller does not say that *people* survived, in these "earth-covered conventional bomb shelters." Such a shelter might survive the firestorm which followed the Hiroshima explosion. It is unlikely, however, that its occupants would survive the heat and lack of oxygen.*

> 1.6 to 3.1 miles [from the ground zeros of Hiroshima and Nagasaki] 98 percent of the inhabitants—283,000 people—survived.

At 1.6 miles from ground zero at Hiroshima and Nagasaki, the peak blast overpressure was less than three pounds per square inch and, at 3.1 miles, the peak overpressure was less than one pound per square inch. These are much lower than the peak overpressures which would be typical in either U.S. or Soviet urban areas during an all-out nuclear war. For the United States, it has been estimated that one-half of the urban population would be exposed to overpressures in excess of 15 pounds per square inch.[8] This corresponds to distances of less than one-half mile from ground zero at Hiroshima and Nagasaki—well within the area of total destruction where only a very small percentage of the population survived.[9]

4. Soviet civil defense could be highly effective.

> The landmass of the USSR is more than twice that of the United States; its urban concentration proportionately much lower.

Urban population density (people per square mile in cities) has nothing to do with national land mass. In fact, because the relative absence of automobiles has allowed much less urban sprawl, the Soviet Union's average urban concentration is about *twice* as high as that of the United States. Even the Soviet *rural* population is relatively concentrated. One-half of the Soviet rural population lives in an area about one-tenth as large as that of United States.[10]

> Under Soviet civil-defense plans, nonessential city workers would be evacuated if the immediate danger of war (or intent for a Soviet first strike) arose. The evacuees would build crude but effective shelters in the countryside according to well-prepared instructions.

This refers to another of the nightmares popularized by Teller and the Committee on the Present Danger.[11] According to this scenario:

---

* Actually, upon further reading, I learned that the fires at Hiroshima did not have the intensity of a true firestorm and that it might have been possible to survive in an underground shelter.

· The Soviets evacuate their cities before a nuclear war. (Much of the population would have to travel on foot since there are few private automobiles and available buses and trucks would be insufficient to evacuate more than a fraction of the urban population.)
· The evacuees build effective underground fallout shelters using only materials locally available in the fields and forests.
· Each shelter is supplied with a two-week supply of water, food, tools, lanterns, a radiation dosimeter and a radio, plus medical, sanitary and other necessary survival supplies.
· The population stays in these shelters for the two weeks or so required for the intensity of the fallout radiation field to decrease to the point where it would be safe to spend significant periods outside.

It seems likely that at least some of the subscribers to *Reader's Digest* might have become skeptical if Teller had described his nightmare at even this level of detail. Indeed, it appears that he might be suspending his own disbelief since he has apparently not bothered to ask himself how, even if the Soviet population survived for two weeks on emergency supplies, it would survive in the longer term with: no fuel for its transport or agricultural machinery; its farm animals dead from radiation; and its urban housing, factories, hospitals, and distribution systems destroyed. Many of those who have looked at the corresponding situation of the United States after an all-out nuclear war, have concluded that the population surviving in the short term would subsequently go into a downward spiral, as stocks of food, fuel, medicines, pesticides and critical equipment were exhausted before the capability to replace them could be restored.[12]

Of course, evacuation of Soviet cities would eliminate the element of surprise, which would be the principal advantage of a first strike. Upon observing the evacuation, the United States would presumably put its land-based missiles on a launch-on-warning status, send every available missile-equipped submarine to sea and put a much larger proportion of its nuclear bombers and nuclear-capable fighter bombers on a high-alert status.

5. Defensive nuclear weapons could protect us.

Extremely important research is being conducted on systems to defend against incoming nuclear missiles. For example, exploding a very small nuclear bomb near an attack missile as it enters the upper-to-middle atmosphere over our nation would have no effects on the ground and negligible effects on the atmosphere, but could totally *disarm* the incoming missile without *detonating* it. Such a system, used to protect our vulnerable missile silos, could be an important first step in improving both our current retaliatory position and directing our policy toward defense. The nuclear-freeze movement would end further work on what could be the best defense systems. (Emphasis in original.)

Here Teller stakes out his traditional position that continuing the nuclear arms race would be safer than stopping it. He claims specifically that antiballistic missiles (ABMs) armed with nuclear warheads may make possible an effective defense for U.S. missile silos. Elsewhere—apparently including a private meeting with President Reagan—he went much further and argued that "third generation" of nuclear weapons might make possible a defense of the *entire nation* against Soviet nuclear attack.[13]

Success in the defense of a missile silo can be defined as preventing the attacker from destroying it in a surprise attack without using more warheads than the silo contains. As has been pointed out above (Myth 2), this condition corresponds, for U.S. missile silos, to an average expenditure of two Soviet warheads per silo destroyed and is already met today without *any* ABM defense. The additional protection offered by such a defense would probably be quite modest. It is doubtful, for example, whether an ABM system would be effective in defending a silo containing a ten-warhead MX missile against an attack involving ten Soviet warheads.[14]

In any case, defense of the entire nation, or even its major cities, against nuclear attack would be enormously more difficult than defending hard missile silos. Silo defense requires only moderate confidence of preventing up to a few nuclear warheads from coming very close to a silo for long enough to allow launch of its missile. In contrast, city defense requires almost perfect success for the duration of the war, keeping thousands of hostile nuclear warheads miles away from targets which themselves cover tens to thousands of square miles. An added complication is the fact that nuclear warheads could be delivered by routes other than through space. Some could even be emplaced in advance, having been shipped as ordinary freight.

6. You can't negotiate with the Soviets.

We have negotiated for 25 years, and the results are readily visible. Why would a totalitarian empire that depends on military force to maintain its power voluntarily disarm itself?

The Soviet Union did not, of course, deploy nuclear weapons in order to maintain internal order in its empire. Furthermore, no foreseeable nuclear-arms-control agreement would come near disarming either superpower. Nevertheless, more limited arms-control agreements could reduce the danger of nuclear war and are achievable because they are in the interests of the Soviet Union as well as all other nations.

Arms-control negotiations between 1957 and 1982 were not entirely fruitless. They included the Limited Test Ban Treaty, the Nonproliferation Treaty, the ABM Treaty and the SALT II Treaty. (The last treaty was signed but not ratified.) Teller opposed many, if not all, of these treaties and has played a leading role in the efforts to prevent the consummation of a comprehensive nuclear test-ban treaty. His assignment to the Soviet Union of the full responsibility for the lack of greater success in nuclear arms control negotiations was therefore excessively modest.

For more than 40 years Edward Teller has promised the American public increased security just around the next corner of the nuclear arms race, using arguments such as those put forward in his *Reader's Digest* article.

Meanwhile, U.S. immunity to destruction by other nations was irretrievably lost, and the nuclear arms race focused on the development and deployment of first-strike weapons—a folly which led to hair-trigger, launch-on-warning postures and possibly irreversible deployment of thousands of easy to hide cruise and other mobile missile systems.[15] Adopting Teller's proposal to deploy extensive ABM systems would violate the ABM treaty and would trigger another futile and destabilizing offense-defense race.

There is no forseeable way in which we can eliminate the existing "balance of terror" by continuing the nuclear arms race. That can only be done by negotiation. Teller's article was apparently motivated by his nightmare that the nuclear weapons freeze movement might force the United States once again into serious arms control negotiations with the Soviet Union. Fortunately, this one of Teller's nightmares came true.

EDWARD TELLER'S RESPONSE

A subject that generates strong emotions also generates strong convictions which are not easily turned around by reason. The March 1983 issue of the *Bulletin of the Atomic Scientists* presented a reprint of my article from *Reader's Digest*, "Dangerous Myths About Nuclear Weapons," and an article by Frank von Hippel, "The Myths of Edward Teller." The controversy to which these articles refer has become so heated that it seems helpful to begin by emphasizing a point on which von Hippel and I agree.

Two of the myths I discuss in the *Reader's Digest* article involve scientific matters much misunderstood by the general public: that nuclear weapons will create radiation or damage to the ozone layer sufficient to create an apocalypse. I am gratified that von Hippel offers not one word suggesting that a nuclear war would be the end of the human race.

In my article, I called attention to an erroneous idea which by repetition has been elevated to the status of myth: "The Soviet and American nuclear stockpiles are close to identical." The Soviets emphasize explosives of high megatonnage which are particularly potent as instruments of terror and are the only ones that constitute any danger to the stratosphere. Incidentally, the only thorough analyses of this latter danger have been carried out in the Lawrence Livermore National Laboratory.[16–24]

The fact is that the Soviet nuclear striking power is much more potent and reliable than ours. The rough quantitative comparison becomes clearer when one examines the available nuclear military forces item by item. In land-based missiles, the Soviets have a five- or six-to-one advantage in explosive power. For us, a first strike is completely excluded, but unfortunately, the same cannot be said about the Soviets, who seem to see such a first strike as a preventive measure. A Soviet first strike could completely disarm our land-based missiles.

In bomber forces, we are superior. However, both the number of bombers that would be able to take off and, more important, the number that would penetrate Soviet air space is very questionable. While we completely lack air defenses against Soviet bombers, Soviet air defense is practically overwhelming—a fact that will not be changed by putting our bombers on alert following indications of tension or impending attack.

In submarine-carried explosives, we are approximately equal. The public assumes that submarines are safe from attack. Indeed, the Navy is keeping existing doubts so secret that even many responsible naval officers remain in ignorance about real dangers that may arise from advanced technology in detecting submarines. Even if submarines remain effective, their weapons are targeted against industrial and—regrettably— civilian targets. A force less oriented against military power than against innocent bystanders is adduced by von Hippel as an effective equalizer, but leaves me wishing for a thorough change.

Nuclear war is not inevitable. I do not believe that the Soviet Union will start such a war, unless they feel sure of overwhelming superiority and indisputable success. I believe this situation does not yet exist. But the Soviets appear to be superior, and surely are making more rapid progress than we.

Perhaps the most important part of my difference with von Hippel is connected with civil defense. His attitude toward civil defense—which would blunt the effects of nuclear war damage—is particularly hard for me to understand. In view of the possibility of nuclear war, the most urgent and important duty seems to me to be to achieve the best possible preparedness of civilian protection. We must remember that our forces going on alert in case of a Soviet urban evacuation will not save a single American life unless this alert succeeds in deterring war.

Two widely, but wrongly held, assumptions are present in the accusation that civil-defense plans are not effective. The first is that inexpensive shelters cannot be well designed, sanitary and safe to a protection factor of 1,000. They can indeed be so designed and constructed.[25] The second is that the conventional bomb shelters held no survivors in the atomic bombings in Japan. In Hiroshima, an all-clear sounded before the bomb was dropped, so there were no people in the shelters. In Nagasaki, the several people in a conventional tunnel shelter *located one-third of a mile from ground zero* survived with minimal or no injury.[26]

The idea that Soviet cities would be evacuated, that individual families would build effective underground fallout shelters, have adequate and appropriate supplies and remain in their shelters for a few weeks has a basis in fact and sound planning.[27,28] Anyone doubtful of the ability of the Soviet transportation system to provide for such an evacuation in a tense situation should examine the Soviet evacuation, not only of personnel but of entire vital industries, which was conducted in 1941 during the fantastic progress of the Nazi invasion.

Radiation is indeed a hazard, and von Hippel, in fact, does not disagree with my quantitative statements on this topic. It should be noted that, while population centers in the Soviet Union could be hit very hard, as von Hippel points out, the greater size of the country and the smaller megatonnage on our side would expose them to a lesser degree of fallout. In fact, this point is indirectly conceded in the discussion of the area that Soviet superbombs would cover with fallout.

It is true that considerable portions of the United States could receive dose rates greater than 1,000 rem per hour in the first few hours after an attack. In a large-scale, civilian-oriented nuclear attack on the United States by the Soviet Union, about one-eighth to one-sixth of the United States, primarily the Great Lakes, Ohio River Valley and the East Coast, will sustain levels above lethal values for an *unsheltered* population. Civil defense would clearly be effective in saving many lives in these areas.[29] The structure of the radiation field in space within this area depends on many factors: number and size of explosives per city, clustering patterns from cities, varying wind conditions, presence or absence of rain. These details cannot be predicted in advance and only gross features can be estimated.

Clearly, a dose rate of 100 rem per hour is lethal within a few hours. The main point of the paragraph which von Hippel attacks was to show how rapidly radiation fields decay. I did not advocate that people leave their fallout shelters soon after attack, when radiation levels are high. In a worst-case situation, involving 10,000 megatons being exploded in contact with the ground over the most densely population one-third of the United States (a somewhat unrealistic scenario), the average radiation in those areas would be 30 to 50 rads* per hour after five days, if no rainfall occurs.

Under these worst conditions, people could at that time come out of their shelters for a very short time each day to perform essential tasks. Some areas would have considerably less radiation, and the population could take refuge in these areas at times determined by radiation dose rate and the availability of transportation and supplies. Most importantly, cleanup operations in urban areas, where fallout is heavy but blast destruction limited, could be conducted for the benefit of whole populations. (Weapons fallout is so composed that vacuuming of streets and sidewalks, possibly by remotely controlled machines, would be effective

* The difference between rads and rem (which arises because this information was drawn from two different sources) is unfortunately smaller than the uncertainty of any estimate of radiation levels.

in lowering the radiation rate.) All this emphasizes the serious need for carefully planned civil defense.

In the final section of his article, von Hippel proposes something new: more negotiations. This suggestion had some novelty a quarter of a century ago. Indeed, the idea is even older. It goes back to the period when Neville Chamberlain, the British prime minister of good will and good intentions, went to Munich with a simple and direct approach to peace and came back with what proved 11 months later to be the complete opposite.

Democracies by their nature will always prefer peace to power. The SALT I Treaty ratified in 1972 did not specify the essential difference between reloadable and nonreloadable silos. Today we know that the Soviet silos are reloadable. The unratified SALT II Treaty tried to rectify this. It is highly doubtful whether, without thorough on-site inspections—which would involve the effective breakdown of the Soviet police state—this deficiency can actually be changed.

There is one final point of agreement. We live in dangerous times with many hazards, deadly not to the human race but to countless individuals and, what is even more important, to the human spirit. In this situation, von Hippel, I and every sane individual agree that we must attempt not only to prevent nuclear war but any war. The disagreement involves not our aim but the practical execution of this aim.

For years, I have tried to counteract the consequences of neglecting military technology in the United States, the consequences of negotiations governed by hopes for "peace in our time" and the results of badly divided counsel. Recently yet another erudite and gifted writer has offered this comment about scientific experts: "All they can tell us is what the weapons are."[30] In view of past and accelerating developments of weapons technology, there is clearly the possibility for technologists to make informed guesses about future weapons which could have surprising and (contrary to widespread opinion) not invariably harmful results. It is regrettable that in our schizophrenic world of two cultures, nontechnical discussions presume without argument that technology has either a static or a steadily more perilous nature. Help could be provided, but if only the rules of secrecy would permit it. Without this permission, we face not only a "window of vulnerability," but an abyss whose depths cannot be guessed.

I have long struggled with the problem. Because of the initiative of brilliant young people, I have discarded many of my old opinions and have come to hope for *defensive* nuclear weapons, directed against the instruments of war in action, rather than against people. I was recently informed that at last I may assert my interest in x-ray lasers, but not my evaluation of whether these can have a place in a defensive arsenal.

Frank von Hippel is the grandson of James Franck, a giant in physics with an understanding heart, who was my mentor and dear friend. A few months ago, I spoke in Chicago at the centennial of his birth. If he and his grandson had been present, perhaps jointly we could have accomplished more than a printed and repetitious controversy.

FRANK VON HIPPEL REPLIES

In Edward Teller's reply to my critique, he does not defend any of the many claims that I showed to be either misleading or false in his *Reader's Digest* article. Instead, he offers nine references to studies on the effects of nuclear explosions on the Earth's ozone layer and five on the effectiveness of subsurface shelters against radioactive fallout.

As Teller acknowledges, his first set of references documents a point in his article that I did not challenge; that a high-yield nuclear explosion set off at the Earth's surface is a much greater threat to the ozone layer than a number of smaller surface bursts with the same total yield. The reason is quite simple: the larger fireball will rise farther into the sensitive layer of the stratosphere.

The references to fallout shelters also are not germane to my principal criticism of Teller's discussion of the value of civil defense in an all-out nuclear war. I did not question that, given the time, transportation, supplies and equipment, and favorable conditions, a well-trained populace could build fallout shelters effective enough to allow survival for a few weeks in areas not directly targeted with nuclear weapons. I did challenge, however, Teller's implied equation of such short-term survival with the long-term survival of the populace of a modern nation whose industrial and transportation systems had been subjected to large-scale nuclear attacks. Teller has not responded to this fundamental criticism.

As far as the future of the nuclear arms race is concerned, the most important issue raised by Teller's *Reader's Digest* article is his claim that "the deterrent effect [of U.S. nuclear forces] has become doubtful." In my critique, I argue that such a statement is indefensible because no first strike could reduce our deployed arsenal of many thousands of protected and deliverable strategic weapons to a size that is less than terrifying. While, in his reply, Teller expresses (in my view greatly exaggerated) concerns about the vulnerability of U.S. strategic forces, I am pleased to note that he comes nowhere near reasserting his original claim.

Finally, I would like to make a point about the importance of secret information in the formulation of public policy concerning nuclear arms. Teller's *Reader's Digest* article began as follows:

Educating people about the nature and actual perils of nuclear weapons would not be easy under any circumstances. It is almost impossible when the elementary facts are guarded by strict regulations of secrecy.

In fact, I believe that my critique and Teller's response show that all of the "elementary facts"—true and false—asserted in his article can be checked, using information available in the public domain.

Indeed, Teller has indicated only one very limited area, relating to the discussion of x-ray lasers, where he has felt restrained by secrecy regulations. Even here, however, the promoters of the technology have found a way around the censors. A relatively detailed description, complete with an artist's conception, of the hopes of these scientists (apparently including Teller) for an antiballistic-missile system in space based on nuclear explosion-powered x-ray lasers, may be found in an article published in the February 23, 1981 *Aviation Week and Space Technology*.

Non-governmental Arms Control Research: The New Soviet Connection

U.S. and Soviet scientists have been holding quiet discussions on nuclear arms control since the first International Pugwash Conference on Science and World Affairs in 1957. Sometimes these discussions have constituted an informal "backchannel" between the governments for consideration of possible arms control initiatives. Thus in conversations between U.S. and Soviet scientists in 1964, U.S. scientists argued that antiballistic-missile (ABM) systems would not be effective against a determined adversary and that their deployment would stimulate an offense-defense arms race; they accordingly proposed a treaty to limit ABM systems. Two high-level Soviet scientists, Lev Artsimovich (who was head of the Soviet fusion program) and Mikhail Millionshchikov (who was vice president for applied physics and mathematics of the Soviet Academy of Sciences), subsequently helped bring their government around to this position, thereby contributing to the achievement in 1972 of the ABM Treaty.[1]

Such informal contacts between U.S. and Soviet scientists have not always been welcomed in government circles. Yet as the history of the ABM Treaty illustrates, they have provided an opportunity to investigate new, experimental ideas that the governments have been loath to explore for fear of reducing political maneuvering room. Such informal discussions also have been convenient forums in which to go beyond the issues of the day and to develop a basis for longer-range planning.

Therefore, despite misgivings, government officials who are interested in the possibility of progress in arms control negotiations have sometimes welcomed the private efforts of independent scientists, seeing them as scouts mapping out technical territory that the armies of government technical experts will be able to secure very quickly once they are permitted to move forward.

During the early 1980s, a period of renewed cold war tension, a number of U.S. scientists began cautiously to cultivate contacts with independent-minded Soviet counterparts such as Evgeny P. Velikhov, the Soviet Academy's current vice president for applied physics and mathematics, and Roald Sagdeev, then the head of the Soviet Institute for Space Research. With the emergence in the mid-1980s of Mikhail Gorbachev as leader of the USSR and the advent of *glasnost*, it became possible to experiment with more open types of exchange, including joint research programs on the technical basis for new arms control policy initiatives. At the same time, some of the Soviet scientists were catapulted into positions of top advisory authority, a situation that involves some risks but also great opportunities.

As some of the Soviet scientists took on greater responsibilities, demands on their time became voracious, limiting their availability for casual discussion. Despite their closeness to power, however, they continued to operate with an activist style.

As a result of various fortuitous circumstances, I have been personally involved in a number of the exchanges with these Soviet scientists, and my professional life became more exciting as a result.

I first met Velikhov at a meeting of the International Physicians for Social Responsibility in the summer of 1983. Earlier that year, a group of Soviet academicians had sent an open letter to the U.S. scientific community asking whether, in light of President Reagan's "Star Wars" speech of March 1983, there had been a change in the professional consensus in the U.S. regarding the feasibility of effective missile defenses. Only the Federation of American Scientists (FAS) responded directly, and that response led to an invitation from Velikhov to visit the Soviet Union to discuss nuclear arms control with Soviet scientists. Despite a partial boycott on bilateral scientific contacts, which the federation had initiated mainly because of the Soviet government's treatment of Andrei Sakharov, the group decided to accept Velikhov's invitation. In November the federation sent a party to the USSR that included FAS President Jeremy Stone, John Pike of the FAS staff, John Holdren of the University of California Berkeley (FAS vice chairman), and myself (FAS chairman).

Immediately thereafter, Velikhov accepted an invitation from Senator Edward M. Kennedy to come to the United States to testify about "nuclear winter". Velikhov came with a party that included Sergei Kapitsa (Vavilov Institute of Physical Problems) and Vladimir V. Aleksandrov (Computing Center of the Academy of Sciences). While in the U.S., Velikhov visited FAS headquarters in Washington, and also Princeton, affording an opportunity for further conversations.

The Committee of Soviet Scientists

In these meetings, Velikhov was acting as chairman of the Committee of Soviet Scientists for Peace and Against the Nuclear Threat, a committee, mostly made up of high-level members of the Soviet Academy of Sciences, that was established in the spring of 1983, in reaction to President Reagan's "Star Wars" speech. Velikhov had succeeded Artsimovich as head of the Soviet fusion program and Millionshchikov as the Soviet Academy's vice president for applied physics and mathematics.

In early 1983, Velikhov had already been involved in discussions with Richard Garwin of IBM and others concerning the possibility of a ban on antisatellite weapons. These discussions took place in the context of meetings between the U.S. National Academy's Committee on International Security and Arms Control and a counterpart group from the Soviet Academy of Sciences that had been taking place since June 1981.

These discussions helped persuade the Soviet government to declare, in August 1983, a unilateral moratorium on the testing of Soviet ASAT (antisatellite) systems. That same month the USSR introduced at the United Nations a draft ASAT treaty that owed a good deal to a model treaty that Garwin and Kurt Gottfried of Cornell had developed in cooperation with the Union of Concerned Scientists.

Velikhov told me that the reason he decided to organize the Committee of Soviet Scientists was to educate a new generation of Soviet scientists, including himself, about nuclear arms control and to reopen the U.S.-Soviet dialogue on strategic defense with the roles reversed. Now it would be the Soviet scientists who would try to convince the U.S. government, with U.S. scientists as intermediaries, that the pursuit of ballistic-missile defenses would be counterproductive.

The Committee of Soviet Scientists (CSS) therefore opened exchanges with scientists representing the full spectrum of U.S. opinion on the strategic defense initiative (SDI)—including, to the surprise of some of us, Edward Teller.

As a result of such exchanges, its own studies and previous Soviet studies, the CSS became quite expert on the technical aspects of SDI, and a group under the leadership of Velikhov, Sagdeev and Andrei Kokoshin (at that time head of the division of military-political affairs of the Institute of U.S. and Canadian Studies) wrote up its conclusions in a book which was printed in 1986 in both Russian and English.

The primary message of the book was that it would be feasible to neutralize space-based defenses with much less expensive countermeasures. The analyses presented were based on descriptions of proposed SDI weaponry that had appeared in U.S. publications, such as *Aviation Week and Space Technology*, and on back-of-the-envelope physics calculations—much in the style of Garwin and Hans Bethe. However, open publication of a technical discussion of possible future weapons systems was an unprecedented event in the Soviet Union and led to a number of letters from irate Soviet citizens demanding that the members of the CSS be prosecuted for revealing how the Soviet Union would neutralize the U.S. Star Wars system. Fortunately, the Soviet government ignored these demands.

In the upshot, the direct impact of the CSS on the U.S. debate over SDI was negligible. But the indirect impact was more important, because it helped persuade Gorbachev, who became General Secretary in early 1985, to announce that the Soviet Union would not compete with the United States in attempting to establish space-based defenses but would instead make an "asymmetric response" based on the types of countermeasures described by the Soviet scientists. This undermined the argument of American SDI proponents, who had said that if the United States did not go full speed ahead, the Soviets would deploy space-based defenses first.

In parallel with its critique of space-based defense, the Committee of Soviet Scientists also sponsored some studies on nuclear winter.[2] Because of the limited capacities of Soviet computing facilities, these studies contributed more to the internationalization of scientific concern about nuclear winter than they did to the understanding of the phenomenon itself.

In-Country Seismic Monitoring

When Gorbachev came into power in early 1985, *glasnost* and a personal relationship between Velikhov and Gorbachev gave the CSS the opportunity to undertake new ventures.

Its first new move was in direct support of Gorbachev's first arms control initiative: the Soviet unilateral moratorium on underground testing that began in August 1985.

In announcing the moratorium, Gorbachev presumably was inspired by the bilateral test moratorium of 1958–1961, with which the U.S. and Soviet governments signaled to each other and the rest of the world that they were seriously interested in ending all nuclear testing. That moratorium led to the Kennedy-Khrushchev Partial Test Ban Treaty of 1963, which ended nuclear testing in the atmosphere, in outer space and in the oceans, but not underground. Now Gorbachev wanted to complete the job by ending all underground testing of advanced nuclear weapons systems.

For many years the U.S. government had been on record as favoring a comprehensive nuclear test ban, but the Reagan administration had backed away from this position. Gorbachev apparently hoped that world opinion would persuade the United States to join in a moratorium. In fact, although the Soviet moratorium was widely praised by advocates of arms control, the public response was far weaker than that to the 1958–1961 moratorium, perhaps because moving testing underground had effectively ended the fallout that had so frightened the public.

One of the major obstacles that had prevented Kennedy and Khrushchev from consummating a comprehensive test ban had been a claim by the U.S. weapons laboratories that the Soviets might be able to continue to develop new nuclear weapons with small underground tests, which seismic sensors beyond the borders of the USSR would be unable to distinguish from earthquakes. The 1958 International Conference of Experts sketched out a verification system involving a worldwide network of seismic stations and on-site inspections at the locations of suspicious seismic events, but in the end, the system that the U.S. government wanted was too intrusive for the Soviets, and the underground part of the ban had to be dropped.

Meetings with Shevardnadze, Scientists

In September 1985, at a meeting in Copenhagen commemorating the centennial of the birth of Niels Bohr, Velikhov suggested to me that the Soviet government might be willing to let an outside group set up a seismic monitoring system in the USSR. I was already aware that one group, Parliamentarians Global Action, was interested in establishing a monitoring system for a bilateral U.S.-Soviet moratorium. (Founded in 1979 by British and Canadian legislators, Parliamentarians Global Action had launched a peace initiative in May 1984—now known as the Five Continent Peace Initiative—with the objective of getting the two superpowers to reopen a constructive dialogue on arms control.) During the next several months, I learned that similar proposals were being made by Jack Evernden of the U.S. Geological Survey and Thomas Cochran, a physicist with the Natural Resources Defense Council (NRDC), an independent organization that does legal and technical work on environmental, energy and arms control policy.

The Parliamentarians were proposing to establish seismic monitoring stations around the U.S. and Soviet test sites to verify a bilateral test moratorium. Evernden was attempting to expand a scientific seismic monitoring agreement between the U.S. Geological Survey and the Soviet Academy to provide information toward the design of a network to monitor a ban of all but very low yield underground tests. The NRDC was interested in detecting low-yield tests that the U.S. and USSR do not announce.

In April 1986, I accompanied a delegation from Parliamentarians Global Action on a visit to Soviet Foreign Minister Edward A. Shevardnadze. The delegation urged the Soviet Union to extend its testing moratorium in the hopes that the United States might still be persuaded to join.

To a physicist unfamiliar with the rituals of diplomacy, the meeting with Shevardnadze seemed very stylized. After we had shaken hands, we sat down and tea and cookies were brought in. Then the spokesman for the Parliamentarians made his statement, and Shevardnadze responded politely. There were one or two additional polite exchanges; then the delegation got up, shook hands with Shevardnadze and left. It was not clear to me that anything had been accomplished, and so I suggested that we find Velikhov.

The meeting with Velikhov could not have been more different. The first thing he asked was, "Do you have any good ideas?" This led to a brainstorming session, at the end of which Velikhov and I agreed to organize a workshop the following month in Moscow to which I would bring representatives of the Western groups that were interested in setting up seismic stations in the USSR.

After the meeting, as we drove away, one of the Parliamentarians said to me in wonder: "You scientists can talk to each other!"

May 1986 Workshop

At the workshop on test ban verification in May 1986 in Moscow, seismic monitoring was discussed. But the monitoring system suggested by the Parliamentarians would have required the Reagan administration to join the Soviet test moratorium, and Evernden's plan also would have required U.S. governmental support. In contrast, the NRDC was able to make an immediate commitment to the project. The workshop therefore resulted in an agreement between the Soviet Academy and the NRDC to set up three seismic stations around the principal U.S. and Soviet underground test sites.

Nevertheless, all three groups made key contributions to the project. The design of the seismic monitoring system was based on that developed by Evernden; the scientific director of the project, Charles Archambeau of the University of Colorado at Boulder, had originally been recruited by the Parliamentarians for their project; and the NRDC undertook to raise funds for the U.S. side of the project and to administer it.

Less than two months later, a team of seismologists recruited by Archambeau and led by Jon Berger and James Brune of the University of California's Scripps Institution of Oceanography were taking data in Kazakhstan, 100 kilometers from the Soviet test site. Cochran organized the overall U.S. effort.

This project had a rather big political impact—perhaps bigger than Gorbachev's unilateral moratorium on testing—because it was the first demonstration of the Soviet government's willingness to accept in-country monitoring of an arms control agreement. The project also had technical merit: It provided data that will be valuable to the design of an in-country monitoring network to verify a low-threshold underground test ban treaty.

International Scientists' Forum in Moscow

A key event in the developing exchanges on possible arms control agreements between Western and Soviet scientists was the International Scientists' Forum on Drastic Reductions and Final Elimination of Nuclear Weapons, which took place in Moscow in February 1987. The Forum was organized by Velikhov with some assistance from Western scientists, including myself.

It was at this meeting that Sakharov reemerged as a public figure in the USSR and argued, in public for the first time, that the USSR should stop conditioning its agreement to a new strategic arms reductions treaty on a U.S. promise not to deploy strategic defenses. Sakharov argued that the SDI program would collapse under its own weight.

There was a workshop at the forum on the idea of clarifying the gray areas of the ABM Treaty by imposing quantitative limits on parameters such as the brightness of lasers directed at objects in space. This idea was subsequently taken up by both the Soviet government and by Paul Nitze, who at that time was Reagan's specially designated arms control expert in the State Department. (Strobe Talbot, *Time* magazine's chief diplomatic correspondent, credits John Pike of the FAS with implanting this idea in both governments.[3])

Also at the forum, a group of West European advocates of "nonoffensive defense," who had been developing their ideas for several years in a series of Pugwash workshops, had the opportunity to present to Gorbachev's advisers their arguments that the best way to stabilize and shrink the conventional-weapons confrontation in Europe would be to preferentially eliminate offensive weaponry such as tanks. Subsequently, three of the West European analysts, physicist Anders Boserup (University of Copenhagen), economist Robert Nield (Cambridge University) and philosopher Albrecht von Mueller (Max Planck Society, Starnberg), and I were invited to write a letter to Gorbachev explaining the idea of nonoffensive defense and its implications for arms control efforts.[4] These inputs helped provide the intellectual basis for Gorbachev's decision in late 1988 to unilaterally eliminate 5,000 tanks from Soviet forces in Eastern Europe (about one-half the total number there) and another 5,000 from the Western USSR.

Finally, it was decided at the forum to launch three new cooperative East-West ventures:

· An international journal, *Science and Global Security*, to publish the results of research pertaining to arms control, disarmament and the environment.
· A five-year Cooperative Research Project on Arms Reductions under the joint auspices of the Federation of American Scientists and the Committee of Soviet Scientists
· An International Foundation for the Survival and Development of Humanity.

Joint Journal on Science and Security

Although a number of American journals, including *Scientific American* and *Physics Today*, publish occasional articles on the technical basis for arms control agreements, and the Forum on Physics and Society of the American Physical Society has published a number of useful collections of articles, there has been no journal with the publication of such work as its primary mission. *The Bulletin of the Atomic Scientists* is used by scientists concerned about the arms race primarily to reach the public and to communicate with one another about political concerns, rather than to make detailed presentations of technical work.

With the creation of *Science and Global Security*, a specialized journal for just that purpose now exists. Harold Feiveson, a Princeton physicist and political scientist who works primarily on arms control, is the U.S. editor, and the publisher in English is Gordon and Breach Science Publishers, which has had a long-standing relationship with Sagdeev and a number of the other leading members of the Committee of Soviet Scientists. The Russian edition is being published by the Committee.

The first (double) issue of *Science and Global Security* appeared in English in October 1989 and contained articles on arrangements to verify nuclear weapon dismantlement, on the verification of limits on sea-launched cruise missiles and on space-reactor arms control.

The Cooperative Research Project

The FAS-CSS cooperative research project, on which Sagdeev (who succeeded Velikhov as chairman of the CSS) and I have been codirectors, has thus far focused principally on developing the technical basis for U.S.-USSR agreements that would impose direct limits on nuclear warheads, ban nuclear reactors in Earth orbit and ban antisatellite laser weapons. On the U.S. side, about 20 analysts, almost all of whom are university and national laboratory physicists, have contributed. On the Soviet side, the contributors have been six physicists from Sagdeev's group at the Space Research Institute and four analysts from Kokoshin's military-political affairs group at the Institute of U.S. and Canada Studies. Funding for the FAS group has been provided by the W. Alton Jones Foundation, the Carnegie Corporation and an anonymous philanthropist.

The focus of our work on the verification of direct limits on nuclear warheads is deliberately complementary to the traditional approach of limiting ballistic missiles and nuclear weapon "launchers"—the approach followed in the 1972 and 1979 strategic arms limitation (SALT) treaties, the 1988 treaty eliminating intermediate-range missiles in Europe (the so-called INF Treaty) and the START Treaty negotiations. Now that the Soviet Union is open to on-site inspections, nuclear warheads are no longer beyond the reach of arms control.

It is now important to have verifiable limits on warheads because nuclear arms negotiations are concentrating for the first time on *reductions*. The INF Treaty eliminated a class of land-based nuclear missiles, and the START negotiations have the objective of reducing by approximately 50 percent the warheads currently deployed on strategic ballistic missiles. But neither the INF Treaty, as ratified, nor the START treaty, as it is being negotiated, include procedures for eliminating the warheads being retired. These warheads and the fissile materials they contain are therefore available for other uncontrolled weapons systems or for a sudden "breakout" from the constraints of arms reductions agreements.

One of the FAS-CSS papers examined possible arrangements for verifiably eliminating warheads and placing their fissile materials under safeguards without revealing warhead designs to the other side. Another explored the problem of verifying declarations of stockpiles of warheads (deployed and nondeployed) and stockpiles of weapons-usable fissile materials in weapons or available for their manufacture.

A major joint FAS-CCS study relating to controls on nuclear warheads examined the applicability and limitations of passive radiation detection and of radiographic techniques for detecting nuclear warheads. This paper provided the theoretical basis on the U.S. side for another Velikhov-NRDC project during the summer of 1989 in which the gamma rays and neutron emissions from a cruise-missile warhead on a Soviet cruiser were measured at short range and at distances up to 70 meters, respectively.

Some of these papers on the technical basis for limits on warheads have been published in *Science and Global Security*. All appeared in *Reversing the Arms Race*, a book edited by Sagdeev and myself.

The FAS-CSS project wrote another set of papers on the technical basis for a ban on nuclear reactors in Earth orbit. One of the indirect results of this effort was the uncovering of the fact, previously kept secret by both the U.S. and Soviet governments, that gamma and positron emissions by Soviet nuclear reactors in Earth orbit had become a major problem for gamma-ray astronomers.[5]

In our joint research, the Soviet scientists have repeatedly shown their independence from official Soviet positions as the following two examples will attest.

· In February 1988 the CSS brought to a joint workshop in Key West a manuscript critiquing the technical basis for Gorbachev's statement two months earlier that the Soviet Union had created "national means for verifying the presence of nuclear weapons on various naval ships . . . without conducting any on-the-spot inspection on board the vessels themselves."

· In May 1988 Sagdeev signed a joint CSS-FAS statement proposing to ban nuclear reactors in Earth orbit. It quickly became clear that this statement did not reflect Soviet policy when the Soviet space-reactor community counterattacked with a *Tass* article arguing the importance of space reactors and subsequently sent a delegation to the annual meeting of U.S. space-reactor contractors in Albuquerque with offers to sell Soviet space reactors to the U.S. The leader of the Soviet delegation, Academician Nikolai N. Ponomarev-Stepnoi, when asked at the meeting about Sagdeev's opposition to space reactors in Earth orbit, said that they had met recently and that Sagdeev "told me his opinion and I told him mine. And we were both so glad that we could tell each other our own opinion in our own country finally."

The International Foundation

At the January 1987 forum, Velikhov proposed the creation of a new foundation dedicated to fostering international cooperative solutions to the arms race, environmental degradation, underdevelopment, denial of human rights and lack of education. This proposal was inspired in part by Velikhov's exposure to U.S. foundations such as the Carnegie Corporation and the MacArthur Foundation, which had supplied prompt support for the NRDC-Soviet Academy seismic monitoring project despite the fact that it was not greeted with universal enthusiasm within the U.S. government. The American who played the greatest part in organizing the foundation was Jerome Wiesner, science adviser to President Kennedy and president emeritus of MIT.

In January 1988, with start-up grants from a number of U.S. foundations and the Soviet Peace Fund, the board of directors of the International Foundation for the Survival and Development of Humanity had its first meeting in Moscow. The name of the foundation, like that of the Committee of Soviet Scientists for Peace and Against the Nuclear Threat, is somewhat awkward sounding to Western ears. But Andrei Sakharov, one of the International Foundation's founding board members, insisted on this name. It appears to be important to declare your purpose in naming an organization in the Soviet Union.

In the area of international security, the Foundation has thus far sponsored workshops and published two reports: 1) a set of recommendations of ways to reduce the dangers of accidental nuclear war, and 2) a technical critique of the arguments put forward by the U.S. and Soviet nuclear-weapon establishments against a comprehensive nuclear-warhead test ban.

The Soviet government has given the Foundation a unique charter that permits it, "for completion of its projects, . . . to create enterprises and organizations." Thus far, the Foundation has used this authority to support a Soviet human rights group sponsored by Sakharov and to create a Soviet chapter of Greenpeace under the chairmanship of Alexei Yablokov, a leading Soviet ecologist.

An Assessment

Cooperative and open research on the technical basis for arms control policy initiatives by independent U.S. and Soviet scientists is a hopeful indication that the pressures driving the arms race may be dissipating. Such cooperation would not be permitted by either country if there were not an increasing consensus that the arms race is more of a threat to both countries than we are to each other.

Of course, the cooperation has a political impact—it strengthens the basis for further cooperation. Therefore, if one thinks that strengthening cooperative relationships between the U.S. and USSR is dangerous because it undermines the will to invest in defenses, one will not welcome these initiatives.

It is often asked whether the types of joint projects discussed here are not better left to the governments. The answer is that governments don't like to sponsor research on questions relating to policy decisions that have not been made yet. Such research may undermine objections they may later wish to make to a policy option. Thus, for example, Colonel Ed Nawrocki, an assistant to former Assistant Secretary of Defense Richard Perle in the Reagan administration, explained their office's opposition to the NRDC-Soviet Academy seismic-monitoring project as follows:

> The NRDC's goals were totally the opposite of our own. They went into this project to prove that a comprehensive test ban [CTB] treaty is verifiable. [And we'd made verification the main public objection to a comprehensive test ban because] verification is such a "show-stopper," as Perle is fond of saying. So the government didn't go much beyond verification as a reason why we shouldn't have a CTB. And the NRDC was out to undermine the verification argument against a CTB.[6]

The NRDC-Soviet Academy project has therefore forced those who oppose a test ban because they think it is important to continue to develop new types of nuclear weapons, to "come out of the closet" and make their arguments before a not completely sympathetic public.

At this time, the future of the Committee of Soviet Scientists is uncertain. Both of its key scientific leaders, Velikhov and Sagdeev, have moved on. Velikhov became a member of the Central Committee of the

Communist Party of the USSR, chairman of the armed forces subcommittee of the Supreme Soviet's Committee on Defense and State Security, and director of the giant Kurchatov Institute of Atomic Energy. After marrying Susan Eisenhower (President Eisenhower's granddaughter), Sagdeev has shifted his base to the Physics Department of the University of Maryland.

In the meantime the CSS has received a charter that allows it to recruit a full-time staff and establish a small "think tank" with 17 full-time researchers working on the technical basis for disarmament. Whether, without its two original leaders, the CSS will successfully make the transition from an *ad hoc* organization of high-level and talented amateurs to a group whose work is done primarily by much less senior full-time professionals remains to be seen.

The Next Generation

A first step to ensure that there will be a next generation of Soviet physicists working on the technical basis for Soviet policy initiatives on global problems was taken in September 1989, when the Committee of Soviet Scientists joined with the Moscow Physical-Technical Institute (MPTI) to sponsor an eight-day International School on Science and World Affairs in a small hotel outside Moscow. There were twenty-four Soviet physics students, ranging from second-year undergraduates to research associates; nine U.S.-postdocs with physics Ph.D.'s; one U.S. graduate student; five physics graduate students from Imperial College, London; and two physics graduate students from Beijing. The U.S. participants were all engaged in arms control research—at universities, with public-interest groups or as congressional fellows. The faculty of the school also was diverse and lectured on global climate as well as arms control issues.

The U.S. postdocs came away from the school quite impressed with the Soviet students and interested in further exchanges. Four of them therefore organized a second summer school in 1990 at Princeton University with the subject matter broadened to include the energy and other global environmental problems. This summer school led directly to the establishment at MPTI of a Center for Arms Control, Energy and Environmental Studies. Also, one of the Soviet participants in the second summer school stayed on at Princeton for a year to do arms-control research. Other U.S.-university arms control research groups have also expressed their willingness to host Soviet postdocs embarking on careers in that area. Obviously the door is wide open for further development of the U.S.-Soviet "connection" in arms control research.

Attacks on Star Wars Critics

The December 1984 issue of *Commentary* contained an article, "The War Against 'Star Wars,' " by Dartmouth College astrophysicist, Robert Jastrow, which attacked two technical critiques of President Reagan's Strategic Defense Initiative (SDI). One of the critiques had been written by a group organized under the auspices of the Union of Concerned Scientists (UCS) and the other by Ashton Carter for the congressional Office of Technology Assessment (OTA).[1]

The *Wall Street Journal* immediately picked up Jastrow's attack, in a December 10, 1984 editorial, "Politicized Science," which attacked the UCS and OTA reports as "less than scientific." The editorial ended with a note of concern: "It would be a shame. . . if the President fails to realize that his plan is supported by men such as Mr. Jastrow who have studied the problem carefully and scientifically." In fact, Jastrow had not himself done any scientific studies, but was merely reporting somewhat breathlessly the criticisms of the UCS and OTA reports by anonymous "experts" at the Lawrence Livermore and Los Alamos Laboratories.

The UCS group and Carter responded with letters to the editor of the *Wall Street Journal*, published on January 2, 1985. A storm of letters supporting the editorial was then published in the January 17 edition. These included letters from: Lieutenant General Abrahamson, the director of the SDI organization; C. Paul Robinson, the principal associate director of Los Alamos National Laboratory; and Lowell Wood, the head of the x-ray laser group at the Lawrence Livermore National Laboratory.

At the technical level, the principal focus of the criticisms of the UCS report* was a calculation of the number of laser battle-stations that would

---

* I discuss here only the debate over the UCS report because the public discussion focused primarily on it. However, on May 8, 1984, General Abrahamson distributed to the press a set of criticisms of the OTA (Carter) report. This was followed on June 4, by a letter from Deputy Secretary of Defense William H. Taft IV to OTA Director John Gibbons, demanding

be required in orbit to destroy Soviet intercontinental ballistic missiles (ICBMs) during "boost phase," the period of up to five minutes after launch while the rocket engine is still burning and before the multiple warheads and decoys are released. According to the *Wall Street Journal*, the original UCS estimate was 2,400 battle-stations, but "defense experts at Los Alamos say only 80 to 100 will do. The initial UCS error would make the difference between estimating a defense cost of, say, $50 billion and estimating at $1 trillion or more."

At the political level, the issue is the credibility of the technical critics of Star Wars. During the 1968-1972 debate over the antiballistic-missile (ABM) system, proposed by the Johnson and Nixon administrations, two of the principal contributors to the UCS report, Richard Garwin and Hans Bethe, helped to turn the scientific community against the proposed system, by showing in a *Scientific American* article how vulnerable it would be to countermeasures.[2]

Obviously, both sides of the Star Wars debate remembered that history. One side hoped to repeat Garwin and Bethe's earlier success in having an impact on the policy debate with a technical critique of the new proposal for a ballistic missile defense. On the other side, advocates of the SDI program, whose leaders included scientists such as Jastrow and Edward Teller, who had supported the Johnson-Nixon ABM system, hoped to render the critics ineffective by attacking their credibility.

The UCS group described a hypothetical battle station, equipped with a hydrogen-fluoride laser producing a beam of infrared (2.7 micron) radiation with a power of 25 million watts. This beam would be aimed by a perfect (10-meter diameter) mirror able to focus the beam on a spot with a diameter of less than a meter at a distance of 3,000 kilometers, with an intensity sufficient to burn through the shell of a booster within about seven seconds.

The number of such battle stations required to destroy all the Soviet ICBMs—assuming they were all launched at the same time—would depend upon a number of factors:

· the total number of Soviet ICBMs—assumed by the UCS group in their original March 1984 report to be the then current number, 1,400;[3]

that the OTA withdraw Carter's report. The OTA issued a sharp rebuttal to Abrahamson's list of criticisms and, on July 13, 1984, after having the OTA report reviewed by three high-level defense experts, Gibbons turned down Taft's request. The Defense Department does not appear to have pursued the matter further.

· duration of the boost phase—assumed to be 100 seconds;
· average distance between battle-station and booster—assumed to be 3,000 kilometers;
· distribution of silos—assumed to be the same as the then current distribution;
· distribution of satellites in orbit—approximated as uniform;
· "slew-and-settle" time required to move the laser beam from one target to another—assumed to be zero.

Some of these assumptions were generous. For example, the Soviets could increase the number of their ICBMs or deploy relatively inexpensive decoys that would mimic ICBMs during their boost phase. They could concentrate their missile silos in a single area, thus minimizing the number of battle-stations within range at any one time. "Fast-burn" boosters could be developed that cut the duration of the boost phase to 50 seconds. And the slew-and-settle time required to focus a 10-meter diameter mirror on a moving booster 1,000 kilometers away would not be negligible.

However, other approximations made in the original UCS calculations were decidedly ungenerous. Most significantly:

· battle-satellites could be placed into orbits which would increase their relative density at the latitudes of Soviet missile fields by a factor of almost three;
· as the density of battle-satellites increased, the average distance between battle-satellites and targets would decrease.

Similarly crude approximations were made in the original Los Alamos calculations, and both groups quickly refined their work. By the time the UCS report appeared as a book and, in a shortened version, in *Scientific American* a few months later, *all* its key assumptions were generous to the Star Wars concept, and the estimated number of battle-satellites had been reduced to 300.

In an analytical paper,[4] however, Garwin highlighted this generosity by pointing out that, were the Soviet Union to deploy 3,000 small, 40-second burn-time boosters in a region of 1,000 kilometers or less in diameter, and if the slew-and-settle time of the laser mirror were as long as one-half second, the calculated number of battle-satellites would increase from 300 to 1,500. In view of the fact that a laser battle station might cost a billion dollars and a fast-burn booster a few million, the cost-exchange ratio would be far from advantageous for the United States.

It should be emphasized that the hypothetical system being debated by the UCS group and its critics was not an officially proposed design. Although such specific designs have been proposed by small groups of Star Wars enthusiasts, the $26 billion that had been requested for the SDI Program at that time was only for the first five years of a 10-year exploratory research program.

In the absence of a specific design, the critics had either to postulate their own—and run the risk of being criticized, as the UCS group was, for ungenerous assumptions—or offer criticisms that would apply to any space-based system. In my view, the more general criticisms of the SDI Program are the most important.

Perhaps the most fundamental technical objection to any Star Wars system would be its susceptibility to countermeasures. Indeed, this point was at the core of the UCS-OTA critique of the Star Wars proposal—just as it was at the core of the Garwin-Bethe critique of the Johnson administration's ABM system. From this perspective, the attempts of Star Wars advocates to focus on the details of the earliest version of the UCS calculations of the number of battle-satellites *in the absence of countermeasures* must be seen as a diversion. McGeorge Bundy, George Kennan, Robert McNamara, and Gerard Smith have made this point particularly well:[5]

> [the] inevitable Soviet reaction is studiously neglected by Secretary Weinberger when he argues in defense of Star Wars that today's skeptics are as wrong as those who said we could never get to the Moon. The effort to get to the Moon was not complicated by the presence of an adversary. A platoon of hostile moon-men with axes could have made it a disaster.

Consider, for example, the battle-satellites' vulnerability to attack. The Star Wars program puts much emphasis on such orbiting satellites because, after the boost phase, the deployment of multiple warheads and decoys could make the defense problem virtually impossible, and almost all boost-phase schemes require battle-satellites.*

* Only one directed-energy beam has been proposed that could be light enough to be "popped-up" into space *after* Soviet ICBM launch had been detected. This is the nuclear-explosion-powered x-ray laser. However, as both the UCS and OTA reports point out, x rays from this weapon could not penetrate far into the atmosphere and a "fast-burn" booster could be designed to release its warheads below this level.

These satellites would be much more vulnerable to attack than their targets. Unlike boosters, which would be available for destruction for only about a minute at an unpredictable time, battle-satellites would be at predictable locations in predictable orbits. These billion-dollar machines could therefore easily be destroyed by ground-based lasers or something as simple as a cloud of small metal pellets put into a counter-rotating orbit. (Because of their high closing-speed, such pellets would deliver hundreds of times as much destructive energy as an equivalent weight of bullets.) Of course, at great expense one could transport thousands of tons of armor to each battle station, but then how could the sensors see and the lasers fire? In any case, this example shows how one simple countermeasure could either incapacitate a battle-station or greatly increase its complexity and cost.[†]

Other countermeasures could neutralize a defensive system, without destroying it. For example, Jastrow proposed a relatively low-cost, but easy-to-counter design, in an article in the *New York Times Magazine*, written in collaboration with Zbigniew Brzezinski, President Carter's national security advisor, and Max Kampelman, one of President Reagan's arms control negotiators.[6] The proposed scheme would involve two layers: the first would consist of 100 satellites, each carrying 150 interceptor rockets. Those few satellites within range would attack Soviet ballistic missiles during their boost phase. The system could be neutralized by "fast-burn" boosters that completed their burn within the atmosphere because the infrared sensors of the homing interceptor warheads would be blinded by friction heat as soon as they entered the atmosphere. The second layer of Jastrow's proposed system, made up of 5,000 ground-based rockets, each of which could intercept a warhead above the atmosphere as it approached its target could easily be overwhelmed by tens to hundreds of thousands of light decoys designed to be indistinguishable from a reentry vehicle above the atmosphere.

There are also fundamental objections to the Star Wars proposal at a political level. Perhaps most importantly, even if a Star Wars system was intended to serve only defensive purposes, the other side would not see it as such. And, in fact, such a system makes much more sense as an adjunct to a first-strike capability than as a shield from a first strike. Because of its inevitable vulnerability, a Star Wars-type system would be

---

[†] After this was written, the SDI program accepted the logic of the critics' case and proposed much smaller and more numerous battle satellites, each carrying a single 50-kilogram "brilliant pebble" interceptor missile. However, the critics pointed out that, among other problems with the new scheme, so few of the interceptors would be close enough to attack fast-burn boosters that the cost-exchange ratio would once again be very unfavorable to the defense.

fairly easy to neutralize at the beginning of a highly orchestrated first strike. But, in the face of a disorganized retaliatory strike by an unprepared *victim* of a surprise attack, it might be more effective. The Star Wars system would therefore tend to destabilize the balance of terror by increasing the advantages of a first strike. The fact that the Star Wars program was launched at the same time that the United States was embarking on a huge buildup of exactly the types of accurate ballistic missile warheads that would be most useful in a first strike must have been particularly disturbing to Soviet strategic analysts. Indeed, Yuri Andropov said as much four days after President Reagan's original Star Wars speech:[7]

> The strategic offensive forces of the United States will continue to be developed and upgraded at full tilt and along quite a definite line at that, namely that of acquiring a first strike capability. Under these conditions the intention to secure itself the possibility of destroying with the help of ABM defenses the corresponding strategic systems of the other side, that is of rendering it unable of dealing a retaliatory strike, is a bid to disarm the Soviet Union in the face of the U.S. nuclear threat.

The Soviet Union will not allow the United States to free itself unilaterally from the U.S.-USSR mutual-hostage relationship. The United States can, however, unilaterally launch a defense-offense arms race which will waste the skills of tens of thousands of scientists and engineers and induce enormous uncertainty and paranoia among worst-case analysts on both sides. Staving off such a defense-offense arms race was, of course, the major achievement of the 1972 ABM Treaty.

The debate over the credibility of the Star Wars critics therefore masked a much more important debate—between those who, knowingly or not, were attempting to launch the nuclear arms race into a far more virulent new phase and those who were trying to help the United States and Soviet Union avoid this danger.

Fissile Weapons Materials

WITH DAVID H. ALBRIGHT AND
BARBARA G. LEVI

Agreements on nuclear-arms control based, like START, on verifiable counts of missiles and other vehicles for delivering nuclear weapons are becoming more difficult to devise. The vulnerability of strategic weapons that has come with precision guidance has stimulated a trend toward smaller mobile missiles that are difficult to count and many weapon systems, such as fighter-bombers and cruise missiles, have been designed to carry either conventional or nuclear explosives, impeding an accurate count of deliverable nuclear warheads.

Clearly a new approach is needed to complement the delivery-vehicle counting rules. We suggest a new look at one of the oldest proposals for restraining the growth of nuclear arsenals: an agreement to cut off any further production of the fissile materials necessary for the construction of nuclear weapons.

Every nuclear weapon contains at least a few kilograms of chain-reacting fissile material. Fission of about one kilogram of uranium-235 demolished Hiroshima. Nagasaki was leveled by the fission of one kilogram of plutonium-239 in another weapon. The development of thermonuclear, or "hydrogen," bombs in the early 1950s did not eliminate the need for fissile materials, because such weapons require a fission explosion to ignite the hydrogen fusion reaction.

Since fissile material is an essential ingredient in all nuclear weapons, a cutoff would place an ultimate limit on the number of weapons that could be produced. Proposals for a cutoff of production of fissile materials have therefore been on the international arms-control agenda virtually since the invention of nuclear weapons.

Between 1956 and 1969 a cutoff was repeatedly put forward by the U.S. as a separate arms-control proposal. Soviet responses were not encouraging, perhaps because at that time the USSR had considerably fewer nuclear warheads than the U.S. By the 1980s, the two stockpiles were comparable, however, and in 1982 Soviet Foreign Minister Andrei Gromyko suggested that the "cessation of production of fissionable materials for manufacturing nuclear weapons" could be made one of the initial stages of a nuclear disarmament program.

A cutoff would be a natural part of any larger package of mutually reinforcing arms-control and disarmament proposals. For example, to be meaningful, any agreement to freeze or reduce the number of warheads would have to contain assurances that new warheads were not being produced.

A cutoff would serve another purpose as well. Continued production of fissile materials for nuclear weapons by the superpowers is severely undermining their efforts to discourage comparable activities by other nations. In the 1950s and 1960s, U.S. proposals for a cutoff were often linked with efforts to persuade non-nuclear states to support the Nonproliferation Treaty. That treaty came into force in 1970 and has since been signed by more than 100 states. That the U.S. and the USSR, the nations that devised the treaty, have not brought their arms race under control has resulted in strong expressions of dissatisfaction with the treaty on the part of the non-nuclear states.

A superpower agreement to cut off the production of fissile materials for nuclear weapons would thus be in the interests of nonproliferation, as well as, superpower arms control.

E ssential background for any discussion of a production cutoff is a description of the nature and availability of the fissile materials themselves. Uranium-235 is the only fissile isotope that exists naturally in more than trace quantities. However, it is not found in a form that can be used directly in manufacturing nuclear weapons. Only 0.7 percent of a typical sample of natural uranium is U-235. The other 99.3 percent is uranium 238, a heavier isotope that cannot sustain a chain reaction. To make a practical weapon, the uranium must be enriched to contain at least 20 percent U-235. U.S. and Soviet weapon-grade uranium contains more than 90 percent U-235.

One technology through which uranium-isotope enrichment is achieved was developed early in the history of the U.S. nuclear-weapon program.

Called gaseous diffusion, it involves diffusing uranium hexafluoride (a gaseous, uranium-carrying compound) through a succession of thousands of porous barriers. The lighter molecules containing U-235 move slightly more rapidly, though the barriers and their relative abundance in the gas therefore increases. In the 1940s and 1950s, the U.S. built three diffusion enrichment plants in Tennessee, Kentucky and Ohio. In the early 1960s, at the peak of U.S. production, these facilities produced about 80 tonnes (metric tons) of weapon-grade uranium—enough to produce thousands of nuclear weapons each year.

By 1964, the U.S. had such a large supply of fissile material that President Lyndon B. Johnson decided to cut back production, explaining that "even in the absence of agreement we must not stockpile arms beyond our needs or seek an excess of military power that could be provocative as well as wasteful." Since then, the U.S. uranium-enrichment complex has produced mainly "low-enriched" uranium used as fuel in most nuclear-power reactors. Although some highly enriched uranium has been produced for use in naval reactors, research reactors, plutonium and tritium production reactors and a few power reactors, the U.S. has added no highly enriched uranium to its nuclear-weapon stockpile since 1964. All weapon-grade uranium used in new warheads has come from the stockpile produced before 1964, or has been recycled from retired weapons.

Another fissile isotope, plutonium-239, is also used in nuclear weapons. To make Pu-239, a "target" of U-238 is bombarded with neutrons in a nuclear reactor. Plutonium-production reactors are basically no different from nuclear-power reactors, except that they are operated to yield plutonium containing more than 93 percent of the isotope Pu-239. Such "weapon-grade" plutonium is more desirable for weapons than grades that contain higher percentages of heavier plutonium isotopes. Plutonium is preferred over highly enriched uranium for modern, compact nuclear warheads because a much smaller quantity—only a few kilograms—is needed to produce a fission explosion.

During most of the period between 1955 and 1964, the U.S. had 13 reactors producing plutonium. Eight were at the Hanford site, near Richland, Washington, and five at the Savannah River site, near Aiken, South Carolina. Together, they produced more than six tonnes of plutonium, enough for more than a thousand warheads, each year.

In the eight-year period following President Johnson's decision to cut back U.S. production, all the original eight Hanford reactors were shut down and two of the five production reactors at Savannah River were mothballed. After the Chernobyl accident, the remaining three Savannah

River reactors were shut down for safety improvements. Another, newer "dual purpose" reactor, completed in 1964 at Hanford, which generated electric power as well as producing plutonium was permanently shut down. Thus the U.S. has virtually shut down unilaterally its production of weapons plutonium as well as weapons uranium.

How much fissile material is in the U.S. and USSR stockpiles? Enough information is publicly available to allow reasonable estimates of the U.S. stockpile, but public information about the Soviet weapon-production complex is much sparser.

According to the records of the Department of Energy, the U.S. has since 1944 bought approximately 250,000 tonnes of natural uranium, containing about 1,800 tonnes of U-235. The best way to estimate how much of this U-235 might have been used for weapons is to examine government reports that list the annual amounts of "separative work," or enrichment, done in the U.S. uranium-enrichment complex and the associated percentages of U-235 that were left in the "depleted uranium" by-product of the enrichment process. We estimate using these data that the U.S. could have produced up to about 750 tonnes of highly enriched uranium for weapons prior to the 1964 cutoff of production. After estimating the nonweapon-related demands for uranium enrichment through 1964 and subsequent demands for highly enriched uranium, we conclude that there are still about 500 tonnes of weapon-grade uranium remaining in the U.S. weapon stockpile. Thomas B. Cochran and Milton M. Hoenig of the Natural Resources Defense Council reached a similar conclusion.

The amount of plutonium in the U.S. weapon stockpile can be estimated from data that have been released by the Department of Energy on the heat outputs of its plutonium-production reactors since 1951. Heat output is directly proportional to the amount of U-235 that has been fissioned in these reactors, which in turn is directly proportional to the quantity of plutonium they have produced. (Approximately 0.9 kilograms of plutonium are produced for each kilogram of U-235 that is fissioned.) On this basis, we conclude that the U.S. weapons stockpile contains about 100 tonnes of plutonium. Once again, Cochran and Hoenig made a similar estimate.

Estimates of the amounts of plutonium and highly enriched uranium produced for weapons by the USSR have not been made available by that government or by the U.S., but Soviet plutonium production can be gauged from the amount of radioactive krypton-85 that has accumulated in the atmosphere. This isotope, which is produced by fission, is released by facilities that reprocess nuclear fuel to recover plutonium. Relatively small amounts are also released by tests of nuclear weapons and by leakage from reactor fuel. Because it is chemically unreactive, Kr-85 accumulates in the atmosphere, through which it spreads relatively uniformly because of its long radioactive half-life (approximately 11 years).

Since about 1954, various groups of investigators throughout the world have made periodic measurements of the atmospheric concentration of Kr-85. The most comprehensive and accurate published measurements have been made by Wolfgang Weiss, Albert Sittkus, Helmut Stockburger and Hatmut Sartorius of the Max Plank Institute for Nuclear Physics in Freiberg, Germany. By estimating the amount of Kr-85 released in weapon tests worldwide and in fuel reprocessing outside the USSR and then subtracting this amount from the total amount of Kr-85 released into the atmosphere, it is possible to estimate how much has been released into the atmosphere by the USSR (see Figure 1.). By this method, we estimate that, through 1984, the USSR had released about as much Kr-85 into the atmosphere as the U.S. If, as in the U.S., most of the Kr-85 was released in reprocessing fuel from reactors that produce plutonium for weapons, then the amounts of plutonium in the two countries' stockpiles, like their estimated numbers of nuclear warheads, are roughly comparable. The rate of plutonium production in the USSR in the early 1980s appears to have been considerably higher than that in the U.S., however.[1]

S uppose the two superpowers agreed to cut off production of fissile materials for weapons. Could each adequately verify that the other had not violated the agreement? For the purpose of this discussion, we define adequate verification as the ability to detect, within a few years, any set of clandestine activities large enough to increase one of the superpower stockpiles at a rate greater than 1 percent per year. This would be a significant limit; it represents a rate of production about one-tenth as large as the peak production rates of the past. The strategic significance of smaller violations would be so minor that it is doubtful either superpower would consider the gains to be worth the risks of detection.

For example, taking our estimates of the U.S. stockpiles as a yardstick, a growth rate of 1 percent per year corresponds to production of about

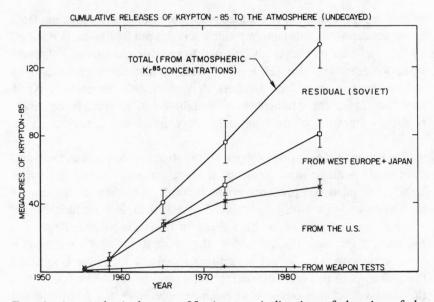

FIG. 1. *Atmospheric krypton 85 gives an indication of the size of the USSR plutonium stockpile. This isotope is released primarily by nuclear-fuel reprocessing facilities and remains in the atmosphere because it is chemically unreactive. The upper curve, which is based on historical measurements of atmospheric Kr-85 shows the total amount of Kr-85 released to the atmosphere worldwide. The lower curves give the authors' estimates of the contributions to this total originating in weapon tests worldwide and in reprocessing facilities outside the USSR The remainder represents an estimate of the amount of Kr-85 released by reprocessing facilities inside the USSR It is comparable to the amount released by those in the U.S. Most releases from the U.S. and the USSR were probably from facilities producing plutonium for weapons, suggesting that the superpowers' stockpiles of weapon plutonium are also comparable. The releases from Western Europe and Japan were mostly from civilian reprocessing activities.*

five tonnes of weapon-grade uranium or one tonne of plutonium. Undetected violations below this level would still provide the wherewithal to produce hundreds of warheads per year and would therefore be quite significant in absolute terms, but with respect to the existing stockpiles such violations would be insignificant.

The problem of verifying a cutoff can be divided into two subsidiary problems. The first is ensuring that significant quantities of fissile material are not diverted to weapons from legitimate activities; the second is ensuring that there is no significant clandestine production.

The U.S. has always assumed that a cutoff agreement would include a system of on-site safeguards against diversion at facilities that process fissile materials for purposes other than weapon production. Since about 1965, official U.S. statements have suggested that the inspection could be assigned to the International Atomic Energy Agency (IAEA), which would use techniques similar to those it employs in safeguarding fissile materials in states that have signed the Nonproliferation Treaty and have committed themselves not to build nuclear weapons.

Indeed, as part of its campaign for the Nonproliferation Treaty, the U.S. offered to put all its own nuclear facilities except those "with direct national security significance" under IAEA safeguards. An agreement between the U.S. and the IAEA making it possible to implement the offer went into effect in 1980. The Soviet Union made no similar move until 1982, when Gromyko announced that the USSR would be willing to place some of its peaceful nuclear installations under the control of the IAEA. A very limited initial agreement was concluded March 1985, under which the IAEA was allowed to safeguard a Soviet power reactor and research reactor. More recently, the coverage of this agreement has been expanded.

IAEA safeguards are designed to detect within days or months the diversion of enough material to make a single nuclear weapon: eight kilograms of plutonium or 25 kilograms of weapon-grade uranium. Diversions of nuclear material would have to be 1,000 times larger to have any potential strategic significance. There is little doubt that IAEA safeguards should be able to detect diversions of less than 1 percent of fissile material flowing through a nation's nuclear-reactor fuel system. For comparison, 5 percent of the flow through the U.S. nuclear-power system, or 15 percent of that through the smaller Soviet system, would have to be diverted before the annual diversion amounted to 1 percent of the fissile material already in the corresponding weapons stockpile.

The task of the IAEA safeguards is to confirm, within a specified accuracy, that any fissile material delivered to, or produced at, a facility is either still there, has been fissioned or has been delivered to another safeguarded location. In this respect, the problem of verifying accounts of fissile-material is similar to the problem of verifying financial accounts. Visiting IAEA inspectors periodically check the consistency between actual and reported inventories. Measurements of radiation are used, along with other nondestructive measurements on randomly selected nuclear-fuel assemblies, to check that there has been no substitution of "counterfeit" fuel.

Where fissile material is in inactive storage, the IAEA simplifies its task by applying tamperproof seals to the containers and storage vaults involved so that their contents need not be checked on each visit. Storage areas that cannot be sealed are monitored for suspicious activities with tamperproof cameras.

The fuel cycle that is currently most common in U.S. and USSR power reactors has low-enriched uranium in fresh fuel and no recovery of plutonium from spent fuel. In such a fuel cycle, there is an additional major barrier to the diversion of fissile material to weapons. Even if enough fissile material could be diverted, a major additional clandestine operation would be necessary to convert it into a form usable for nuclear weapons: fresh reactor fuel would need enrichment to higher levels and spent fuel would need reprocessing to separate plutonium from the highly radioactive fission products. These barriers to diversion will exist as long as the superpowers refrain from shifting their nuclear-power systems to fuel cycles involving the use of plutonium or highly enriched uranium in the fresh fuel.

U nder a cutoff, U-235 would still be used as a fuel in naval-propulsion reactors as well as nuclear-power reactors. The U.S. and the USSR each have more than a hundred ships propelled by nuclear reactors. U.S. naval reactors are fueled by weapon-grade uranium and are currently supplied with a total of about five tonnes of U-235 per year. Since the total estimated shaft horsepower of the Soviet nuclear navy is about the same as that of the U.S., and since Soviet ships are at sea a much smaller percentage of the time, it is likely the Soviet navy's demand for U-235 is smaller.

Neither navy is likely to allow international inspectors on its ships or in facilities that produce fuel for naval reactors. One alternative arrangement would be for the superpowers to agree on the amount of U-235 each would be allowed to produce for use in its naval reactors. Under this arrangement, the U-235 would be produced entirely at safeguarded plants and an equivalent amount of irradiated enriched uranium would have to be turned in at another safeguarded facility within a certain period of time. These measures would prevent the cumulative diversion of significant quantities of naval U-235 for use in weapons.

The U.S. has about as many research reactors as it has naval power reactors, but their total demand for U-235 is about one-tenth as large. We have no reason to think the corresponding demand in the Soviet Union is much larger. This is a small flow of material (about half a tonne per year) compared with the amount that would constitute a significant violation. In any case, the IAEA has developed thorough safeguards to detect diversions from research reactors.

The final class of reactors whose fuel cycles would have to be safeguarded are tritium-production reactors. Tritium provides the neutrons that initiate the fission chain reaction and "boost" the fission efficiencies in U.S. nuclear weapons. It is also the source of most of the neutrons produced by the "neutron bomb." Tritium is produced by allowing lithium-6 to absorb neutrons in the same way as plutonium is produced when U-238 absorbs neutrons.

Because of its 12-year radioactive half-life, tritium must be replenished even if stockpiles are frozen. This would not call for a very large-scale effort, however. An amount of tritium equal to that currently in the U.S. stockpile could probably be maintained by a reactor with the capacity of one of the Savannah River reactors. Such a reactor, like any other, could be safeguarded against clandestine production of fissile materials for weapons.

I f legitimate reactors and their fuel cycles can be safeguarded against significant diversion of materials to nuclear weapons, what are the prospects of a country successfully constructing a clandestine production facility? Under early U.S. proposals for a cutoff of production of fissile materials, each superpower would have deployed roving teams of inspectors to search the other's territory. That approach was unacceptable to the Soviet Union. It was therefore highly significant when, in 1969, the U.S. completely dropped the demand. What brought about such a major change in position?

Part of the answer is that surveillance satellites had given the U.S. government confidence that it could detect large-scale clandestine production from space. Routine surveillance of the Soviet Union by satellites began in 1961, and by 1969 it had become possible to subject the exterior of every structure on the Earth's surface to detailed inspection.

Today, indications of the energy intensity of hidden activities can be obtained as well, by telescopes that are sensitive to the infrared radiation emitted by warm surfaces. When the data from satellite surveillance are analyzed in combination with information culled from internal reports, from intercepted radio and microwave transmissions and from interviews with émigrés, the integrated product is stunning. This has been demonstrated convincingly in the Department of Defense's annual publication, on "Soviet Military Power."

It is unlikely that either superpower could conceal from such scrutiny the existence of a program large enough to produce one tonne of plutonium or five tonnes of highly enriched uranium per year. There would be many opportunities to discover such a program. For example, the construction of plutonium-producing reactors and their associated fuel-reprocessing facilities would be the equivalent of multibillion-dollar projects. In view of the many thousands of workers who would be involved, it would be extremely difficult to conceal the nature of an effort on this scale.

A great deal of uranium, roughly a thousand tonnes of natural uranium per year, would be needed as well. Although this is not a physically large amount of material, it does correspond to a significant fraction of the projected uranium flow in either of the superpowers' nuclear-power systems. It is likely that the diversion of so much newly mined uranium would be difficult to hide, particularly if the uranium mills at which uranium is recovered from ore were subject to some level of on-site safeguards.

The detection of clandestine production facilities through their associated mining and milling activities has limitations, however, because a clandestine production program could be supplied for years with uranium from a previously established stockpile. The U.S. has built up a stockpile of hundreds of tonnes of U-235 in low-enriched natural and depleted uranium. Similar stockpiles probably exist in the USSR. It is all too easy to imagine that a stockpile of uranium containing up to perhaps 100 tonnes of U-235 could be hidden before a cutoff agreement went into effect.

Another way to detect clandestine production plants would be to search for emissions characteristic of their operation. The best example of such an emission is the enormous amount of heat generated by plutonium-production reactors. A set of clandestine reactors capable of producing one tonne of plutonium per year would have an average output of about three million kilowatts of waste heat. Such an amount is equal to the heat generated by a U.S. city of 300,000 people. It would be hard to dispose of so much heat without detection—sensors exist that can detect from space the presence or absence of ceiling insulation in a single-family house.

The least conspicuous facilities currently able to produce weapon-grade fissile materials are probably the so-called centrifuge enrichment plants. This technology involves spinning cylinders of uranium-carrying gas in centrifuges. Considerably fewer stages are needed in order to reach a given level of enrichment in a centrifuge plant than in a diffusion plant. In addition, centrifuge plants are smaller and consume less energy. The appearance of gas-centrifuge plants is much less distinctive than that of diffusion plants, and it might not be possible to identify them from satellite photographs alone. A larger intelligence effort would probably be able to identify them, however, by picking up indications of the enormous effort required to manufacture and install the tens of thousands of centrifuges needed today to produce five tonnes of highly enriched uranium per year.

The U.S. Department of Energy has announced that its future uranium-enrichment facilities will employ a new technique called laser-isotope separation. This technology exploits the fact that the atomic energy levels of U-235 and U-238 electrons are slightly different because of the difference in the sizes of the atoms' nuclei. To separate the isotopes, a set of lasers are tuned to produce energy that can be absorbed by U-235 atoms (each of which loses an electron in the process) but not by U-238. An electric field then separates the charged U-235 ions from the uncharged U-238 atoms.

An enrichment plant based on laser-isotope separation would be smaller than a centrifuge plant; it would therefore be even more difficult to identify from satellite photographs. Nevertheless, a laser enrichment plant capable of producing five tonnes of weapon-grade uranium per year would still cost the equivalent of hundreds of millions of dollars to construct and would incorporate unusual, high-powered, rapidly pulsed lasers. These features and others would facilitate the detection of such a plant by a larger intelligence effort.

Although each of the means of detection we have discussed in theory could be eluded, clandestine production of fissile materials would require that the construction and operation of all major facilities involved be concealed successfully for a period of several years. Detection of one suspicious facility by any of the available means of surveillance and intelligence would threaten the entire enterprise.

Ambiguous evidence of clandestine production activities could be brought to a body organized along the lines of the Standing Consultative Commission, established to discuss questions concerning compliance with the 1972 SALT I treaty. In the absence of satisfactory explanations,

on-site inspections could be requested. Systematic obstruction of efforts
to obtain answers to legitimate queries would, of course, bring into
question the continuation of the cutoff agreement.

The reward for successful concealment of a clandestine production
program would hardly be spectacular; it would be a small increase in the
size of a stockpile of fissile material already unnecessarily large.[2]

I f the superpowers reach an agreement banning further production of
fissile materials for nuclear weapons, it will be natural to try to extend
the ban to include the other states with nuclear-weapon capability and to
states without nuclear-weapon capability who have not signed the Nonproliferation Treaty. A verifiable production cutoff would also lay the
basis for verifiable reduction in the quantities of fissile materials already
in the arsenals of the nuclear-weapon states.

The obvious ways to dispose of surplus fissile materials and fissile
materials recovered from warheads being eliminated would be to "burn"
them in existing nuclear-power reactors. Weapon-grade uranium would
be useless for nuclear weapons after it was diluted with depleted or
natural uranium, down to the low enrichment level used in power-reactor
fuel. Weapon-grade plutonium would have to be disposed of with greater
care, since there is no natural isotopic denaturant for plutonium. One
method would be to use the plutonium as fuel in a relatively few heavily
safeguarded reactors operated in a "once through" mode (that is, without
reprocessing the fuel). Ten large reactors could in this way dispose of all
the plutonium currently in U.S. or Soviet weapons in a decade.[3]

Since the superpowers can probably estimate each other's stockpiles of
fissile materials reasonably well, there is no obvious reason why they
could not, on the basis of these estimates, negotiate reductions of 50
percent or so in their weapon stockpiles. As stockpiles were further
reduced, small violations would become potentially more important, and
so a greater exchange of information and more refined analyses would be
necessary to lay the basis for further reduction agreements.

There is no reason, however, to delay actions that could be taken
immediately. If the superpowers are willing to accept safeguards on their
nuclear activities not related to weapons, both a cutoff in production of
fissile material for nuclear weapons and substantial reductions in the
quantities of fissile materials already in weapons could be satisfactorily
verified.

A Low-Threshold Nuclear Test Ban

WITH HAROLD A. FEIVESON AND CHRISTOPHER E. PAINE

The testing of nuclear weapons is currently banned in all environments, except underground, by the Limited Test Ban Treaty of 1963. Furthermore, the Threshold Test Ban Treaty of 1974 limits the yields of U.S. and Soviet underground tests to no more than 150 kilotons.

When, the Soviet Union undertook an 18 month unilateral testing moratorium, from July 1985 to February 1987, it dramatized its interest in banning *all* underground nuclear explosions. But the Reagan administration, supported by the Joint Chiefs of Staff and the nuclear weapons laboratories flatly rejected a Comprehensive Test Ban (CTB). In February 1987, at the end of the Soviet moratorium, the Reagan administration summarized its position on a CTB as follows:[1]

> As long as we depend on nuclear weapons for our security, we must insure that those weapons are safe, secure, reliable and effective. This demands some level of underground nuclear testing as permitted by existing treaties.

Other opponents of comprehensive ban added that it is also important to be able to use underground nuclear explosions to test the resistance of military systems to nuclear weapons effects.

Within Congress, however, strong interest was expressed in the possibility of lowering the yield limit on underground testing, as far as verifiability by seismic means will allow. In August 1986, the U.S. House of Representatives voted an amendment (later dropped in Senate–House conference) which would have withheld funding for U.S. testing above 1 kiloton, provided the Soviet Union reciprocated and cooperated with the U.S. in establishing in-country seismic monitoring stations.[2] In May 1987, the House again attached this amendment to its version of the Fiscal Year 1988 Defense Authorization Bill while, in the Senate, a modified version of the amendment containing more detailed verification provisions and a small quota for tests up to 15 kilotons was introduced with bipartisan sponsorship.

This essay explores the extent to which a Low-Threshold Test Ban (LTTB) approach deals with the concerns raised by the Reagan administration.[3] It also examines the possibility of allowing a small quota of tests at higher yields to deal with the concerns raised about maintaining reliability.

The discussion is based entirely on public information, together with insights from simple physics calculations. Although we have not had access to the secret literature on nuclear weapons design, we have been assured by several reviewers that none of our basic conclusions are invalidated by it. Lack of access has offered one important advantage: the freedom to discuss what we *do* know publicly.

The Debate over Nuclear Testing

For more than two decades, the most prominent arguments against a Comprehensive Test Ban centered on verification questions. These questions became particularly difficult after 1959, when CTB opponents showed that it was possible theoretically to muffle small nuclear explosions in large underground caverns[4]—a possibility that was subsequently confirmed by experiment.[5] This conclusion meant that nonseismic means, such as satellite photography, would need to be depended upon to detect preparations for such tests, or in-country seismic monitoring would be required to detect their seismic vibrations. For many years, the Soviet Union was unwilling to permit in-country monitoring.

During the Carter administration, however, the Soviet Union agreed, in principle, to allow deployment of unmanned seismic monitoring stations within its borders. Then, in July 1986, the USSR allowed a private U.S. group to set up three manned seismic stations around its principal test site in Eastern Kazakhstan. Much analytical work has been done in assessing the potential capabilities of in-country seismic monitoring networks. There is now general agreement within the expert community that, given

25–30 carefully sited seismic stations within both the U.S. and USSR, even muffled nuclear explosions could be reliably detected and identified down to yields of a few kilotons[6] or less.[7]

As the ability to monitor testing limitations has improved, however, test-ban opponents have begun emphasizing various other reasons why the U.S. needs to continue testing. The reasons are discussed below, under the headings of effectiveness, reliability, safety and security, and weapons effects. Effectiveness is discussed first because it relates to the need to develop new nuclear weapons, the primary purpose of underground testing today.

Effectiveness of Nuclear Weapons

In the U.S., technical concepts for new types of nuclear weapons are usually developed at two nuclear weapons laboratories: the Lawrence Livermore National Laboratory in California and the Los Alamos National Laboratory in New Mexico. These technical concepts are then developed into weapons concepts by the weapons labs and the military, and finally into specific production programs for new nuclear weapons which are proposed to Congress. The weapons labs participate at each stage in planning and have also played a leading role in opposing limitations on nuclear testing.

The weapons-laboratory perspective on the importance of the continued development of new nuclear weapons has been presented repeatedly to Congress. An example is the following statement, taken from the 1985 congressional testimony of C. Paul Robinson, then Principal Associate Director for National Security Programs at Los Alamos National Laboratory:[8]

> All our experience at Los Alamos convinces me that continued research, development, and testing of nuclear weapons is essential if the United States is to continue to rely on the nuclear deterrent as we know it. . . . a CTB . . . would prevent us from validating the development of weapons that would allow us to respond to new requirements such as those which may derive from the changes that are occurring in the targets we must hold at risk in the Soviet Union. These requirements might include using maneuvering reentry vehicles (MaRVs) to counter Soviet defenses; developing earth penetrating weapons to hold at risk extremely hard, buried targets (missile silos, deep underground facilities) and developing effective means to hold at risk mobile and imprecisely located targets. . . . To

ensure that we could destroy buried or hardened Soviet C^3 [command, control, and communications] assets or missile silos, we need to know more about cratering, ground shock, source-region electromagnetic pulse, and other phenomena associated with nuclear explosions. To be able to hold at risk mobile Soviet weapons and support capabilities, we need to know more about the generation of microwave radiation by nuclear explosions.

This excerpt refers to one "third-generation" weapons concept—the use of nuclear weapons to generate microwave radiation to destroy the electronics of mobile targets. Another third-generation concept, often mentioned by testing advocates, is a nuclear-explosion-pumped X-ray laser that could be used to attack ballistic missiles and satellites in space. Indeed, the development of third-generation nuclear weapons already consumed about one-half of the $1 billion U.S. budget for exploratory research on nuclear weapons in fiscal year 1988, with the other half primarily focused on improving second-generation warheads designed to attack Soviet nuclear forces.[9]

Statements such as Robinson's should not be misunderstood to mean that weapons scientists necessarily believe that nuclear weapons could be used successfully to fight and win wars. However, most proponents of new nuclear weapons *do* believe that the U.S. can best protect its own security and that of its allies by continuing to improve the U.S. arsenal of strategic "counterforce" weapons—weapons specifically designed to attack the Soviet nuclear arsenal and its command and control system.

There is an opposing view about the value of counterforce weapons, however, which sees the possession of counterforce weapons by the U.S. and USSR as creating incentives both to strike first and launch on warning of attack. It is therefore argued that new counterforce weapons such as the earth-penetrating warhead and enhanced microwave warhead advocated by Robinson would be crisis-destabilizing and should not be developed. Nuclear weapons designed to destroy space targets are also seen as destabilizing since they, too, might be used most effectively by the side that strikes first.

Of course, the value that one assigns to the deterrent effects of U.S. counterforce capabilities, relative to their crisis-destabilizing effects, depends heavily upon one's assumptions concerning the psychology of the Soviet leadership. Official views on this question can also be found in congressional testimony. For example, Richard L. Wagner, then Assistant to the Secretary of Defense for Atomic Energy, made the following statement in 1983 concerning the psychological impact of new nuclear weapons on the probability of war:[10]

> What it comes down to in the end is to keep [the Soviets'] image of themselves inferior to their image of us, so that if a crisis comes they will have a gut feeling that they won't measure up against us. It is often said that Soviet leaders are conservative. They are when they feel inferior. . . . our job is to keep them feeling inferior and thus conservative. . . . I believe that our level of technology in itself, quite apart from exactly how it is built into fielded systems, affects their overall image of themselves and of us, and thus can have a significant deterrent effect. . . . By the [19]90s we'll need some really new technology to keep the image ratio in our favor. The technology of nuclear explosive design is an important part of our overall technological capability.

This statement was unusual more for its bluntness than for the views expressed, which are widely held among government officials who believe in the strategic value of continuing efforts to refine nuclear-weapons technology.

Test-ban advocates typically express quite a different view of the value of continued development of new nuclear weapons. This view is that, once a country obtains even one-tenth of the high levels of survivable destructive power that the United States and Soviet Union both currently possess, it has bought most of the deterrence that nuclear weapons can provide. Beyond that point, trying to give the nuclear threat more credibility is like a man who has filled up his house with dynamite continually inventing new triggering mechanisms to convince potential burglars that the house really will blow up if they break in. In this view, the nuclear weapons modernization process simply fosters a nuclear warfighting approach to deterrence which dehumanizes the other side, undermines diplomatic steps toward Soviet-American reconciliation, and weakens the ability of the U.S. and USSR to persuade other nations not to develop nuclear weapons.

Another frequently claimed benefit of continued testing—reduction in the destructiveness of the nuclear arsenals—has been described in a White House strategy document as follows:[11]

> . . . the United States does not target population as an objective in itself and seeks to minimize collateral damage through more accurate, lower yield weapons.

In fact, despite dramatic increases in accuracy, the W-87 warhead for the MX missile has twice the yield of the original warhead on the Minuteman III missile which it replaced and the yield of the W-88 warhead for the Trident II missile is about 10 times as great as the yield of the warhead on the first MIRVed submarine-launched missile, the Poseidon.[12]

Temperatures and Yields

Modern strategic nuclear warheads release their energy in two main "stages." In the primary stage, most of the energy release is caused by fission. Energy from this primary explosion then compresses and heats the fuel in the secondary stage to the point at which thermonuclear reactions are ignited. Typically, a considerable amount of additional fission energy is also released in the secondary stage.

In the primary stage, a mass containing a few kilograms of "fissile" (chain-reacting) plutonium-239 and/or uranium-235 is "imploded" into a denser configuration by surrounding chemical explosions. As the spacing between the nuclei in the imploding mass decreases, the probability increases that any free neutron traveling through the mass will be captured by a fissile nucleus, causing a fission and the release of two to three new neutrons. At some point, the capture probability rises through the threshold above which an exponential fission chain reaction can be sustained. In this domain, the compressed mass is termed "supercritical."

The total energy released by a fission chain reaction initiated in such a configuration is proportional to the number of fissions that occur before the pressures developed by the energy release reverse the implosion and return the density to a subcritical level. The time scale for the entire explosion is much less than a microsecond (a millionth of a second) with the energy release growing from tons to kilotons of TNT equivalent in the last one-hundredth of a microsecond.[13]

Although the complete fission of only about 60 grams of fissile material releases an amount of energy equal to that released by 1,000 tons (one kiloton) of standard chemical explosive, even the lowest-yield fission warheads in the U.S. nuclear arsenal weigh tens of kilograms. Most of this weight is associated with the implosion system. Much of the refinement of fission explosives has therefore been devoted to the reduction of this extra weight, thereby increasing the yield to weight ratio of nuclear explosions.

A major contribution to the increase of the yield-to-weight ratios of fission primaries has occurred through the introduction into the fissile core of a small quantity (probably a few grams) of deuterium-tritium gas. The rapid increase in temperature during the fission explosion ignites the thermonuclear reaction, releasing a burst of high-energy neutrons which give a final "boost" to the chain reaction just as expansion is causing the mass to become subcritical. Since a deuterium-tritium fusion releases only one-tenth as much energy as a fission event, the fusion reactions make only a relatively minor direct contribution to the total energy of the explosion, but their neutrons make a large indirect contribution through the extra fissions they cause.

The deuterium-tritium reaction rate becomes significant on the very short time scale involved in a fission explosion only when the temperature in the core becomes of the order of 100 million degrees Kelvin.[14] At these temperatures, the collisions of the deuterium and tritium nuclei become violent enough so that they can penetrate each other's electrostatic shields, allowing short-range nuclear reactions to take place. In order to achieve such a temperature, at least 1 percent of the material in the core must fission.[15] If we assume that the minimum amount of fissile material required to make a practical primary is two kilograms of weapon-grade plutonium,[16] the fission of 1 percent of this material would release about 0.4 kilotons of energy. This estimate of the minimum amount of fission energy release required in practice to reach the threshold for boosting is consistent with the statement by Theodore B. Taylor, a former weapons designer, that "[i]t is difficult to imagine militarily attractive boosted weapons with yields less than one kiloton or so."[17]

The thermonuclear reactions in the "secondary" are ignited by compression—apparently caused by the energy carried by the black body x-rays radiated by the hot primary.[18] High efficiency in the conversion of fission energy into x-ray energy is therefore a key *desideratum* in a primary. This efficiency is a function of the primary's yield-to-weight ratio. In the approximation that the temperature of the core and surrounding implosion mechanism is uniform after the completion of the release of the energy in the primary, the fraction of the primary's energy going into x-rays increases rapidly with yield-to-weight ratio until it exceeds 50 percent at yield-to-weight ratios above about 0.1 kilotons per kilogram (see Figure 1).[19]

Based on the yield-to-weight ratios of pure fission warheads, a primary with a yield-to-weight ratio of 0.1 kilotons per kilogram would weigh about 100 kilograms and have a yield of about 10 kilotons.[20] The fact that a significant portion of U.S. testing occurs in the yield range of 5 to 15

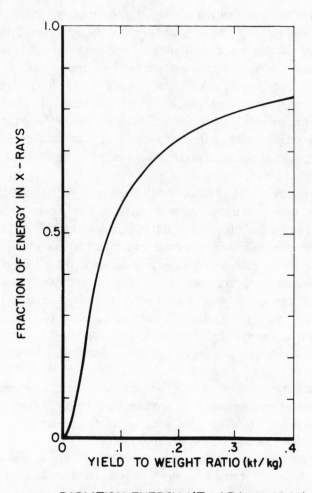

RADIATION ENERGY / (Total Primary Yield)

FIG. 1. *In a strategic nuclear weapon, the x-rays produced by a "primary" fission explosive carry the energy that causes the compression and heating of the thermonuclear fuel in the "secondary." This graph suggests that, in order to be efficient producers of x-rays, primaries would have to have yield-to-weight ratios of 0.1 kt/kg or greater. Such yield-to-weight ratios are achievable at about 10 kt. The graph shows, as a function of yield-to-weight ratio, the fraction of the energy released by a fission weapon that is in the form of x-rays. The residues of the explosive are assumed to be fully ionized and at a uniform temperature, and the x-ray radiation field inside the weapon casing is assumed to be in thermal equilibrium with these residues at the original bomb density of 2,500 kg/m³.*

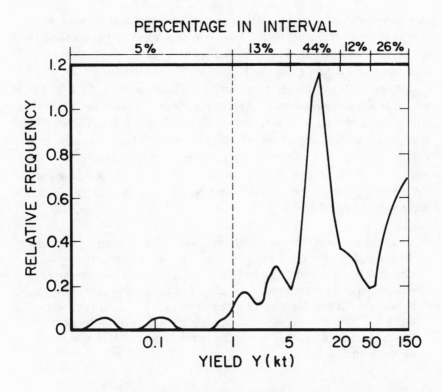

DISTRIBUTION OF U.S. EXPOSIVE YIELDS (1980–1984)

FIG. 2. *This figure shows the yield distribution of U.S. tests for the period 1980–1984. Equal areas under the curve correspond to equal relative frequencies of testing. The relatively high frequency of testing in the 5–15 kiloton yield range is probably mostly due to the tests of the fission "primaries" of thermonuclear weapons. The peak at higher yield reflects the influence of the U.S.—USSR Threshold Test Ban Treaty, which constrains all U.S. and Soviet nuclear explosions to yields of not more than 150 kilotons.*

kilotons (see Figure 2)[21] suggests that U.S. strategic weapons have such "hot" primaries.

This analysis gives us our second temperature-related point of nuclear yield. Note that both of these points relate to the performance of boosted primaries: the first, at about one kiloton, relates to the onset of thermonuclear reactions in the primary, and the second, at about ten kilotons, relates to the capability of the primary to ignite thermonuclear reactions in a high-yield secondary. (This does not mean that it is impossible for a thermonuclear explosive with a low-yield secondary to have a total yield lower than ten kilotons. The so-called "neutron bomb," which has a yield of about one kiloton, is an instance of such an explosive.)[22]

The fact that primaries account for a significant portion of the weight of all but the highest-yield modern thermonuclear warheads has made them a principal target for weight-reduction efforts. It probably accounts for the relatively high frequency with which they are tested and may also be one reason why virtually all concern expressed about the reliability of U.S. nuclear weapons focuses on primaries. It is certainly the message carried by the most explicit public statement to date on this subject from the weapons laboratories:[23]

> It is by now no secret that the large majority of reliability problems discovered in the US stockpile over the years have involved the physical process known as boosting. . . . [L]aboratory experiments have been and continue to be incapable of accurately predicting the results of nuclear tests of boosted devices. . . . This is a fact of particular importance when those devices are used as triggers for thermonuclear weapons, where the permissible range of yields may be quite small.

Reliability

Concerns raised about the possibility that U.S. nuclear weapons might become unreliable in the absence of testing played a key role in derailing President Carter's efforts to achieve a Comprehensive Test Ban.[24] The technical basis for this concern was immediately challenged in a letter to Carter from a former weapons laboratory director and two former weapon designers.[25] However, spokesmen for the weapons laboratories continued to insist that reliability remained a real concern.

The most precise official statement of which we are aware regarding the use of nuclear weapons tests to maintain stockpile reliability is the following: "More than one third of all weapons designs introduced into the stockpile since 1958 have encountered reliability problems. Of these 75 percent were discovered and/or corrected as a result of nuclear testing."[26]

Several of these instances of reliability problems were publicly discussed by Jack Rosengren, a former weapons designer, as evidence of the need for nuclear weapons testing to maintain confidence in the weapons stockpile.[27] But Ray Kidder, another former weapons designer, reviewed the Rosengren study and concluded that:

> none of the examples cited . . . support[s] the thesis that nuclear explosive testing is necessary to maintain confidence in the reliability of the *existing* U.S. nuclear stockpile of *thoroughly tested* nuclear weapons. . . .[28]

Kidder's critique elicited a rebuttal from Rosengren, which Kidder rebutted in turn.[29] Finally, at the request of the U.S. House of Representatives' Committee on Armed Services, Kidder prepared a detailed analysis of the historical data bearing on the relationship between nuclear testing and warhead reliability and the leadership of the Lawrence Livermore National Laboratory issued a rebuttal.[30]

It may be impossible for outside observers to come to a final conclusion on the reliability issue, based on such fragments of the debate declassified by the weapons labs. However, the following three key facts *have* been established:

1) Prohibitive numbers of nuclear tests would be required to maintain confidence in the continuing reliability of the stockpile with random nuclear tests. The principal way in which problems in the stockpile are detected and rectified today is by disassembly and inspection and by non-nuclear tests.

2) During the period 1970–1985, only eight underground nuclear explosions were justified by the need to "correct defects in stockpiled weapons."[31] A comparable number were probably carried out to determine the seriousness of problems detected during routine disassembly and inspection. The resulting total of an average of about one reliability test per year should be compared with the average of a total of approximately 20 U.S. nuclear tests per year during this same period.

3) As has already been noted, almost all reliability problems concern the primary. Those who argue that reliability tests are required therefore only argue for tests up to the full yield of the primary—which we have concluded is typically less than 15 kilotons for U.S. primaries. This situation may account for the willingness of former Livermore Director and Secretary of Defense Harold Brown in 1986 to endorse a threshold test ban with a yield limit at five kilotons.[32] It may also account for the statement in 1977 by Harold Agnew, then Director of Los Alamos National Laboratory, that "I don't believe testing below

say five or ten kilotons can do much to improve (as compared to maintaining) strategic posture. . . . "[33]

It would appear that a quota of about one test per year at a yield of about five to ten kilotons could satisfy the concerns that have been raised about the need for reliability tests.[34]

It appears quite possible that an independent review, with full access to the relevant information, would establish that even this small number of tests would be unnecessary, or could be phased out within a few years, if no new weapons designs were introduced into the weapons stockpile.*

Alternatively, a consensus could probably be achieved to forgo reliability tests if the U.S. were to abandon its emphasis on counterforce. A high degree of reliability is significant only to those who believe that it would be possible to destroy thousands of military targets in the Soviet Union with nuclear explosions without inflicting "unacceptable" damage to the civilian population.[35]

Safety and Security

Another technical reason given for continued testing is the need to improve safety and protection against unauthorized use.

With regard to safety, U.S. nuclear weapons are already designed to be "one-point safe"—not to explode with a significant nuclear yield even if a segment of the chemical explosives in the nuclear trigger is detonated by the penetration of a bullet or by fire.[†] Current work on safety improvements is therefore focused on the much less serious problem of reducing

---

* A listing of reliability tests declassified after this was written shows that, during the period 1961–1987, there were 39 nuclear explosive tests conducted for the purpose of correcting problems in stockpiled weapons—an average of 1.5 per year. [See Table 2 in *Nuclear Weapons Tests: The Role of the University of California-Department of Energy Laboratories* (University of California, July 1987).] Curiously, all of these tests occurred in two periods: 1961–1964 (28 tests) after a three-year testing moratorium and 1980–1987 (11 tests). More relevant to the question of a low-threshold test-bam treaty, however, is the fact that only in the case of one warhead was a reliability test conducted more than four years after the weapon entered the stockpile. [For warhead initial production dates, see table 1.2 in Thomas B. Cochran, William M. Arkin, R. Stan Norris, and Militon M. Hoenig, *U.S. Nuclear Warhead Production* (Ballinger, 1987).] In the absence of the introduction of new warheads, therefore, we would expect that the rate of required stockpile confidence tests would quickly drop to a *very* low level—probably zero.

† Since this was written, the U.S. nuclear-weapons laboratories have made public the fact that three-dimensional calculations using supercomputers have revealed that not all U.S. nuclear-warhead designs are one-point safe. See Sidney D. Drell, John S. Foster and Charles H. Townes, "Report of the Panel on Nuclear Weapons Safety" in *Nuclear Weapons Safety*, Committee Print of the Committee on Armed Services of the House of Representatives (U.S. Government Printing Office, Washington, D.C.: 1990).

the likelihood of dispersal of toxic plutonium as a result of the accidental detonation of the chemical high explosives. An important advance in this regard has been the introduction in new nuclear weapons of "insensitive high explosives" (IHE), which are much less subject to accidental explosions. The introduction of IHE into the U.S. arsenal was motivated primarily by the need to reduce risks associated with the movements of airborne and land-mobile weapons.[36] Modern nuclear bombs containing IHE are now available with a full range of yields and the warheads of all U.S. cruise missiles contain IHE. The warhead for the MX, which contains IHE, could be used on the proposed land-mobile "Midgetman" intercontinental ballistic missile as well.[37]

In many cases where new warheads containing IHE have not been developed, there are institutional or technical reasons. Thus, for example, the Navy elected *not* to put IHE in the warhead for its Trident II ballistic missile because warheads containing IHE are somewhat heavier and the substitution would therefore reduce either the range or number of warheads that could be carried by the missile. If the Navy changed its mind, the Trident II could use the same warhead as the MX. In the case of artillery shells, the problem is technical: since a larger volume of IHE is required to release a given amount of energy, the small diameter of artillery shells makes them difficult to convert. Finally, replacement warheads are not being developed for some tactical weapons that are being phased out in favor of precision-guided conventional weapons.[38]

Virtually all other safety improvements are focused on the mechanical and electrical designs of the triggering systems and can therefore be adequately tested without a significant nuclear explosion. One way in which this is done is by removing the fissile material from the primary and replacing it with nonfissile material such as U-238. The progression of the implosion is then followed with imbedded sensors and flash x-ray pictures. Even more sensitive tests are sometimes conducted by partially removing the chain-reacting material, leaving only enough so that the result is a nuclear explosion with a yield equivalent to the explosion of less than one kilogram of TNT. Production of neutrons from such a "zero-yield" nuclear test provides an extremely sensitive measure of the degree of compression that has been achieved by the chemical implosion. Such tests were used by the U.S. to explore safety problems during the 1958–1961 U.S.-Soviet nuclear testing moratorium.[39]

Permissive-action links (PALs), the electronically coded locks that are used to secure U.S. nuclear weapons from unauthorized use, have already gone through several generations of improvements. The primary issue today is not further technical refinement but rather the fact that many weapons in the U.S. stockpile, including the weapons on ballistic-missile submarines, still have no PALs at all. A test ban would not prevent the introduction of modern (category D, six-digit code) PALs into currently unprotected weapons or weapons with earlier-generation PALs because this type of PAL works on components that do not require nuclear tests to certify their performance.[40]

Nuclear Weapons Effects

The final use of nuclear weapons tests is to examine the ability of military equipment—especially nuclear warheads—to withstand the effects of nearby nuclear explosions. For this purpose, the Limited Test Ban already imposes significant constraints on our ability to obtain further knowledge of such key nuclear weapons effects as the electromagnetic pulse from nuclear explosions in near space or on cratering by large surface-burst explosions. Much of the knowledge obtainable from underground tests can be gleaned from low-yield explosions, and therefore the need for effects tests is not a strong argument against an LTTB. For example, about the same radiation intensities can be achieved 40 meters from a 1-kiloton test as 500 meters from a 150-kiloton test. For this reason, and because tests involving smaller-yield explosions are less expensive, most U.S. nuclear weapons effects tests are already conducted at quite low yields.[41] If a small number of 5 to 15 kiloton tests were allowed, they could be used for those few applications where a higher-temperature source is advantageous.

Effects of a Low-Threshold Test Ban

A one-kiloton threshold test ban would severely impede the development of all new nuclear directed-energy weapons other than those with yields of a few kilotons or less.[42]

However, a low-threshold test ban would not by itself prevent development and deployment of new strategic and tactical nuclear delivery systems. New delivery systems could be developed with nuclear warheads as fixed rather than variable parameters in their design. For example, the already tested MX warhead could be mated to the mobile single-warhead Midgetman missile.*

* Former weapons designers R.L. Garwin, J.C. Mark and H.A. Bethe have wryly observed that, "It might need shock alleviation mounting for a mobile Midgetman subject to nuclear attack, but the demand for a new nuclear warhead is analogous to requiring that one redesign an astronaut before launching him or her into space. Careful attention to packaging will do.

A low-threshold test ban would also meet the concerns that have been raised with respect to the effects of a test ban on nuclear weapons safety and security and on our ability to collect information about nuclear weapons effects.

The addition of a quota of about one test per year at a yield of 5 to 15 kilotons would allow the continuation of reliability tests at their previous rate. To the extent that a small permitted quota of 10-kiloton tests were exploited for weapons development rather than reliability tests, some slow progress could also be made on the development of new weapons with yields up to perhaps 30 kilotons.[43] Since the certification for deployment of even a modestly improved version of an already existing type of warhead currently typically requires about 10 tests, however, the development of qualitatively new weapons types would be greatly impeded.

A disadvantage of a Low-Threshold Test Ban relative to a CTB is that it would still allow the development of exotic new types of subkiloton weapons and the exploration of the underlying physics and technology that could be used to develop higher-yield weapons if the treaty limits were to break down. For this reason, some arms-control experts advocate still more stringent limitations on nuclear weapons testing. Richard Garwin, for example, would only permit "explosive releases of nuclear energy" sufficiently small that they could safely take place "in permanently occupied above-ground buildings. . . ."[44] This might be taken as a reasonable definition of a comprehensive test ban.

We share the hope that, after in-country seismic monitoring systems are fully established and tested, it will become politically possible to lower the threshold to below one kiloton and eventually to near zero as a result of increased public confidence in nonseismic means of verification. Only then will the nuclear-testing nations be in a position to present the treaty for signature by nonweapons states—thereby obtaining a meaningful technical barrier to the proliferation of thermonuclear weapons and an additional moral and political barrier to the spread of all nuclear weapons.*

[*Public Interest Report* (Federation of American Scientists, Washington, D.C., December 1986, p. 11).]
* Since we wrote this, I have become convinced that the pursuit of intermediate goals short of a CTB is a prescription for indefinite delay in a CTB and that the strengthening of the legitimacy of the non-proliferation regime requires a CTB by 1995. See Don Fenstermacher, Nikolai Kapranov and Frank von Hippel, *Toward a Comprehensive Nuclear Warhead Test Ban* (International Foundation for the Survival and Development of Humanity, Washington, D.C.: 1991).

The Nuclear Laboratories Versus a Test Ban

WITH JOSEPHINE ANNE STEIN

The United States committed itself to seek a comprehensive nuclear weapons test ban in 1963 in the Limited Test Ban Treaty and in 1970 in the Nuclear Nonproliferation Treaty. Negotiations between Washington, Moscow and London in the late 1970s established agreement on the technical basis for effective verification, including detailed arrangements for incountry monitoring. Congress urged President Reagan to negotiate a ban. The Kremlin showed its seriousness with an 18-month unilateral moratorium on testing, and offered to extend it indefinitely if America refrained from testing, but America didn't. Why is there no agreement?

One of the most important reasons is opposition from the nation's two principal nuclear weapons design laboratories, at Livermore, California and Los Alamos, New Mexico. On the two occasions when U.S. and Soviet negotiators appeared closest to an agreement on a ban, the laboratories raised objections that dashed hopes of obtaining the two-thirds Senate majority required for treaty ratification.

In 1958, President Dwight D. Eisenhower and Premier Nikita S. Khrushchev halted nuclear testing and began negotiations on a permanent comprehensive test ban. Almost immediately, weapons scientists associated with Livermore argued that the Soviet Union might be able to cheat by testing in an underground cavern. Now, verification experts at Livermore agree that a modern seismic system could detect underground explosions, even if muffled in a cavern, down to a few kilotons—about 1 percent of the yield of today's strategic weapons.

Nonetheless, the laboratories engendered enough doubts about verifiability so that when President John F. Kennedy and Khrushchev signed the Limited Test Ban Treaty, it still permitted underground explosions.

In 1977, under the Carter administration, when both superpowers were again close to agreement, the heads of both laboratories claimed that, in the absence of nuclear testing, the reliability of our stockpiled weapons would decline. Independent experts responded that thorough non-nuclear testing of the warhead components and periodic rebuilding of the warheads to their original design specifications could maintain our stockpile's reliability indefinitely. But it would have been virtually impossible to persuade the Senate to ratify a treaty over the laboratories' opposition, and President Jimmy Carter decided not to try.

The key rationale for continued testing under the Reagan administration also emerged from the laboratories. Early in President Reagan's first term, Edward Teller, Livermore's founder, met with him to promote a nuclear-explosion-powered x-ray laser as a way to protect the U.S. from nuclear-armed ballistic missiles. These talks helped convince Reagan to launch the Strategic Defense Initiative.

Most recently, during the Bush administration, after the x-ray laser weapon proposal had lost its credibility, the weapons laboratories have begun to argue that U.S. nuclear weapons are not sufficiently safe and that new safer designs must be developed and tested.

The laboratories' changing technical arguments against a ban may conceal a deeper motivation for their opposition. When he was director of the lavishly funded nuclear weapons program at Los Alamos, Paul Ribinson articulated a possible reason—the intellectual challenge. "At present, the nuclear weapons program in total, both in offensive uses, defense suppression, as well as defense, is more exciting than I've ever known it." Apparently the weapons designers were enjoying developing methods for penetrating and destroying the defenses they are inventing.

However, nuclear arms, inherently weapons of mass destruction, are unusable for fighting war. Continued nuclear testing is a waste of precious resources. The enormous technical talent at Los Alamos and Livermore should be redirected to meet other pressing national needs. America should fulfill its treaty obligations by negotiating and ratifying a comprehensive test ban.

Reducing the Confrontation*

The Soviet Union and the United States each possesses 10 to 100 times the destructive power required to destroy either as a modern society. These levels of destructive power make the nuclear arms race a concern of the entire world. They also create opportunities for reductions by as much as 90 percent and provide the leaders of the United States and the Soviet Union with great freedom to experiment with unilateral initiatives as a way to build support for disarmament.

The pervasive fears of disarming surprise attacks that help drive the arms race are greatly exaggerated: a large fraction of the nuclear weapons on each side remain safe because they are well hidden in the ocean, can escape attack in aircraft, or are on land-mobile launchers. As a result, a surprise attack by either side could only succeed in reducing the total destructive power of the other by perhaps one-half—an insignificant result, given the levels of destructiveness both would possess, even after 90 percent reductions.

It is also critical to realize that an attempt at a disarming attack would kill tens of millions of people—making it both a crime against humanity and probably the first step toward the end of civilization.

With regard to the possibility of defense, an effort by either side to protect itself against nuclear attack by building defenses appears hopeless. The leaders of both the United States and Soviet Union accepted this reality in 1972 when they signed the treaty limiting antiballistic-missile systems. The integrity of this Treaty remains critical, since it stands in the

* This essay was delivered as a speech to General Secretary Mikhail Gorbachev and other senior officials of the Soviet government, in their meeting with the 1,500 participants in eight parallel "International Forums on Drastic Reductions and the Final Elimination of Nuclear Weapons" at the Kremlin Palace, February 16, 1987.

way of a still more wasteful and dangerous arms race. The deployment of large-scale antiballistic-missile systems would also dangerously reduce strategic stability.

Some suggest, however, that space-based weapons systems are so obviously foolish that they will probably never be deployed. They argue that resolution of the controversy should not delay reductions agreements that may be achieved now. It could be made clear that such reductions might be reversed if, in fact, the Antiballistic-Missile Treaty was abandoned.*

A much more stable balance could be achieved at a 90 percent reduced level of nuclear weapons—primarily through the elimination of two large classes of offensive nuclear weapons. The first class is multiple-warhead ballistic missiles. These have been acquired by both sides primarily because of their abilities to attack nuclear weapons of the other side. This creates a particularly dangerous instability. Most multiple-warhead ballistic missiles should therefore be eliminated or replaced by single-warhead missiles.

The other weapons that should be eliminated are so-called "tactical" nuclear weapons, designed for battles between military forces on land or sea. These are destabilizing because there could be pressure to use them even in small conflicts and, once used, the barrier to large-scale use would be broken.

The proliferation of nuclear-armed cruise missiles is also a serious problem and they should be strictly limited.

Although there is no insuperable technical barrier to drastic reductions, further developments are required before we can determine how to take the final step to the complete abolition of nuclear weapons. The goal of abolition is, however, an essential part of a more hopeful future for humanity. This objective should be a central part of our research agenda.

The threat of non-nuclear war must also be reduced in parallel to that of nuclear war. Military forces in Europe must be restructured to appear less threatening. Advocates of such a reconstruction call it "nonoffensive" or "nonprovocative" defense and believe that it could contribute to a second wave of détente in Europe. The Soviet Union and the United

* This was Andrei Sakharov's position, which he put forth publicly for the first time at the International Scientists' Forum on Drastic Reductions and the Final Elimination of Nuclear Weapons in Moscow in February 1987. The Soviet government finally adopted this position in November 1989.

States should both become more seriously involved in discussions of the possibility of less provocative defensive postures in Europe.

Finally, a continuing commitment to an open and democratic future for the Soviet Union could, in the long term, be the greatest contribution that the Soviet citizenry and government can make to the ending of the nuclear arms race.

Civilian Casualties from Counterforce Attacks

WITH BARBARA G. LEVI,
THEODORE A. POSTOL
AND WILLIAM H. DAUGHERTY

T he ratification of the agreement between the U.S. and the Soviet Union to ban all intermediate-range nuclear missiles and the progress toward completion of the Strategic Arms Reduction Talks (START), which have as their primary aim a 50 percent cut in the number of long-range ballistic-missile warheads to approximately 5,000 on each side, have given many observers reason to be optimistic about the prospect for further reductions in the nuclear arsenals, which will still include about 20,000 strategic and tactical nuclear warheads deployed on each side. Further reductions, however, will require the U.S. and the Soviet Union to reassess many of the military missions they have planned for their nuclear forces in the event of war.

The missions that would be most affected by further nuclear-arms reductions are generally known as counterforce missions. Their purpose is to destroy the military capabilities of the opponent, including nuclear and non-nuclear forces, as well as the industrial base on which the forces depend. Since the opponent's strategic forces represent the greatest threat, they are considered to be the highest-priority targets for counterforce missions. Because there are thousands of potential targets for a strategic counterforce mission, plans for comprehensive attacks result in nuclear arsenals of vast size.

Counterforce attacks could not significantly limit the damage that the U.S. or the USSR could do in a retaliatory attack (see Figures 1 and 2).

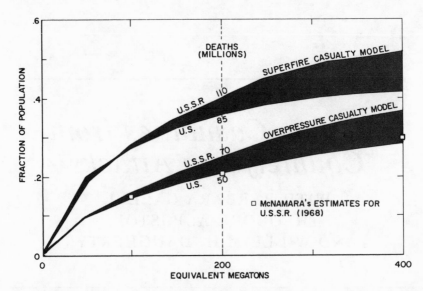

FIG. 1. *How many nuclear weapons does it take to deter a nuclear attack? According to the "assured destruction" criterion first laid out in the 1960s by Secretary of Defense Robert S. McNamara, the capability of detonating—in a retaliatory attack—200 equivalent megatons over Soviet cities would effectively deter the USSR. The authors' calculations show that such an attack on the United States or on the Soviet Union would result in prompt fatalities amounting to as much as 40 percent of the population (about 100 million people) if the lethal effects of the superfires are taken into account.*

However, many defense analysts argue that threatening to destroy a variety of military targets deters limited aggression more effectively than threatening to attack cities, because such threats are less likely to elicit a devastating counterstrike against the cities of the attacker and can therefore be made more credibly. In addition the country that first executes such missions might hope to destroy many more of the other side's warheads than it employs in carrying out the attack. Such a lopsided exchange is made possible in part by modern nuclear missiles that carry multiple warheads, each of which is capable of destroying a different target. Unfortunately, the perception that one might gain instability, with each side tempted to preempt the other's attack if nuclear war appears possible. The START Treaty will not eliminate this instability since it allows each side to retain its most modern multiple-warhead missiles.

Both sides are reluctant to eliminate these accurate multiple-warhead missiles because they are crucial to the execution of strategic counter-

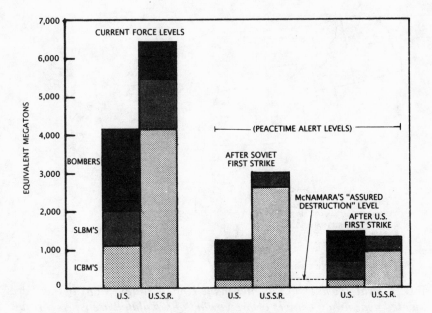

FIG. 2. *Both the U.S. and the USSR have substantially more equivalent megatons in their respective strategic arsenals than are necessary to meet McNamara's assured-destruction criterion—even after their strategic forces have suffered a "worst case" nuclear attack. The excess weapons are justified largely on the grounds that they are required to execute "counterforce" attacks on military facilities, in particular those associated with the nuclear forces of the other side.*

force attacks—especially against the silo-based multiple-warhead missiles of the other side. But does the U.S. or USSR need to rely on a strategic counterforce mission to prevent aggression? Does a counterforce capability really provide a more credible deterrent by threatening military targets and not civilian ones? Our calculations suggest a negative answer: they show that a large-scale attack on strategic forces would cause so many civilian casualties that it would be difficult to distinguish the resulting catastrophe from that which would be caused by a deliberate attack on the population.

Curiously enough, the number of civilian deaths that counterforce attacks would cause remains a relatively neglected topic in the nuclear-weapons policy debate. Even during the 1980 presidential cam-

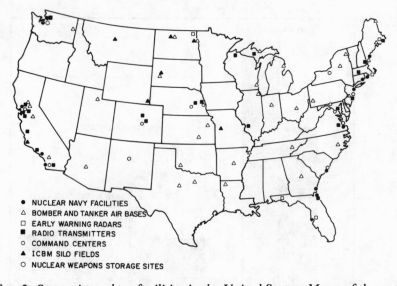

• NUCLEAR NAVY FACILITIES
△ BOMBER AND TANKER AIR BASES
□ EARLY WARNING RADARS
■ RADIO TRANSMITTERS
○ COMMAND CENTERS
▲ ICBM SILO FIELDS
○ NUCLEAR WEAPONS STORAGE SITES

FIG. 3. *Strategic nuclear facilities in the United States. Many of these are located near urban centers or are upwind of populated areas. As a result there are likely to be tens of millions of civilian deaths from the blast fire and radioactive fallout from a counterforce attack, even though only military facilities (and not cities per se) are the targets.*

paign, when the vulnerability of U.S. ICBMs became a political issue, the civilian casualties that would result from an attack on the ICBMs was not even mentioned. Indeed, we know of only one public discussion of the subject by the U.S. Department of Defense—and that took place in 1975.[1]

In our calculations we considered the consequences of attacking with nuclear weapons 1,215 strategic nuclear facilities in the U.S. and 1,740 strategic nuclear facilities in the USSR (see Figures 3 and 4). All but approximately 100 of the targets on each side are either missile silos or their associated launch-control centers. The disparity between the numbers of targets is due to the fact that the Soviet Union has more missile silos than the U.S. Other targets on the lists are bases for long-range bombers, and ports for ballistic-missile submarines, aircraft carriers and ships carrying long-range, nuclear-armed cruise missiles. We assumed that early-warning radar installations and key command-and-communication facilities would also be struck by nuclear weapons, in order to effect the maximum surprise and blunt the effectiveness of any retaliatory attack.[2]

The list of targets in the U.S. includes major nuclear-weapon depots and bases for the tanker aircraft that would refuel U.S. bombers on the

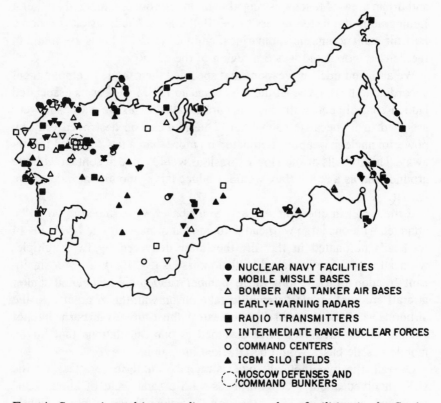

FIG. 4. *Strategic and intermediate-range nuclear facilities in the Soviet Union.*

way to and from their targets in the Soviet Union. The list of targets in the USSR includes antiballistic-missile launchers around Moscow and bases for mobile intermediate-range missiles and nuclear-armed bombers, which could be employed to attack facilities of the North Atlantic Treaty Organization in Europe.

A review of the listed targets indicates that many of them lie in or near major urban areas. In the U.S., for example, tanker aircraft are based at airports near Chicago, Milwaukee, Phoenix and Salt Lake City; Navy bases for nuclear armed vessels are situated in San Francisco Bay and at Long Beach near Los Angeles (and one is planned for Staten Island in New York Harbor); the Washington D.C. urban area contains key command posts and Navy radio transmitters are located in or near Jacksonville, Sacramento and San Diego.

In the USSR there is a similar colocation of strategic-weapon facilities and urban areas: Moscow is ringed with underground command bunkers; Leningrad is the headquarters of the Baltic fleet; Vladivostok is a home port for ballistic-missile submarines, and many ICBM fields are found in the densely populated western region of the country.

We assigned nuclear weapons and specified their mode of employment according to target type. If the target was an ICBM silo, or its associated launch-control center, the most accurate ballistic-missile warheads were assigned to it, because such "hard" targets can be destroyed only by powerful nuclear weapons detonated no more than a few hundred meters away. The fireballs of such low explosions would come in contact with the ground, and as a result they would produce large amounts of radioactive fallout.*

If the target in question was a U.S. air base, we assumed it would be attacked with one large warhead detonated at or near ground level plus 14 warheads detonated in the air, the latter delivered by two multiple-warhead submarine-launched ballistic missiles (SLBMs). Since a significant fraction of U.S. long-range bombers and their associated tanker aircraft are kept on alert, ready to take off on warning of an attack, the airbursts would be targeted so as to destroy those already airborne but not yet out of the area. We have assumed in our calculations that Soviet mobile-missile bases would be attacked in a similar way.

Overall, the hypothetical Soviet strategic counterforce attack on the U.S. involved about 3,000 warheads with a total yield of about 1,300 megatons, whereas the U.S. attack on the Soviet Union involved slightly more than 4,000 warheads with a total yield of about 800 megatons.† Such attacks are well within the capabilities of each nation, even after the reductions envisioned in the START negotiations. The greater number of warheads and lower total megatonnage of the U.S. attack on the Soviet Union result from respectively the greater number of Soviet missile silos and the smaller average yield of U.S. strategic warheads.

I n calculating the number of civilians who might die or sustain injury as a result of a large-scale strategic counterforce attack, we considered only the direct effects of nuclear explosions: blast, fire and radioactive fallout.

---

* In keeping with standard military planning, such facilities were targeted with two nuclear warheads each in case one of the warheads failed to arrive.
† A megaton is defined as an amount of energy equivalent to that released by the detonation of a million tons of standard chemical explosive.

The standard method applied by the U.S. Defense Department and the Federal Emergency Management Agency (FEMA) for estimating casualties from blast and fire relies on extrapolating the consequences of the relatively small-yield (0.015 megaton) explosion over Hiroshima to the much more powerful nuclear explosives in modern strategic arsenals. To be specific, the government's extrapolation, which we call the "overpressure model," assumes that the casualty rate would be the same as the rate observed in Hiroshima for a given value of the peak blast over-pressure: the maximum air pressure (above the ambient level) produced by the explosion's blast.

Yet some of the casualties at Hiroshima were a consequence of a fire that developed approximately 20 minutes after the explosion and covered a roughly circular area having a radius of about two kilometers. The area was small enough so that most of the people who had not been trapped under collapsed buildings or otherwise incapacitated were able to escape before the environment in the fire area became lethal. Studies done for the Defense Nuclear Agency by Harold L. Brode and Richard D. Small of the Pacific-Sierra Research Corporation suggest that detonation of nuclear warheads over U.S. and Soviet cities and suburbs could result in much larger "superfires": huge conflagrations fanned by hurricane-force winds. Given the typical yield of today's strategic nuclear weapons (at least 10 times greater than the Hiroshima weapon), the conflagration area would be so large that people would not be able to escape before they succumbed to the combined effects of heat, smoke and toxic gases. On these grounds one of us (Postol) suggested in 1985 that the Defense Department and FEMA might be seriously underestimating the potential fatalities from the direct effects of nuclear explosions.[3]

The conditions that would prevail in a superfire caused by a nuclear explosion resemble the conditions during the fire storm that developed in Hamburg after an intense Allied incendiary attack in July 1943. In that case, basement shelters provided little protection from the lethal effects of carbon monoxide and the extreme temperatures generated by the overlying smoldering debris. The area destroyed was about 12 square kilometers (about the same as the area of conflagration at Hiroshima) and the death toll was estimated at between 50,000 and 60,000 (also comparable to that at Hiroshima).

Although any prediction about the extent of urban fires caused by nuclear explosions is uncertain, we believe the probability of lethal superfires is great enough so that casualty estimates should take them into account. We have done so by making casualty estimates using both the traditional overpressure model and our own superfire model. The respective results define the lower and upper end of a range of uncertainty.

T he other direct cause of death associated with nuclear explosions is fallout: soil and debris sucked up into the fireball of a low-altitude nuclear explosion that eventually falls back to the ground heavily contaminated by fission products. The fallout that settles downwind from a nuclear explosion can create of zone of gamma radiation so intense that people without adequate shielding would die of severe radiation sickness. In estimating the casualties caused by radioactive fallout, we adapted a government computer model designed to predict the way fallout would be dispersed and drew on government databases for wind patterns and population distributions.

We also considered the possibility that the resistance of human beings to ionizing radiation under wartime conditions might be much less than has been traditionally assumed. This possibility has been suggested by analysis of the data on the casualties at Hiroshima.

Since World War II, the standard assumption made in government analyses has been that an exposure to 4.5 grays* of gamma radiation within a period of less than two weeks constitutes the so-called LD-50 dose: the lethal dose that causes death by radiation sickness in 50 percent of an exposed population within about 60 days. That assumption was based primarily on experimental data from animals, but it seemed to be consistent with the human data from Hiroshima.

In 1982, however, investigators at the Lawrence Livermore National Laboratory discovered that the estimated radiation exposures in Hiroshima were too high. This led a group of Japanese investigators to reexamine the fates of more than 3,000 Hiroshima inhabitants who had not suffered severe blast or burn injuries from the bomb's explosion, but were near enough to ground zero to be exposed to direct gamma radiation. When the new Lawrence Livermore results were applied to determine the radiation doses for each individual in the Hiroshima group, a surprisingly low estimate for the LD-50 was obtained: just 2.5 grays.

The Hiroshima victims, of course, did not benefit from the modern treatment for radiation sickness, which involves placing the victim in a sterile environment and administering heavy doses of antibiotics. Yet modern medicines and hospital care would probably be as unavailable to

* A gray is the metric unit for measuring doses of ionizing radiation. A rad, the unit of radiation dose that is most commonly used in the U.S., is one-hundredth of a gray.

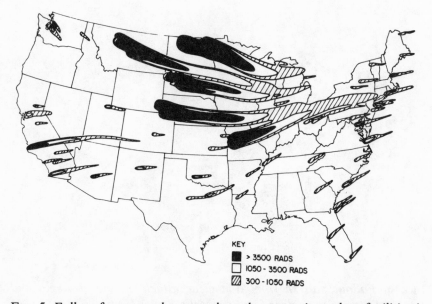

FIG. 5. *Fallout from a nuclear attack on the strategic nuclear facilities in the United States would expose millions of people to lethal doses of gamma radiation. If the median lethal dose is taken to be 3.5 of the units called grays, most people who were not in the shelters within the outermost radiation-level contours would suffer severe radiation sickness. Even people sheltered in windowless cellars would die within the innermost contours.*

survivors of a large-scale nuclear attack today as they were to the survivors of Hiroshima. We therefore tested the effects on our casualty estimates of values of the LD-50 ranging from 2.5 to 4.5 grays.

The number of casualties estimated for the attacks also depends on the strength and direction of the winds at the time of the attack, because it is the wind that disperses radioactive fallout. Of the four seasonal wind patterns we considered, we found that the strong winds typical of February produced the highest number of deaths in both the U.S. and the USSR (see Figures 5 and 6).

The doses from fallout radiation could be reduced to a certain extent by taking refuge in shelters. Every shelter can be assigned a protection factor: the number by which the open-air fallout-radiation exposures would have to be divided in order to give the actual radiation dose in the shelter. We assumed that the population of both the U.S. and the USSR would be equally divided between a group that did not spend much time in underground shelters (and therefore had an average effective protection

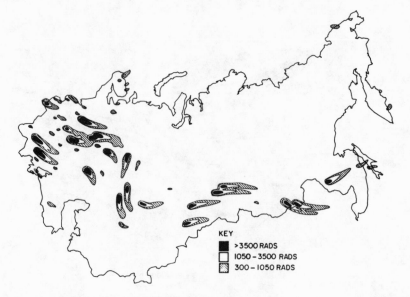

FIG. 6. *Fallout pattern from a nuclear attack on the strategic and intermediate-range nuclear facilities in the Soviet Union.*

factor of about three) and a group that did spend most of its time in shelters (and therefore had an average effective protection factor of about ten).

Fallout shelters with higher protection factors do exist, but it would be difficult for people in them to reduce their average radiation dose to levels substantially lower than we assumed. The reason is that most of the sheltered population would have to emerge within a few days to replenish supplies or seek help, and even a short period spent outside the shelters would greatly increase their radiation dose. Average radiation doses would also be increased within a relatively short time as many people began to consume water and food contaminated by radioactivity.

Our calculations indicate that the direct effects of the blast, fire and radioactive fallout of a Soviet attack on U.S. strategic nuclear facilities could kill between 12 and 27 million people. The corresponding U.S. attack on Soviet strategic nuclear facilities could kill between 15 and 32 million. We also estimate that the survivors of the attacks would suffer between one and eight million additional deaths from cancer over their remaining lifetimes as a result of their exposure to fallout radiation.

The numbers at the low end of our ranges, which were derived by applying the overpressure model and assuming an LD-50 of 4.5 grays, are consistent with the estimates presented by the Defense Department in 1975. The numbers at the upper end of our ranges were obtained from the superfire model and an LD-50 of 2.5 grays.

In our results, deaths from blast and fire are roughly comparable in number to those from fallout. Although the percentage of the area of the U.S. subjected to lethal levels of fallout radiation was found to be larger than that for the USSR, there would be comparable numbers of casualties from the radiation in both countries, since much of the fallout over the Soviet Union would descend on the heavily populated European region of the country.

Limiting the attack to any subset of counterforce targets, such as missile silos, bomber bases, naval bases, weapon storage depots, command-and-communication facilities or intermediate-range forces (in the case of the USSR) would cause at least a million deaths in all cases but one (see Figure 7). Hence one could not hope to reduce the casualties below many millions by eliminating one or two classes of targets. Our casualty estimates for the USSR, for example, would be only about 10 percent lower if we had not included as targets the intermediate-range missiles eliminated by the 1987 Intermediate-range Nuclear Forces Treaty. In fact, the effect of the elimination of the Soviet intermediate-range missile will be approximately offset by the replacement of Trident I warheads with more powerful Trident II warheads on U.S. ballistic-missile submarines.

Our casualty estimates for both sides would have been considerably higher if we had included other classes of plausible military-related targets. For example, we estimated separately the civilian casualties that would result from an attack with one-megaton airburst warheads on a group of 101 factories identified as being among the highest-priority targets in an attack on U.S. military-industrial capability. These factories manufacture such items as missile-guidance systems, automatic guns for aircraft, antitank missiles, radars and command-and-control systems. We found that the attack would kill between 11 and 29 million people. The toll is so high because most of the military-industrial targets are in major urban areas, such as those surrounding Boston, Detroit and Los Angeles.

Finally, it should also be kept in mind that we have considered only the casualties that would be caused by the direct effects of nuclear explosions. Tens of millions of additional deaths might result from exposure, famine and disease if—as seems likely—the U.S. or the Soviet Union suffered economic and social collapse after a nuclear attack. The popu-

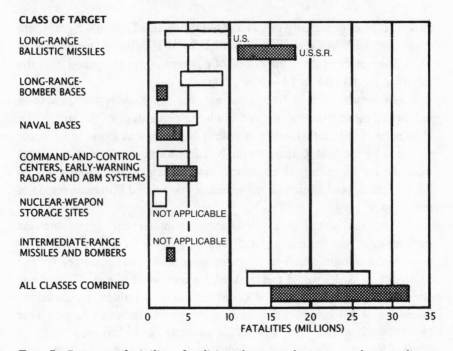

FIG. 7. *Ranges of civilian fatalities that can be expected as a direct consequence of counterforce attacks on various classes of military targets. The fatalities associated with a counterforce attack on all targets do not equal the sums of the fatalities for attacks on individual classes of targets, because there is some overlap in the areas affected and because the lower and upper values of the fatality ranges apply to different months in different attacks.*

lations of other nations around the world would also suffer indirectly from the manifold economic and environmental effects of such an attack.

Our results reaffirm an assertion made in 1961 by the chairman of the Joint Chiefs of Staff, General Lyman L. Lemnitzer, when he briefed President John F. Kennedy on the U.S. nuclear war plans:[4]

There is considerable question that the Soviets would be able to distinguish between a total attack and an attack on military targets only . . . . Because of fallout from attack of military targets and colocation of many military targets with [cities], the casualties would be many million in number. Thus, limiting attack to military targets has little practical meaning as a humanitarian measure.

Yet for the past two decades the U.S. and the USSR have continued to develop increasingly elaborate counterforce targeting strategies, ignoring the fact that the large-scale application of nuclear weapons against military targets is not qualitatively different from their application against civilians. In view of the massive civilian casualties counterforce attacks would entail, threatening to execute such attacks can be no more credible than threatening to destroy cities.

It is clear that eliminating counterforce weaponry by treaty would be preferable to eliminating them by use on one another. Yet it is the continuing reliance on counterforce strategies by policy makers that blocks stabilizing nuclear-force reductions beyond those currently being considered in the START negotiations.

Beyond START

WITH HAROLD A. FEIVESON

Even after the strategic nuclear arsenals of the United States and Soviet Union are reduced to the levels envisioned for the Strategic Arms Reductions Treaty (START), each will contain more than 6,000 warheads with a total destructive power equivalent to more than 50,000 Hiroshima bombs. The use of only a few percent of these weapons could destroy either country as a modern state. The equivalent of 50 one-megaton warheads exploded over the urban areas of either country could destroy its infrastructure and kill 25–50 million people by direct effects alone.[1]

Recent extraordinary changes in the Soviet Union and Eastern Europe, which have transformed the Soviet threat to the United States and its allies, give hope that these oversized arsenals can be reduced substantially in post-START negotiations.

Prior to the events of 1989, it was still possible to point to the Warsaw Pact forces in Eastern Europe as a major potential threat to Western Europe. NATO planners, uncertain—and at times downright pessimistic—about NATO's ability to withstand an all-out attack by the Warsaw Pact forces, insisted on a credible threat of U.S. nuclear use, if necessary, to stop the invasion. Credibility was thought to require the ability to target, with "counterforce" nuclear weapons, many thousands of Soviet nuclear and other military facilities.

Today, the non-nuclear threat from the Warsaw Pact is rapidly disappearing. The Soviet Union is unilaterally reducing its military personnel and withdrawing about one-half of its forces from its former Eastern European satellites and, in the negotiations on Conventional Forces in Europe (CFE), has agreed to further substantial asymmetric reductions.

Still more important, dramatic political changes in Eastern Europe are dissolving the Warsaw Pact effectively as a real military alliance and are likely to result in the withdrawal of virtually all Soviet military forces from the former "satellite" nations of Eastern Europe.

Partly in response to the changed situation in Europe, there are great pressures in the United States and the USSR to cut their military budgets in order to free resources to deal with urgent national problems.

Under these circumstances, it seems reasonable to suggest that whatever small increment of deterrence (if any) that has been achieved with the huge U.S. nuclear counterforce arsenal can be foregone, and that the United States and the Soviet Union can agree to reduce to less excessive and costly strategic forces. Indeed such reductions would not be inconsistent with the requirements laid out for the strategic forces in NATO's May 1989 statement on its "comprehensive concept":[2]

> Strategic nuclear forces . . . must be capable of inflicting unacceptable damage on an aggressor state even after it has carried out a first strike. Their number, range, survivability and penetration capability need to ensure that a potential aggressor cannot count on limiting the conflict or regarding his own territory as a sanctuary.

Much smaller strategic forces could have all of these capabilities.

Let us consider, as a next step beyond START, the feasibility of reducing the U.S. and Soviet strategic nuclear arsenals each to a highly survivable force of about 2,000 warheads. Such forces can be considered "finite-deterrence,"[3] rather than "minimum-deterrence" forces, because they would still be far larger than the minimum required to maintain the U.S.–Soviet mutual nuclear hostage relationship. They could probably be cut again by a factor of two, without much affecting stability and verification concerns. However, it would probably be impossible to reduce to less than 2,000 warheads on each side without involving other nuclear-weapon states in the negotiations.

A key design criterion for the finite-deterrence forces is that at least several hundred deliverable warheads should survive any conceivable first strike. This survivability should be sufficiently enduring—at least a few days—that each side could adopt a "ride-out and then decide" posture in which the remaining elements of the national leadership of the attacked side would be able to reestablish communications and decide how to respond. With such postures, the U.S.–Soviet mutual-hostage relationship would become much less susceptible to accidental and unauthorized actions. Current postures rely excessively on the ability to launch under attack, allowing only very short decision times after first warning of a possible attack.[4]

Below, we consider the justifications given for the current size of the U.S. strategic nuclear arsenal, conditions that would make possible bilateral reductions to finite-deterrence levels, a specific realization of finite-deterrence forces for the United States and Soviet Union, the stability of the resulting balance, and the ways in which the reductions could be verified.

Rationales for Large Strategic Forces

Why would one want more strategic warheads than a finite-deterrence force would contain? The official reason given is the need for forces capable of destroying all of the targetable strategic and other military forces on the other side. Thus, in 1989, General John Chain, Commander-in-Chief of the Strategic Air Command (CINCSAC) and Director of the Joint Strategic Target Planning Staff (JSTPS), described the target list for the post-START forces as follows:

> One needs to understand the target set that I am responsible to be able to go against.
>
> Targets fall into different categories . . . . First are hard targets . . . . They fit in the categories like ICBM silos; they have command posts; and they have launch-control facilities.
>
> A second group of targets is soft targets or area targets—things like their radar sites, their surface-to-air missiles, their airfields, their submarine bases, their naval facilities, factory complexes, communications centers, and economic types of targets.
>
> The third set is what we refer to as mobile targets or relocatable targets . . . . [These include] train-borne ICBMs in the form of SS-24s . . . ; road mobiles in the form of SS-25s . . . ; their surface navies, once they leave ports; their armies, once they leave garrison.[5]

General Chain argued that he needed all of the warheads permitted under START to cover these targets.[6] His statement contrasts starkly with the repeated Gorbachev-Reagan statement that "nuclear war cannot be won and must never be fought."[7]

Most of the targets mentioned by Chain are military but, in fact, an attack on thousands of such targets would almost inevitably kill tens of millions of civilians directly[8] and tens of millions more indirectly as a result of loss of infrastructure and ensuing exposure, famine and disease.[9] Therefore, in effect if not intention, the civilians consequences of such counterforce attacks would not differ significantly from attacks with hundreds of warheads directed at the civilian population and its support infrastructure.

Smaller attacks against up to a few hundred fixed facilities—army and navy bases, airfields, transportation centers, power plants, oil refineries, etc.—might be distinguishable in their effects from counter-civilian attacks, but such attacks could be mounted by finite-deterrence forces as well as by the four-times-larger post-START strategic forces. Therefore, reductions to finite-deterrence levels do not imply an intention to destroy cities should deterrence fail—although some critics argue that this is so.

Benefits from Reductions

What would the United States and Soviet Union gain by reducing to finite-deterrence levels? First, fears of large-scale counterforce attack would be minimized. With either the current or post-START strategic forces, there is danger that, in a crisis, either the leadership or commanders with physical control over nuclear weapons, fearing nuclear attack, believing they had only a few moments' decision time, and thinking only of the military consequences, might actually launch a nuclear attack such as that described by General Chain. Properly designed reductions to finite-deterrence forces would eliminate most of the excess weapons which lead to such dangerous postures.

A second benefit of reductions to finite-deterrence levels would be budgetary savings for both the United States and Soviet Union. These would come from the smaller operating budget of the finite-deterrence forces as well as from the cancellation of new strategic weapons systems, such as the B-2, which are justified by fantastic strategic counterforce targeting plans.[10] William Kaufmann has estimated that the adoption over a ten-year period of a force structure similar (though not identical) to that proposed here would result in a reduction in annual outlays for U.S. strategic forces from $52 billion in Fiscal Year 1990 to about $20 billion annually by Fiscal Year 1999.[11]

The ideas behind finite deterrence have been advocated for decades by a small group within the arms-control community. In 1961, for example, President Kennedy's science adviser, Jerome Wiesner, went so far as to suggest that an adequate U.S. deterrent force would be "two hundred relatively secure missiles . . . even in the absence of an agreement limiting force size and permission for inspection."[12] However, such proposals have always been brushed aside in the nuclear policy-making process by the dominant counterforce school. Today, with the changed situation in Europe, much deeper reductions than were envisioned when the START negotiations were launched appear politically possible.

Preconditions for Finite Deterrence

Deep cuts in offensive ballistic-missile warheads will be possible only if the Antiballistic Missile (ABM) Treaty is preserved in something like its present form. In the past, the United States and Soviet Union have each expressed fears that the other might deploy a ballistic-missile defense (BMD) as a shield to ward off a "ragged" retaliatory strike after launching a first strike. The Soviet Union, therefore, has responded to U.S. consideration of large-scale BMD by making preservation of the ABM Treaty an implicit condition for even the cuts in ballistic-missile warheads being negotiated under START. It is likely that the United States would, for similar reasons, be uninterested in negotiating reductions in ballistic-missile warheads if deployment of an ambitious Soviet BMD system was threatened.

Most of the undertakings leading to finite deterrence could be carried out bilaterally by the United States and the Soviet Union. However, the final stages of the reductions might also require that limitations be accepted by China, France, and the United Kingdom. If current British and French plans to deploy submarine-launched ballistic missiles (SLBMs) with multiple independently-targetable reentry vehicles (MIRVs) are completed, these "middle nuclear powers" could have a combined total of about 1,500 strategic warheads by the late 1990s—approximately the same as the number of warheads assumed for each of the "superpower" finite-deterrence forces.[13]

We do not know what the plans of the middle nuclear powers might be beyond the year 2000 but, on broad strategic grounds, in the context of a U.S.–Soviet agreement to reduce the superpower strategic arsenals to 2000 warheads each, France, Britain and China should be willing to limit their arsenals to 200–500 warheads each.[14] The French and British have founded their strategic forces on ballistic missile submarines (SSBNs) and China is also constructing its future strategic deterrent on submarines. The ability of these forces to hold Soviet targets at risk would be virtually guaranteed by the continued absence of significant ballistic missile defenses. Furthermore, the political weight of the middle power forces depends in part on their size relative to those of the "superpowers"; this relative size would be increased free of cost by superpower reductions.

The Soviet Union could sweeten the deal still further by eliminating the Moscow ABM system[15]—a system that currently degrades the threat of the middle nuclear power forces against Moscow only marginally, but continues to serve as a major talking point for advocates of large increases in these forces as well as for U.S. advocates of ballistic-missile defense.

Cuts in planned buildups of French and British SLBM warheads could be implemented, even if their MIRVed SLBMs are deployed. Perhaps the best way would be to reduce the number of launch tubes per submarine, as recommended below for the ballistic-missile submarine components of the U.S. and Soviet finite-deterrence forces. Alternatively, the number of warheads per SLBM could be reduced with on-site verification arrangements of the type agreed to by the United States and Soviet Union for verification of ballistic-missile warhead limits under the START treaty. Either approach could preserve the number of ballistic-missile submarines at sea.

The Design of Finite-Deterrence Forces

Table 1 shows illustrative examples of U.S. and Soviet 2,000-warhead finite-deterrence forces. It compares them with the strategic forces in 1989, and with projections of what these forces might look like in the mid-1990s, after a START agreement, assuming continued deployments of the ICBMs, SLBMs and strategic bombers currently in production or advanced development, and a compensating phase-out of older systems.[16]

In constructing the finite-deterrence forces, we have assumed that, only for institutional reasons and because of the inherent value of diversity, both sides would continue to deploy all elements of the traditional strategic "triad": land-based intercontinental ballistic missiles (ICBMs), SLBMs, and air-launched weapons carried by long-range bombers. We have assumed that the United States would continue to favor SLBMs, and that the Soviet Union would similarly continue to favor ICBMs.

We have eliminated MIRVed intercontinental ballistic missiles in the finite-deterrence force. Other things being equal, dispersing a fixed number of warheads over a large number of missiles increases their survivability. For the same reason, the number of warheads carried by submarines have been reduced by a larger factor than the number of

TABLE 1. U.S. and Soviet Strategic Nuclear Arsenals in Late 1989 and Hypothetical START and Finite-Deterrence (FD) Forces in the Mid-1990s[a]

	Delivery vehicles			Warheads		
	1989[b]	START[c]	FD	1989[b]	START[c,d]	FD
U.S. FORCES						
ICBMs						
Minuteman II	450	0	0	450	0	0
Minuteman III/IIIA	500	200	0	1,500	600	0
MX	50	50	0	500	500	0
Midgetman	0	344	492	0	344	492
Total ICBMs	1,000	594	492	2,450	1,444	492
SLBMs						
Poseidon	224	0	0	2,240	0	0
Trident I/II	384	432	126	3,072	3,456	1,008
Total SLBMs	608	432	126	5,312	3,456	1,008
Missile totals	1,608	1,026	618	7,762	4,900	1,500
Bombers						
B-52 *ALCM*	194	90	0	3,480	1,800 (900)	0
B-1/2	97	150	125	1,536	2,400 (150)	500[e]
Strategic totals	1,899	1,266	743	12,778	9,100 (5,950)	2,000
SOVIET FORCES						
ICBMs						
SS-11/13	409	0	0	409	0	0
SS-17	108	0	0	432	0	0
SS-18	308	154	0	3,080	1,540	0
SS-19	320	0	0	1,920	0	0
SS-24	58	80	0	580	800	0
SS-25[f]	171	336	1,020	171	336	1,020
Total ICBMs	1,374	570	1,020	6,592	2,676	1,020
SLBMs						
SS-N-6/8/12/17	538	0	0	538	0	0
SS-N-18	224	0	0	1,568	0	0
SS-N-20	100	120	0	1,000	1,200	0
SS-N-23	80	256	120	320	1,024	480
Total SLBMs	942	376	120	3,426	2,224	480
Missile totals	2,316	946	1,140	10,018	4,900	1,500
Bombers						
Bear	85	0	0	310	0	0
Bear-H *ALCM*[g]	75	87	75	450	522 (696)	300[e]
Blackjack	10	50	50	120	600 (400)	200[e]
Strategic totals	2,486	1,083	1,265	10,898	6,022 (5,996)	2,000

TABLE 1. Continued

NOTES

a. The following yields have been assumed for the warheads in the START and finite deterrence forces: Minuteman III, 0.335 megatons; MX, 0.3 megatons; Midgetman, 0.5 megatons; Trident II, 0.1 megatons for one-half of the missiles, 0.475 for the other half; U.S. ALCM, 0.15 megatons; U.S. bombs and SRAMs, 0.5 megatons; SS-18, 0.5 megatons; SS-24, 0.2 megatons; SS-25, 0.5 megatons; SS-N-20, 0.1 megatons; SS-N-23, 0.1 megatons; Soviet ALCMs, 0.15 megatons; Soviet bombs and SRAMs, 0.5 megatons. See also the yields quoted in Cochran, T. B.; Arkin, W. M.; and Hoenig, M. M.; *Nuclear Weapons Databook, Vol. 1: U.S. Nuclear Forces and Capabilities*. Cambridge, Mass.: Ballinger, 1984; *Arms Control Reporter*. p. 611.B.571. Brookline, Massachusetts: Institute for Defense and Disarmament Studies, 1989; and Cochran; Norris, R. S.; and Sands, J. I. *Nuclear Weapons Databook*, Vol 4: *Soviet Nuclear Weapons*. New York: Ballinger, 1989.

b. The numbers for 1989 are from *Strategic Nuclear Forces of the United States and the Soviet Union*. Washington, D.C.: Arms Control Association Fact Sheet, September 1989.

c. For the United States, we assume that, after the START treaty is signed, the number of 24-launcher Trident ballistic-missile submarines will grow to 18, while the remaining 16-launcher Poseidon/Trident I ballistic-missile submarines are retired. We assume also that 53 of the 132 B-2 penetrating bombers proposed by the U.S. Air Force will be bought and that the entire fleet of 97 B-1B penetrating bombers and 90 B-52H cruise missile carriers will be retained.

   For the Soviet Union, we assume that the program of building 20-launcher Typhoon submarines carrying 10-warhead SS-N-20 missiles halts at six submarines, and that the number of 16-launcher Delta submarines carrying four-warhead SS-N-23 missiles will increase to 16, while the older Yankee and Delta submarines are phased out. We assume also that the production of Bear-H ALCM carriers and Blackjack bombers will stop at 87 and 50, respectively.

   Eight alternative U.S. START forces were described in a *Report to the Congress on the Analysis of Alternative Strategic Nuclear Force Postures for the United States Under a Potential START Treaty*, submitted by President Bush on July 25, 1989. All forces included 50 MX missiles, 87 B-52 ALCM aircraft, 97 B-1B, and 132 B-2 bombers. The number of Trident II warheads varied from 2,880 to 4,224. The forces differed primarily in their assumed mix of Minuteman II, Minuteman III, and mobile single-warhead ICBMs.

d. Numbers in parentheses assume a START counting rule of 10 warheads each for U.S. ALCM bombers and of 8 warheads each for Soviet ALCM bombers, and the counting rule agreed at the December 1987 Washington summit of 1 warhead for each non-ALCM bomber. According to information released by the U.S. Air Force on October 16, 1989, a standard load for the B-2, like the B-1, would be eight SRAMs and eight B-61 gravity bombs (Scarborough, R. *Washington Times* October 17, 1989, p. 1). A full loading on a B-52G (-H) is eight (twelve) ALCMs plus eight SRAMs and bombs. We assume that all the remaining B-52s in the START force are B-52Hs.

e. Four ALCMs per long-range nuclear bomber.

f. For the finite-deterrence case, we assume that the SS-25 or a follow-on single-warhead missile will be put into either a hardened-mobile launcher or silo.

g. Evidently the "heavy-bomber exhibition" (at Urin air base in the Soviet Union in April 1990), during which the U.S. was allowed to inspect the Bear-H bomber, indicated that the Bear-H could carry only six ALCMs in an internal rotary launcher. This is what we assume for the 1989 and START forces. See Thomas K. Longstreth and Richard Scribner, "Verification of Limits on Air-launched Cruise Missiles" in Frank von Hippel and Roald Z. Sagdeev, eds., *Reversing the Arms Race: How to Achieve and Verify Deep Reductions in the Nuclear Arsenals* (New York: Gordon and Breach Science Publishers, 1990).

submarines, and the number of bomber-carried warheads by a larger factor than the number of bombers or bomber bases.

Sea-based Forces

At sea, the hypothetical U.S. finite-deterrence SLBM force described in Table 1 is based on 21 Trident submarines (up from 8 in 1989), while the 26 1960s-vintage Poseidon ballistic-missile submarines remaining in service as of 1989 (12 of them carrying Trident I missiles) would be retired. We have assumed that each U.S. ballistic-missile submarine would carry 48 warheads, the equivalent of six 8-warhead SLBMs. This would make it necessary to reduce either the number of launch tubes per submarine or the number of warheads per SLBM. Both possibilities have been suggested by the Bush administration as a way to prevent the number of warheads on the growing Trident submarine force from outgrowing the Navy's share of the proposed START limits.[17] In the longer term, smaller ballistic-missile submarines carrying small low-MIRV SLBMs should replace the current systems.

We have similarly assumed that the hypothetical Soviet finite-deterrence SLBM force, which would carry 480 warheads, would be based on twenty submarines, each carrying 24 warheads (the equivalent of six 4-warhead SS-N-23 missiles).[18] The existing Typhoon submarines could be re-equipped with SS-N-23 missiles or phased out. (Reportedly, no new Soviet Typhoon ballistic-missile submarines are currently being built.)[19]

Although not essential to the stability of the balance between finite-deterrence forces, it would be desirable to ban heavy SLBMs such as the Trident II (D-5) and SS-N-20, because, as with the heavy Soviet SS-18 ICBM, the extra throw-weight of these missiles makes them potentially powerful counterforce weapons. Their reported launch weights are about 60,000 kilograms, almost twice the launch weight of the Trident I (30,000 kilograms), and 50 percent more than the estimated launch weight of the SS-N-23.[20] Indeed, one variant of the Trident II has been explicitly designed to attack very hard targets, and the higher yield of the warheads on that variant would also make it two to three times as effective as the Trident I in a barrage attack against bombers or mobile-missile carriers scattering from their bases.

We have assumed that neither side would choose to deploy any of the 2,000 warheads in its finite-deterrence force on nuclear-armed sea-launched cruise missiles (SLCMs). The range, speed, and ability of ballistic missiles to penetrate defenses are all superior to those of SLCMs. However, nuclear attack submarines could become alternative launch platforms for strategic cruise missiles if, for some reason, airborne cruise-missile launchers became vulnerable, either at their bases or in flight.

Intercontinental Ballistic Missiles

Ballistic-missile submarines at sea are the only strategic launchers that would be virtually guaranteed to survive for longer than a day. This superior survivability does not mean, however, that the entire finite-deterrence force should be placed on nuclear submarines. Such a decision might create its own type of instability. For example, the threshold would be somewhat lower for a war of attrition at sea, in which one side could try to disarm the other by hunting down its ballistic-missile submarines over a period as long as months.[21]

We assume that the ICBM component of the finite-deterrence force would be made up of single-warhead missiles that could be deployed either in silos or on hardened mobile launchers. Although even super-hardened fixed missile silos could be destroyed by super-accurate warheads, more than one warhead would have to be used for each warhead destroyed. The exchange ratio could be made even more unfavorable by the use of deceptive basing, with more than one silo or shelter for each missile.[22]

If the single-warhead missiles were based on hardened mobile launchers, these launchers could be parked by twos ready to dash on warning. The U.S. ICBM would be the Midgetman, and the Soviet ICBM would be a hardened version of the road-mobile SS-25. Although hardened mobile-missile launchers would be highly survivable, they could not assure long-duration mobility such as provided by the submarine force. The Midgetman missile launcher, for example, is designed to protect its missile, but not its crew, from the blast of nearby nuclear explosions and the lethal levels of radioactive fallout that could be deposited downwind from more distant explosions. During an attack, therefore, it would be parked and the crew would seek shelter; the missile could later be launched remotely from underground or airborne command posts.

Strategic Bomber Forces

Both the U.S. and Soviet hypothetical finite-deterrence forces are assumed to contain 125 long-range nuclear bombers on 13 bases. Each bomber would be equipped on average with four air-launched cruise missiles (ALCMs). As the carrying capacity of current strategic bombers could not be verifiably limited to four nuclear ALCMs each, verification of the ALCM limits would have to be accomplished through separate limits on the nuclear-armed cruise missiles themselves (discussed below). The ALCMs would have a high probability of penetrating the other side's air defenses. Small cruise missiles can be made much less detectable than the large B-2 "Stealth" bomber, which the U.S. Air Force argues could fly with relative impunity into the most heavily defended regions of Soviet airspace.[23]

If the yields of SLBM warheads were limited to the estimated 100 kilotons of the Trident I, SS-N-20, and SS-N-23 warheads, the total destructive powers of the U.S. and Soviet finite-deterrence forces would be about 700 and 900 equivalent megatons (EMt) respectively.[24] In order to prevent increases in the yields of future warheads from offsetting the effect of the reductions in their numbers, it would be desirable to have a limit on warhead yield imposed through warhead weight and volume limits.

Getting to Finite-deterrence from START

The finite-deterrence forces could evolve relatively smoothly out of the START forces shown in Table 1:

· Multiple-warhead ICBMs would be phased out as the hardened mobile single-warhead ICBMs are phased in;
· The United States and Soviet Union could keep their modern ballistic-missile submarines, with the number of warheads per submarine reduced; and
· An agreed number of the existing strategic bombers on each side could be kept with reduced loads of ALCMs.

If the United States and Soviet Union were to make early decisions to move toward such less counterforce-oriented forces, they could save funds in the following ways:

· The United States could halt its B-2 program, abandon its program of making the MX rail mobile, and abandon its program to replace the Trident I with the Trident II SLBM; and
· The Soviet Union could stop deploying the 10-warhead SS-24 ICBM[25] and upgrading the hard-target capabilities of the 10-warhead heavy SS-18 ICBM.[26]

Stability of the Finite-Deterrence Balance

In order to minimize dependence on strategic warning, a finite-deterrence force could operate at relatively high day-to-day alert and dispersal levels:

- U.S. Trident submarines already spend about 65 percent of their time at sea. We assume that, in a finite-deterrence force, both the U.S. and Soviet ballistic-missile submarines forces would maintain at least a 50 percent at-sea rate.
- We assume that, in a finite-deterrence force, both U.S. and Soviet bombers would maintain at least a 50 percent runaway alert rate—greater than today's 30 percent rate for U.S. bombers.
- Mobile missiles could be kept dispersed in ones or twos—either, like the bombers, ready to dash on tactical warning, or moving more frequently than the other side's retargeting time.[27] We assume that 80 percent of each side's mobile-missile launchers would be dispersed and on alert at all times.

Crisis Stability

Given these alert and dispersal assumptions, more than half of the warheads in the U.S. and Soviet forces either would already be dispersed or would be able to disperse quickly on warning of ballistic-missile attack. In the case of modern quiet submarines, dispersal at sea means a high probability of survival for at least a matter of weeks.[28]

In principle, even after they had begun to scatter, bombers and mobile missiles might be vulnerable to "barrage attacks," delivered by submarine-launched ballistic missiles during the minutes while the escaping bombers or missile carriers would still provide relatively concentrated targets. According to our calculations, however, except for U.S. bomber bases in coastal areas, where SLBM warheads could impact within 10 minutes after launch, the number of attacking weapons expended per weapon killed (the "exchange ratio") would be highly unfavorable to the attacker. Bombers and mobile missiles at inland bases could be expected to have 15–18 minutes warning time of attacks by warheads launched on minimum-energy trajectories from plausible launch areas, 2,000–3,000 kilometers away.[29] Assuming that the bombers or missile launchers began to scatter 8 minutes after the initial warning, they would be widely dispersed and not susceptible to barrage by the time the SLBM warheads arrived. For example, an attack with a 15–18 minute warning time on five bombers scattering from an airbase,[30] each carrying 4 nuclear warheads, would require 48–117 attacking 100-kt warheads (or 16–40 500-kt warheads) per warhead destroyed. For a parking place with two alert mobile-missile carriers, destruction of one warhead would require 15–30 100-kt warheads (or 5–10 500-kt warheads).[31]

Barrage attacks would appear somewhat more feasible if the barraging SLBM warheads were launched on depressed trajectories along which the warheads could travel 2,000–3,000 kilometers in about ten minutes instead of the 15–18 minutes assumed in our calculations.[32] Fortunately, neither the United States nor Soviet Union seems yet to have tested SLBMs on such trajectories, and a formal ban on depressed-trajectory tests has been proposed by the United States.[33]

Perhaps the most important source of crisis instability in the current balance is the vulnerability of the command and control systems to a "decapitating attack." However, unlike current strategic forces, which are designed to be able to launch a "time-urgent" attack against the other side's strategic forces, the finite-deterrence force would only have to be able to attack a variety of fixed targets on the other side within a period of days. The command and control systems for finite-deterrence forces therefore need only be reconstitutable within such a period.

Breakout Stability

The balance between the finite-deterrence forces shown in Table 1 would be quite stable against "breakout," that is, a rapid increase in the number of warheads deployed by either side. Even a doubling of the number of deployed ballistic-missile warheads would not significantly affect the survivability of submarines at sea, because their locations would be too uncertain for them to be barrage-attacked by any credible number of warheads.[34] A doubling of intercontinental-range ballistic-missile warheads would also not greatly increase the barrage threat to alert bombers and mobile missiles, because of the relatively long warning times for attacks by ballistic-missile warheads fired from intercontinental distances. Nor, because of their long flight times, would the stability of the nuclear balance be sensitive to a rapid increase in the number of deployed air-launched and sea-launched cruise missiles.

A breakout threat which requires more careful consideration, because of the potentially short SLBM flight times, is the possibility of a rapid increase in the number of warheads carried by ballistic-missile submarines. We have assumed in the finite-deterrence force that the number of warheads carried by each Trident submarine would be reduced from 192 to 48, and that the numbers carried by each Typhoon and Delta IV submarine would be reduced from 200 and 64, respectively, to 24. This would be accomplished by reducing the number of launch tubes per submarine or the numbers of warheads per SLBM. If the reduction process were readily reversible, then Soviet SLBM warheads could be quickly increased from 480 to 2,096 and U.S. warheads from 1,008 to 4,032.[35] However, these numbers of warheads still would be far short of the 20,000–45,000 100-kt warheads required to barrage the 13 air bases and 246 mobile missile parking places of the U.S. hypothetical finite-deterrence force, or the 28,000–60,000 100-kt warheads required to barrage the 13 air bases and 510 mobile-missile parking places of the hypothetical Soviet finite-deterrence force (always assuming 15–18 minute flight time).

Nevertheless, it would be desirable to have arrangements that would make it very difficult to increase the number of SLBM warheads rapidly and which would provide early warning of any attempt to do so (see below). Furthermore, as mentioned above, if the arsenals are to remain at finite-deterrence levels for decades, the current generation of ballistic-missile submarines should be replaced by submarines designed from the beginning with fewer launch tubes, or by submarines with launch tubes so small that they could not accommodate heavily MIRVed SLBMs.

Arms-race Stability

One of the original justifications for equipping U.S. ballistic missiles with multiple warheads—and for the associated buildup of the number of U.S. ballistic missile warheads from less than 2,000 in 1970 to about 8,000 in 1990—was to guarantee the U.S. ability to overwhelm any BMD system that the Soviet Union might deploy. A reduction of the number of U.S. and Soviet ballistic-missile warheads to perhaps 1,500 each in their finite-deterrence forces would bring them back to approximately the U.S. number in 1970. Would that make a breakdown of the ABM Treaty and a new offense-defense arms race more likely?

This appears doubtful. The several-year-long debate over President Reagan's Strategic Defense Initiative (SDI) program has shown how robust the ABM Treaty regime has become. The Soviet government and the majority in the U.S. Congress fought hard to preserve the treaty, and the technical critics of SDI in the United States and the Soviet Union invented relatively cheap countermeasures for every BMD technology that the SDI Organization proposed. Although defending against 1,500 ballistic-missile warheads may appear less of a challenge than defending against today's huge arsenals, the challenge would still be enormous, and the time required to deploy the defensive system would still provide ample warning for the other side to deploy penetration aids and, if necessary, more offensive missiles.

Certain test bans could further buttress the arms-race stability of the strategic balance. One prime candidate would be an agreement to ban flight testing of maneuverable reentry vehicles designed to home in on mobile targets.[36] Another would be a test ban that would block development of destabilizing new types of nuclear warheads, such as one that could blanket a large area with a microwave pulse designed to paralyze mobile-missile launchers and command posts.[37]

Verification

Many of the limits involved in reductions to finite-deterrence levels could be verified using procedures established under past and existing arms control agreements. Monitoring of numbers and types of deployed ballistic-missile submarines, ICBM silos, and strategic bombers could be accomplished—as under SALT I and SALT II (Strategic Arms Limitation Talks)—principally through "national technical means" using imaging satellites. MIRV and throw-weight limits on ballistic missiles could be verified largely using satellites, radar, and telemetry interception to monitor ballistic-missile flight tests, as under SALT II. The elimination of missiles and launchers, and bans on the production of prohibited ballistic missiles could be verified by on-site inspection procedures similar to those established by the Intermediate-range Nuclear Force (INF) Treaty.

The principal new tasks essential to verification of reductions to finite deterrence levels (including analogous tasks being worked out in the START negotiations) would be to verify limits on numbers of: warheads deployed on ballistic-missile submarines, deployed mobile ballistic missiles, nuclear-armed cruise missiles, nondeployed ballistic missiles, and nondeployed nuclear warheads. In each case the technical basis for effective verification procedures exists.

Verifying Limits on Warheads Carried by Ballistic-missile Submarines

Reductions in the numbers of warheads carried by individual ballistic-missile submarines could be accomplished either by eliminating launch tubes or by reducing the number of warheads per SLBM.

In the case of future submarines or submarines in early stages of construction, the approach should be reduction in the number of launch tubes. For existing submarines, the number of launch tubes should be reduced, by requiring, if possible, that the section containing the extra tubes actually be physically cut out of the submarine, as has been done by the Soviet Union in ballistic-missile submarines converted to other missions. If this is impractical, the operation of filling the extra launch tubes with concrete and sealing them should be observed by inspectors from the other side. Inspectors could take ultrasonic images of welds, and arrangements could be established to allow subsequent short-notice checks of welds any time a submarine was in port.

Less satisfactory, because it could probably be more quickly reversed, would be to reduce the number of warheads per SLBM. The United States and Soviet Union have agreed to develop "procedures . . . that enable verification of the number of warheads on deployed ballistic missiles of each specific type."[38] It appears that the most likely procedure will be to pick a small number of deployed missiles at random and remove the nose cones to allow direct inspection. Reentry vehicles may be covered with shrouds, if certain design details are considered sensitive.

If there are circumstances in which opening up the missiles is considered unacceptable, existing counting techniques might not require the removal of the nose cone. One method is low-resolution x-ray radiography of the nose cone to reveal the number of masses of dense fissile material inside.[39] The percentage of the missiles sampled and the frequency of the sampling would be negotiated by balancing the complications caused by the inspections against the rate at which breakout could occur and its military significance.

Verifying Limits on Land-mobile Missiles

Verification of limits on the numbers of mobile-missile launchers and their canisterized missiles can be greatly facilitated by using "tags." Tagging identifies every treaty-limited item with a unique noncounterfeitable intrinsic pattern, or tag, that cannot be removed or transferred to another missile or launcher without telltale evidence. Such tags would be placed on already deployed systems in an initial inventory and on subsequently produced systems at special portals at final assembly facilities. Thereafter, the observation of any untagged systems would be equivalent to the detection of a violation of the agreement.[40]

Verifying Limits on Nuclear-armed Cruise Missiles

Long-range ground-launched cruise missiles are already banned under the INF Treaty. However, ALCMs are part of U.S. and Soviet finite-deterrence forces; and although nuclear-armed sea-launched cruise missiles (SLCMs) might be banned, conventionally-armed SLCMs probably will not.[41]

The START treaty will limit the numbers of deliverable nuclear-armed air-launched cruise missiles by limiting bombers equipped to launch ALCMs. Since the number of ALCMs per bomber permitted in our finite-deterrence forces (we have assumed four ALCMs) is much less than the carrying capacity of current strategic bombers, and since virtually any long-range aircraft can be converted into an ALCM carrier, it will be desirable to supplement restrictions on ALCM carriers by direct controls on ALCMs. Since SLCMs may be interchangeable with ALCMs, it will be necessary to have a compatible control system covering both ALCMs and SLCMs. And because large short-range cruise missiles might be upgraded to long range, it will be helpful to include, under this control system, all nuclear-armed cruise missiles of greater than an agreed minimum size.

A control system on long-range cruise missiles could include monitors at the portals of ALCM and SLCM production facilities. Each cruise-missile canister leaving a production facility would be checked with a radiation detector or by radiography for the presence of a nuclear warhead, and the nuclear cruise missiles would be tagged. Nuclear-armed cruise missiles which had already been produced would also be tagged. Storage and deployment sites for nuclear and conventional cruise missiles would then be declared; agreed random on-site inspections of storage and deployment sites and challenge inspections elsewhere would deter the deployment of undeclared nuclear-armed cruise missiles. Detection of a cruise missile entering or leaving an undeclared facility would reveal a violation.[42]

The U.S. Navy has been reluctant to permit on-ship inspections to verify SLCM limits. However, spot checks of launchers and submarine torpedo rooms for untagged nuclear SLCMs could be relatively unintrusive. There are very few places on warships, other than aircraft carriers, where an object as large as a SLCM canister could be hidden.[43]

Verifying Limits on Nondeployed Ballistic Missiles

In a 1988 critique of the emerging START Treaty, the House Armed Services Committee raised the concern that spare and test ICBMs could be clandestinely equipped with nuclear warheads and placed on "unhardened above-ground sites prepared covertly for a first strike."[44] Secretary of Defense Frank Carlucci responded that the scenario was "improbable" and that it "would take years to accomplish."[45] In any case, the concern could be dealt with relatively easily if each side agreed to have its spare and test ballistic missiles tagged and stored at a few central locations where the other side would be able to check periodically that the missiles were all accounted for and that none was equipped with a nuclear warhead.[46]

Verifying Limits on Nondeployed Nuclear Warheads and Fissile Material

Sooner or later nuclear arms control will have to include explicit controls on nuclear warheads and on the fissile materials from which they are produced (ordinarily, plutonium and highly enriched uranium). Such controls would add another layer of verifiability to limits on the numbers of warheads deployed on ballistic missiles and cruise missiles, and would provide a means for limiting weapons systems, such as nuclear-armed fighter-bombers and nuclear artillery, which are differentiated from non-nuclear versions of the same systems primarily by the presence of the nuclear warheads.

A comprehensive system for implementing and verifying warhead reductions would include verified arrangements for: a cutoff in the production of fissile materials for weapons; dismantlement of warheads being retired and placement under safeguards of the fissile material recovered from them; and declarations of total nuclear-warhead arsenals, of the amounts of fissile materials that they contain, and of other fissile materials not under safeguards.

A FISSILE-MATERIAL PRODUCTION CUTOFF.   A cutoff in the production of fissile materials for weapons is an essential prerequisite for verifiable reductions in nuclear warheads and fissile materials because, without a cutoff, dismantled nuclear warheads could be replaced with warheads made with newly produced fissile materials.

On-site arrangements to track fissile material have been developed for most types of nuclear facilities in connection with the International Atomic Energy Agency (IAEA) safeguards, which, in 1987, were in force at over 900 facilities in 57 countries.[47] These arrangements would have to be extended to some new types of facilities in the nuclear-weapon states: shut-down plutonium-production reactors and their associated chemical fuel reprocessing plants, gaseous-diffusion uranium-enrichment plants, and the nuclear fuel cycles for naval propulsion reactors and any reactors producing tritium for nuclear weapons. However, such extensions appear to be relatively straightforward. To be significant, a diversion under a

U.S.–Soviet fissile-material cutoff agreement would have to be at least hundreds of times larger than the standard of significance for a diversion from IAEA safeguards (the amount of fissile material required to make a single crude nuclear explosive).

Similarly, clandestine production activities on a militarily significant scale should be detectable using national intelligence means supplemented by challenge inspections.[48] If the United States and the Soviet Union agree to allow overflights of their territories by each other's instrumented aircraft ("Open Skies"), traditional types of surveillance could be supplemented by systems able to detect the gamma, neutron, and radioactive-isotope emanations characteristic of fissile-material production facilities.

WARHEAD DISMANTLEMENT.   Once the inflow of new fissile material into the production complexes is halted, verifiable reductions could be accomplished by moving agreed amounts of fissile material out of the nuclear-weapons complexes and placing it under safeguards. The most obvious method of doing this in the case of strategic weapons systems would be through the verified dismantlement of warheads that are being retired.

During the INF Treaty ratification hearings, U.S. administration spokesmen were asked why verifiable warhead dismantlement was not included in the INF Treaty. They cited their concern that verification arrangements would compromise the design secrets of U.S. nuclear weapons.[49] However, former U.S. nuclear-weapons designer Theodore B. Taylor has outlined a comprehensive approach to verification of nuclear-warhead dismantlement which would not reveal sensitive warhead design information.[50]

Highly-enriched uranium recovered from nuclear warheads could be diluted with natural or depleted uranium to the low-enrichment levels used in the fuel of most nuclear power reactors. Recovered plutonium could either be stored under safeguards for possible future use as start-up fuel in plutonium breeder reactors, or could be disposed of, like the plutonium in unreprocessed spent nuclear fuel, with high-level radioactive waste.[51]

STOCKPILE DECLARATIONS.   As reductions proceed, each side might become concerned about uncertainties in its estimates of remaining numbers of warheads and quantities of unsafeguarded fissile material possessed by the other side. Therefore, it would be desirable for each side to declare their inventories and to verify their declarations.

Verification of fissile-material stockpile declarations would require an exchange of records of past production activities, coupled with analyses of the mutual consistency of these records and their consistency with contemporary satellite photographs and other intelligence information. It would also require examination of physical evidence, including certain key components of production facilities and perhaps residues, such as depleted uranium and high-level radioactive wastes from past production activities. It might be possible to verify declarations of past fissile-material production and consumption with an accuracy of about ten percent.[52]

Verification of warhead declarations could most simply be accomplished by declaring actual locations of warheads, with arrangements for spot checks and challenge inspections. While such declarations and inspections might seem extraordinary, the United States and Soviet Union have already committed themselves in their START negotiations to on-site inspection arrangements to verify the declarations of the numbers of warheads on their deployed strategic missiles. A comprehensive warhead declaration would simply extend such arrangements to all strategic nuclear warheads and to tactical nuclear warheads as well. The U.S. Navy's unwillingness to confirm or deny the presence of tactical nuclear weapons on its ships could be most directly dealt with by simply agreeing to eliminate such weapons.[53]

The mutual consistency of the warhead and fissile-material declarations could be verified by putting weighted samples of the declared warhead stockpiles through the nuclear-warhead dismantlement facilities and assaying the amounts of fissile materials recovered.

There would remain the possibility, because of measurement uncertainties, that many hundreds of nuclear warheads, or their equivalent in fissile material, might be hidden from the verification system. For this reason, a warhead control system should be considered an important complement to delivery-vehicle control, not a stand-alone alternative.

Even a combined verification system, covering delivery vehicles and warheads, would leave irreducible uncertainties. However, these uncertainties should be tolerable because finite-deterrence forces would be highly survivable, even against first strikes by much larger forces.

Conclusion

If the U.S. and Soviet governments decided, in a post-START strategic-arms reduction agreement, to accept the infeasibility of counterforce missions requiring thousands of warheads, it would be possible for them to agree on very much smaller strategic forces.[54] To keep the strategic forces as large as is envisioned in the START agreement would be both provocative and clearly unnecessary in view of the changed situation in Eastern Europe and the Soviet Union. These forces could be designed to maintain a stable and adequately verifiable mutual nuclear hostage relationship within which both sides would continue to be deterred from attacking each other's vital interests.

AUTOMOBILE ENERGY EFFICIENCY

Automobile Fuel Economy

WITH CHARLES L. GRAY, JR.

The U.S. is coming out of an era in which economic growth was stimulated by an abundance of cheap petroleum and going into a difficult period in which energy, particularly in the form of liquid fuel, will be much costlier and in limited supply. That this will be a dangerous period is already clear from the anxiety expressed by U.S. officials about the security of the nation's continued access to the world's largest-known reservoirs of underground oil, those in the Persian Gulf region. Consumers are therefore being urged to conserve energy while government and industry focus on developing costly new domestic supplies. Useful as these measures may be, the possibility of making a successful economic transition to the postpetroleum era depends on a much more determined effort by both government and industry to increase the efficiency with which energy is utilized in those sectors of the economy that depend on liquid fuel, starting with the single largest consumer: the automobile.

The automobile has given Americans an extraordinary degree of personal mobility. Today there are about 100 million passenger cars and 30 million light trucks (mostly privately owned pickup trucks and vans) registered in the U.S., nearly one for every adult. In 1980, this vast fleet of vehicles consumed about six million barrels of petroleum products per day, the approximate equivalent of all U.S. imports or about 60 percent of U.S. domestic production.

A few years earlier, such facts would have seemed only mildly interesting. In 1972, before the Arab oil embargo, there had been no gasoline shortages, and the total cost of U.S. oil imports was only $5 billion. By 1980, the cost of importing not much more oil had escalated to

$80 billion, or roughly $1,000 for every American household. With the cost rising rapidly and the future availability of petroleum uncertain, some people began to ask if U.S. citizens can continue to enjoy the luxury of the private automobile.

One of the most effective and least expensive ways to reduce U.S. dependence on foreign oil in the years beyond 1990 is to make it a matter of national policy to redesign the automobile so that it will be much more energy-efficient and to provide prudent financial aid to U.S. industry in achieving that goal. It should be possible to reduce the fuel consumption of the American light-vehicle fleet by two-thirds to about two million barrels per day. The saved oil "produced" by the automobile industry in this way would be much lower in cost than an equivalent amount of oil produced synthetically from coal or shale. The environmental impact would also be much less.

Average fuel economies of more than 60 miles per gallon may seem unrealistic, but we believe they are not. The enormous potential for efficiency improvements in today's automotive technology arises from the possibility of combining changes both in the average physical characteristics of automobiles and in the efficiency of their power plants and drive lines (the mechanisms for delivering the power plant's output to the wheels). Such changes were introduced piecemeal between 1975 and 1985 as carmakers began to respond to the new market for efficient light vehicles, but the full potential of the possible changes acting synergistically, rather than one at a time, remains to be widely appreciated. We shall therefore describe a hypothetical fleet of light vehicles that have been redesigned to achieve much higher fuel economy.

In vehicles designed for high energy efficiency, the power required at the drive wheels could be less than half that of present vehicles because of reductions in weight, in aerodynamic drag and in the rolling resistance of the tires. The vehicles would be powered by significantly more efficient versions of today's internal-combustion engines, with the transmissions and the peak power of the engines being optimized for fuel economy.

All the technology required for such a highly efficient fleet exists today in production vehicles or in near-commercial prototypes. We are confident that the vehicles we propose can be designed not only to achieve high fuel efficiency but also to be acceptably safe, to meet reasonable emission standards and to be only slightly costlier, if at all, to operate than current vehicles.

The road to improved fuel economy combines a number of related and interacting paths: weight reduction, reduction in aerodynamic drag, reduction in rolling resistance, more efficient engines and more efficient transmissions. There has already been a substantial drop in the weight of American automobiles and in the average size and power of their engines without any significant loss of useful interior space. For example, one of the Chrysler "K cars," the five-passenger 1981 Plymouth Reliant, was designed to weigh 1,070 pounds (30 percent) less than the 1980 Plymouth Volaré with a sacrifice of only four cubic feet (4 percent) in the volume of the passenger compartment and one cubic foot (6 percent) in the trunk space. As a result of this weight reduction, it was possible to reduce the engine horsepower from 120 to 84 and the miles per gallon were increased from 17 to 24. A major feature of the weight-reduction program in the Reliant, as in many 1980 and 1981 models, was a changeover to front-wheel drive with the engine mounted transversely. This change made it possible to shorten the engine compartment and to eliminate the long, heavy drive shaft that called for a large tunnel through the passenger compartment. The elimination of the rear-axle differential gear also made possible a shorter, deeper luggage compartment.

Weight reductions in the U.S. light-vehicle fleet could also be accomplished by shifting toward a mix of vehicles better matched with the way we use them. The American passenger car was developed in the era when fuel was cheap, when families with four to six members were common and when few households could afford more than one car. The standard six-passenger car made both personal and commercial sense. Similarly, light trucks were originally developed as work vehicles. Today, the average household has fewer than three people, and most households with two or more members own at least two cars or a car and a light truck. Well over half of American light trucks (vehicles with a gross weight when fully loaded of less than 10,000 pounds) have been bought for personal use and serve mainly as passenger cars. It is clear that today the American automobile fleet has a great deal of carrying capacity that is used only infrequently.

It was not until after the gasoline price rise of 1979 that the U.S. public took advantage of the large fuel savings that could be achieved by shifting to a fleet better suited to modern patterns of usage. As a result, sales of five- and six-passenger cars and the larger light trucks dropped sharply. In the first half of 1980, four-passenger cars captured 45 percent of the passenger-car market, compared with 33 percent in 1978. Even this shift, however, leaves vehicle capacity and actual transportation requirements badly mismatched. Surveys show that on about 80 percent of all trips U.S. cars carry no more than two people and that in a little more than half of all trips the driver is alone. Therefore it is likely that, if inexpensive, fuel-efficient two-passenger cars become available, many will be sold.

Further major reductions in weight could be achieved by replacing steel with aluminum, fiber-reinforced plastics and foam-filled structures, an evolutionary process already under way. The ultimate weights that can be achieved by such substitutions will probably be close to 40 percent less than those that are being achieved in today's cars.

The concern has sometimes been expressed that the savings in fuel that can be realized with lightweight materials might be offset by increases in the energy needed for their fabrication. This is not the case. Very roughly, a reduction of 1 percent in the weight of a passenger car can yield a reduction of 0.7 percent in the car's lifetime energy consumption. Since passenger cars today consume about 10 times their weight in fuel over a lifetime of 100,000 miles, a one-pound reduction in weight implies a fuel saving of about seven pounds. This is several times the penalty in manufacturing energy resulting from the substitution of lightweight materials.

Let us now turn to a specific hypothetical four-passenger lightweight vehicle whose aerodynamic drag and rolling resistance are reduced significantly below those of today's vehicles. Consider first the engine. The efficiency of an automobile engine is quite low, when operating at a small fraction of its peak rated output. It is therefore important to equip vehicles with engines that are not unnecessarily powerful. The peak power requirements of an automobile engine are dictated by its ability to accelerate, climb hills and pull loads. We have chosen minimum performance requirements that reflect the importance of fuel efficiency. We assume that light vehicles must be able to accelerate from zero to fifty miles per hour in about 13 seconds. Although this acceleration capability is below the average of the 1980 fleet (from zero to 50 miles per hour in about 10 seconds), it is better than the performance of a number of models that are currently popular. We assume also that the car must be able to maintain a speed of 55 miles per hour while climbing a 5 percent grade. (Only 3 percent of the driving in the U.S. is up steeper grades.) The car must also have extra power for accessories such as air conditioning and (in some vehicles) enough extra power to tow a trailer of the same weight up a 5 percent grade at 40 miles per hour.

L et us now consider the implications of these performance requirements for the engine of our hypothetical vehicle, which will have a "test weight" (the curb weight plus 300 pounds, representing the average load in urban driving) of 2,200 pounds. This weight is comparable to the test weight of the lighter four-passenger cars being sold in the U.S. today. With continued effort toward weight reduction, 2,200 pounds could easily become a typical test weight for future U.S. five- and six-passenger cars. (The five-passenger Reliant already has a test weight of only 2,600 pounds.)

Although the frontal area of our hypothetical vehicle will be about the same as it is for current cars (two square meters, or 21.5 square feet), the coefficient of aerodynamic drag will be at the low end of today's range: 0.4. (The coefficient of aerodynamic drag is a relative measure of the air resistance of a body with respect to that of other objects with the same frontal area. A flat square plate has a coefficient of drag of 1.17. A value of 0.4 is still considerably higher than what has been achieved with aerodynamically shaped but still "practical" prototype cars.)

The tire-rolling resistance of the hypothetical vehicle is equivalent to 1 percent of the downward pull of gravity. This is also at the low end of the current range. Prototype high-pressure tires exist, however, that have values of rolling resistance about 20 percent lower than those of any commercial tires available today.

In order to arrive at the engine horsepower needed for the hypothetical vehicle it is necessary to consider the efficiency of the transmission that delivers power to the wheels. This is a complex technical area. In today's cars the gearing of transmissions usually provides for the selection of only two or three specific rotational speeds of the engine for a given road speed. As a result, in acceleration from zero to 50 miles per hour with a manual transmission, the average engine power output is usually limited to about 80 percent of the peak output.

The current inability to harness the engine's peak power at all road speeds should be remedied with the introduction of transmissions that are continuously variable. Such a transmission in combination with some simple gearing, makes it possible to choose a continuous range of engine speeds. As a result, for most road speeds, any power output up to the full rated output of the engine can be made available. Even more important for achieving fuel economy, is the fact that the most efficient engine speed associated with a given power output can be selected automatically by a microprocessor.

W e shall therefore assume that our hypothetical lightweight vehicle is equipped with a continuously variable transmission and that the engine can thus be operated at its most efficient speed over the full range of road speeds at which significant amounts of energy are expended. We shall also assume that the combined power losses in the drive line (the transmission itself, the ancillary gearing, the wheel bearings and the brakes) will be 10 percent of the engine power delivered to the transmission. (This loss is about the same in one of today's passenger cars equipped with a manual transmission or with one of the newer fuel-efficient automatic transmissions.) In addition we assume that, in periods of peak power demand, the power drawn by the car's accessories can be limited to 0.5 horsepower.

With these assumptions, our hypothetical vehicle will require an engine with a peak rated output of about 36 horsepower. This is 25 percent less than the horsepower of the diesel engine in the slightly heavier 1980 Volkswagen Rabbit. Because of its smaller size, the 36-horsepower engine would be much more efficient than today's large engines in the five- to fifteen-horsepower range, where it would operate most of the time in ordinary driving. For those drivers who want to pull a heavy trailer or for light trucks, optional engines with an additional 20 to 30 horsepower would have to be available, as they are today.

So far, we have not mentioned potential improvements in the thermal efficiency of the engine itself, that is, the efficiency with which the engine converts fuel energy into mechanical energy. Today's most efficient engine for transportation is the diesel, in which the fuel is burned in the form of an aerosol of small droplets. One of the inherent advantages of this engine is that the efficiency falls more slowly at reduced power output than the efficiency of engines, in which fuel vapor and air are uniformly mixed before combustion. Another advantage is that, unlike carbureted engines, they do not have to be fed extra fuel when they are started cold.

The current generation of automotive diesels, however, is still far from being optimized for fuel economy. Various compromises with fuel economy were made to obtain engines that would operate at high rotational speeds (for high peak power), would be easy to start, would make little noise and would meet mandated emission standards. The most important of the compromises was the addition to each cylinder of a small "prechamber" into which fuel is injected and begins to burn. The prechamber makes the fuel efficiency of automotive diesel engines between 10 and 15 percent lower than that of large truck diesels, which have direct cylinder injection. Engine designers have been seeking ways to eliminate the prechamber in automotive diesels without unacceptable performance or emissions. They now appear to be quite close to doing so.

The average efficiency of automotive engines could also be increased by the adoption of another technology that is standard on large truck diesels: turbocharging. The turbocharger is a combination of a turbine and a compressor. The turbine is spun by the exhaust gases; the compressor, which is on the same shaft, pushes extra air into the cylinder and thereby allows additional fuel to be burned on each power stroke. Turbocharging makes it possible to raise the peak power output of an engine of given displacement or, what is equivalent, to reduce the size of the engine for a given peak power. A reduction in engine size is beneficial because smaller engines ordinarily have smaller friction and other losses. Turbocharging automotive diesels has made possible fuel-economy advances of between 10 and 15 percent.

In calculating the fuel economy of hypothetical future light vehicles, we have assumed that the vehicles will be equipped with direct-injection turbocharged engines and with continuously variable transmissions under the control of a microprocessor capable of choosing the most efficient point on a "map" describing the engine's efficiency. In such a map, the thermal efficiency of the engine is plotted as a function of the engine's rotational speed and the amount of energy delivered per revolution (see Figure 1.

The efficiency is low when little energy is delivered per revolution because most of the work done by the expansion of the combustion gases goes to overcoming internal engine friction. Power output is proportional to the product of energy delivered per revolution times revolutions per minute, so that the curves of constant power output on the efficiency map take the form of hyperbolas. Inspection of the efficiency map shows that when only a small fraction of the engine's peak output is needed, maximum efficiency is achieved by holding the engine revolutions constant at the lowest practical level (1,000 revolutions per minute) and adjusting the energy delivered per revolution as it is needed. When more than a certain fraction of the peak engine output is needed (more than 20 percent in the example in Figure 1), additional power can be obtained at maximum efficiency by holding the energy delivered per revolution constant at a high level and increasing the engine's rotational speed.

Once the weight, aerodynamic drag, tire-rolling resistance, accessory power requirements, driveline losses, transmission characteristics, engine size and operating map of an automobile have been specified, it is not too difficult to calculate the vehicle's fuel economy on any specific driving cycle. In our computations, we have used the Environmental Protection Agency (EPA) city-and-highway driving cycles and have expressed the

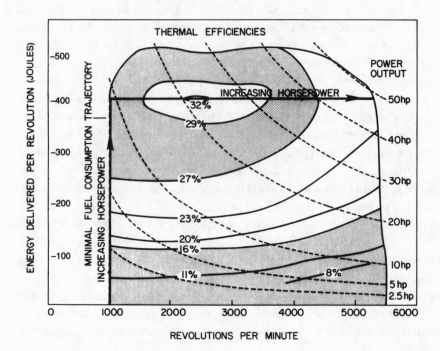

FIG. 1. *Efficiency "map" for diesel engine in a Volkswagen Rabbit relates revolutions per minute (r.p.m.), energy delivered per revolution, power output and thermal efficiency (solid contour lines), Power output is proportional to the product of energy delivered per revolution times r.p.m., so that the contours of constant power output are hyperbolas (dashed lines). In a car with a continuously variable transmission a microprocessor could select for any power output the point along the hyperbola where the engine is most efficient. Broad line is the approximate locus of points of maximum efficiency. Below 10 horsepower a constant 1,000 r.p.m. is best.*

results in terms of the standard "composite" weighted average consisting of 55 percent city driving and 45 percent highway driving.

In order to arrive at a hypothetical fleet of vehicles attainable within 15 years, we have extrapolated from the specifications of average and "best" vehicles of different models available in the 1980 model year. The extrapolations involve vehicle weight, frontal area, coefficient of aerodynamic drag, tire-rolling resistance, type of transmission and drive-train thermal efficiency. Two sets of values are projected: those attainable with the "best" 1980 technology and those we believe could reasonably be attained with the advanced technology available by 1995 (see Table 1).

TABLE 1.   **Projected Attributes of Fuel Efficient Vehicles**

Factor	Approximate Values in U.S. for 1980 Model Year		Projected Feasible Average	
	Average	Best	Current Best Technology	Advanced Technology
Test Weight (pounds)				
2-Passenger	2,900	2,250	1,500	1,050
4-Passenger	2,700	2,000	2,000	1,400
5/6-Passenger	3,700	2,500	2,500	1,750
Light Trucks	4,200	2,500	2,500	1,750
	(all)		(personal)	(personal)
Frontal Area (square meters)	2.0	1.8	1.8	1.8
Aerodynamic-drag Coefficient	0.5	0.4	0.4	0.3
Tire-rolling Resistance (pounds resistive force per 1,000 pounds weight)	14	10	8	7
Transmissions	3-Speed	5-Speed	Continuously Variable	
Average Drive-train Thermal Efficiency (percent)	12	20	25	25

Attributes of fuel-efficient vehicles have been projected on the basis of 1980 best technology and of advanced technology that might reasonably become available. The "average" and "best" values for vehicles built in the 1980 model year are shown for comparison. The main difference between the two projections is in weight and aerodynamic drag: vehicles incorporating advanced technology could have curb weight and aerodynamic drag reduced by about a third. This would yield a large gain in fuel economy.

Here are a few examples of what we believe can be done. In 1980, the average and the lightest four-passenger cars sold had respective weights of about 2,700 and 2,000 pounds. In about 15 years, an average test weight of 2,000 pounds should be achievable for these vehicles with the best 1980 technology. With advanced technology, an average test weight as low as 1,400 pounds (1,100 pounds curb weight) might be practical. At the upper end of the weight range, personal light trucks that in 1980 weighed 4,200 pounds (the average) and about 2,400 pounds (the lightest) could be reduced to an average of 2,500 pounds and perhaps to as little as 1,750 pounds. The weight of five- and six-passenger cars could be similarly reduced. We believe that two-passenger cars, averaging 1,500 pounds, could be made available and that weights as low as 1,050 pounds (750 pounds curb weight) might be practical for such vehicles with advanced technology.

Although the frontal area of the fuel-efficient vehicles might not be much smaller than it was in 1980, we project possible reductions of from 20 to 40 percent in the average coefficient of aerodynamic drag from the 1980 value of about 0.5. The rolling resistance of tires can also be reduced significantly. Reductions in weight, aerodynamic drag and tire-rolling resistance are all important because braking, air resistance and tire losses

TABLE 2. Fuel Economy Estimates

	Frontal Area (square meters)		Engine Size (horsepower)		Fuel Economy (miles per gallon gasoline equivalent)	
Vehicle class	1980 Best Technology	Advanced Technology	1980 Best Technology	Advanced Technology	1980 Best Technology	Advanced Technology
2-Passenger	1.7	1.6	25	18	81	113
4-Passenger	1.7	1.7	31	23	70	96
5/6 Passenger and Personal Light Trucks	2.0	1.9	38	28	58	82

Fuel-economy estimates have been calculated for hypothetical 1995 vehicles with continuously variable transmissions and advanced diesel engines. The body and tires incorporate either the current best technology or advanced technology. The lower weight of advanced-technology vehicles allows a reduction of 27 percent in engine size. Because of reduced weight and improved aerodynamics and tires, advanced-technology vehicles are 40 percent more fuel-efficient than those built with the current best technology. Fuel-economy estimates are adjusted downward by 10 percent because diesel fuel holds 10 percent more energy per gallon than gasoline.

account for about equal amounts of fuel consumption in average driving. With the advanced engine and transmission described above, we calculate that it should be possible to approximately double the drive-train thermal efficiency (the percentage of the energy in the fuel that is delivered to the wheels as driving power) from the 1980 average of about 12 percent to 25 percent.

In calculating the fuel economies of these possible future vehicles, we have assumed that they would meet the performance specifications we listed that led to a 36-horsepower engine in a hypothetical four-passenger car. We have also assumed that on the average 0.5 horsepower is required from the engine to operate the accessories. On the basis of all the foregoing assumptions, we calculate that with the 1980 best technology the entire fleet of light vehicles should be able to achieve a fuel economy of more than 58 miles per gallon. Given a plausible mix of sizes, for example 20 percent two-passenger cars (at 81 miles per gallon), 40 percent four-passenger cars (at 70 miles per gallon) and 40 percent larger cars and light trucks (at 58 miles per gallon), the average fuel economy of the light-vehicle fleet would be about 65 miles per gallon. Increasing the average horsepower of the fleet by 15 percent would reduce the average fuel economy by one mile per gallon. Such an increase would give 20 percent of the fleet a towing capability or alternatively would give the entire fleet an average zero to 50 miles per hour acceleration time of less than 12 seconds. With advanced technology, a fleet of the same composition could conceivably attain a fuel economy of 90 miles per gallon (see Table 2).

The gap between these projections and the estimated fuel economy of 18 miles per gallon for the 1980 U.S. fleet (if light trucks are included) may well prompt the reader to ask: Is the gap understandable, and are the projected numbers believable? Perhaps the simplest way to understand the large factor of potential improvement project is to recognize that reductions in the propulsion energy required at the wheels of a vehicle and improvements in the average thermal efficiency of its drive train have multiplicative effects. Therefore, if the average thermal efficiency of the drive train were to be kept constant at the 1980 value of about 12 percent, the combined effect of all the other improvements in weight, aerodynamic drag and tire-rolling resistance would increase the fuel economy of the fleet based on the best 1980 technology to only 31 miles per gallon and of the fleet based on advanced technology to only 43 miles per gallon. Such numbers would not seem unreasonable in view of the fact that the lightweight (1,950 pounds test weight) 1981 Toyota Starlet, which is equipped with a conventional engine, achieved 39 miles per gallon on the EPA city cycle and 54 on the highway cycle, or 44 miles per gallon on the composite cycle we have adopted for our projections.

A lternatively, if the average test weight (3,300 pounds), aerodynamic drag and tire-rolling resistance of the 1980 fleet were held constant and the average thermal efficiency of the drive train were simply doubled from 12 to 25 percent, the average fuel economy of the fleet would rise only from 18 miles per gallon to about 37, again a number that does not seem intuitively unreasonable. It is only when the effects of decreased power requirements and increased drive-train efficiency are compounded that we arrive at the initially surprising fuel-economy projections in the range of 65 to 90 miles per gallon.

The best demonstration of the validity of our projection would involve a prototype vehicle with the features we have described. Although no publicly disclosed prototype includes all these proposed features, two experimental cars incorporate enough of them to validate our calculations. The first is a Volkswagen Rabbit, with a turbocharged diesel engine built in 1976 for the U.S. Department of Transportation. The vehicle, which has a test weight of 2,400 pounds, achieved a composite fuel-economy score of 60 miles per gallon of diesel fuel. Since diesel fuel holds 10 percent more energy per gallon than gasoline, the prototype's 60 miles per gallon is equivalent to 54 miles per gallon for a gasoline-fueled vehicle.

The second prototype is a more recent experimental vehicle for four passengers, the VW-2000, also built by Volkswagen. Powered by a direct-injection diesel, the vehicle has also achieved a gasoline-equivalent composite city-highway fuel economy of about 60 miles per gallon. The prototype has a fuel-saving feature that we have not included in our projected fleet but that is in the advanced development stage: a flywheel that can be disengaged from the engine. This makes it possible to have the engine stop automatically when the vehicle is stopped or decelerating and then restart automatically and instantly with the energy stored in the flywheel when the accelerator is pressed again.

In our projections, we have not ignored the fact that the EPA testing procedure yields estimates of composite city-highway fuel economy considerably higher (by 15 to 20 percent) than most cars have actually delivered on the road. Fortunately for the purposes of this discussion, however, the vehicles whose characteristics come closest to those we have been describing, namely front-wheel-drive diesel-powered vehicles, achieve on-the-road fuel economies that are much closer to the EPA ratings than vehicles of conventional design.

So much for the technological potential. The discussion cannot, however, end here. Before the U.S. can select a fuel-economy goal, it must understand the relation between fuel economy on the one hand and safety, clean air and cost on the other.

A frequently expressed concern is that passengers in smaller, lighter vehicles are exposed to greater risk of serious injury or death in an accident. Statistics collected for the National Highway Traffic Safety Administration in the mid-1970s show that this is indeed the case. The risk of serious injury or death in an accident increased with decreasing vehicle weight. At the extreme, occupants of the lightest cars were at almost exactly twice the risk of those in the heaviest cars. The study also showed that use of seat belts reduced the risk in all vehicles by more than half. As a result occupants of the lightest cars who fastened their seat belts were at lower risk than those in the heaviest cars who forfeited such protection.

The increased injury risk in light cars is partly offset by the statistical fact that, mile for mile, drivers of subcompact cars appear to have between 10 and 30 percent fewer accidents than the drivers of larger cars. Moreover, one of the major sources of the increased hazard associated with driving small cars, namely collisions with heavy cars, is steadily being reduced as large cars get lighter. The shift toward lighter cars nonetheless makes it imperative that automobile makers improve the crashworthiness of their products at the same time that they redesign them for better fuel economy.

New passenger cars sold in the U.S. are expected to be able to meet a 30-mile-per-hour crash-test standard. Work done by the National Highway Traffic Safety Administration has indicated, however, that there is still much room for improvement in the crashworthiness of light four-passenger cars. The safety of lightweight two-seat city cars may present a special challenge, one that is only partly diminished by the fact that such cars are meant to be driven predominantly in city traffic, where the average vehicle speed is only about 30 miles per hour. We would urge that an international cooperative program be undertaken to demonstrate safe designs for such vehicles.

A second area of major concern in redesigning the automobile for high fuel economy is air pollution, particularly from the increasingly popular diesel engine. Diesel emissions are high in two troublesome pollutants: nitrogen oxides (which contribute to respiratory ailments and to the formation of smog and acid rain) and small particulates that lodge deep in the lungs and carry chemicals that are known to be mutagenic and may prove to be carcinogenic. For equal power output, current diesel engines emit more of these two pollutants than gasoline engines.

It is known that cars powered by prechamber diesel engines, particularly in the smaller sizes, will be able to meet the U.S. federal limit on nitrogen oxide emissions (one gram per mile) that has been applied to gasoline-powered vehicles since 1981. It is expected, but less certain, that the more efficient direct-injection diesels will eventually be able to meet the same standards.

A s for the particulate emissions, it seems probable that small diesel engines will be able to meet the limit of 0.2 gram per mile the EPA has established for 1985 vehicles. Even if they do, however, an emission of 0.2 gram per mile will be about 20 times higher than the quantity of particulates emitted by a comparable gasoline-fueled vehicle. Although the consequences for human health of the mutagenic material carried by diesel particulates remains an unresolved issue, a rising fraction of diesel-powered cars in American cities would add to the quantity of diesel fumes that most people find objectionable and would also generally reduce visibility in these areas. Although the pollution problems of the diesel may not be insuperable, they should motivate a continuing search for efficient automotive power plants that are inherently cleaner.

It is worth noting in this connection that there is one variant of the gasoline-fueled engine that is both efficient and relatively clean and would not require a major break with traditional automotive technology. This is the direct-injection stratified-charge engine. The distinctive feature of such engines is that the charge, or fuel-air mixture, in their combustion chambers is stratified, or made inhomogeneous, at the instant combustion is initiated. As a result, formation of nitrogen oxides is sharply suppressed. Stratification also makes it possible to burn fuel-air mixtures so lean in fuel that they would not burn if the fuel were uniformly mixed with the air. As a result, direct-injection stratified-charge engines have efficiency advantages comparable to those of the diesel. Stratified-charge engines are also capable of burning fuels other than gasoline.

Another possible alternative to the internal-combustion engine is the battery-driven electric motor. Because of the limitations of present storage batteries, electric cars are now primarily of interest for short trips. The driving of electric vehicles has the effect of conserving petroleum and natural gas because only about 15 percent of the nation's electricity is generated from these premium fuels. In developing an automotive strategy for the postpetroleum era, however, one will want to compare the overall efficiency of converting coal or plant material into methanol for internal-combustion engines with the cost of converting the same materials into electricity for charging the batteries of electric vehicles. With current technology, it appears that the methanol route would be the more efficient utilization of the primary fuel.

L et us now address the matter of cost. How large an expenditure on development and retooling is justified in order to achieve a particular level of fuel economy? Here the principle of diminishing returns enters. One can draw a simple curve relating fuel economy, in miles per gallon, to the consumption of fuel over the typical automobile lifetime of 100,000 miles. Such a curve shows that increasing the fuel economy of a 15 miles-per-gallon vehicle by 10 percent to 16.5 will save 600 gallons of fuel over the vehicle's lifetime whereas increasing the fuel economy of a 70 miles-per-gallon vehicle by 10 percent to 77 will save only 130 gallons.

Strictly speaking, the difference between the purchase price of the 77 miles-per-gallon vehicle (for example) and that of the 70 miles-per-gallon vehicle should not exceed the value of the 130 gallons of fuel saved. At some point, defined in the short run by the importance to international stability of reducing U.S. oil imports and perhaps in the long run by the cost of alternative nonpetroleum-based fuels, the cost of the saved energy will become so high that it will no longer be cost-effective to invest in further fuel-economy improvements.

Many cost-benefit analyses have been made, and there seems to be fairly general agreement that the value of fuel savings will exceed their cost at least until the industry is tooled up to build vehicles with a fleet average of 40 miles per gallon. The analysts have not yet reached a consensus, however, on the economic value of going much beyond 40 miles per gallon. Our own belief is that most cost-benefit analyses tend to overstate the cost of making fuel-economy improvements because they do not adequately take into account synergistic effects such as those between the reduction of the power needed at the wheels and the consequent reduction in the size of the engine. We have calculated that, as a result of such effects, the cost to new-car buyers of each additional fuel-economy improvement should be less than $1 per gallon of fuel saved until average fuel economies in the range of about 60 miles per gallon have been achieved (see Figure 2).

This does not necessarily mean, however, that U.S. citizens will be adequately motivated by rising fuel costs to buy the kinds of fuel-efficient vehicles we have described. For example, the difference in fuel consumption between a 40-mile-per-gallon car and a 60-mile-per-gallon one is 0.0083 gallons per mile, which even for fuel costing $2 per gallon amounts to a saving of only 1.6 cents per mile (compared with the total cost of about 25 cents per mile in 1980 to own and operate a light vehicle). Even if the 60-mile-per-gallon car cost no more than the 40-mile-per-gallon one, it is easy to imagine that a new-car buyer would be willing to forgo such a small saving (about $170 per year) for the pleasures of having, for example, a much more powerful engine. If the 60-mile-per-gallon car costs a few hundred dollars more, the temptation would be greater still, even though the fuel savings would pay back the extra cost in about two years. This, of course, is what has happened historically. Even in Europe, where in the mid-1970s gasoline prices were already close to $2 per gallon in 1980 dollars, average passenger-car fuel economy did not exceed 25 miles per gallon.

The automobile industry, for its part, should not be expected to move to the production and promotion of more fuel-efficient vehicles unless the "invisible hand" of the market forces it to. Although, ultimately, it may not cost any more to produce a light, fuel-efficient vehicle than it does a heavy, powerful fuel waster, retooling to manufacture a new generation of cars will cost tens of billions of dollars beyond routine refurbishing costs.

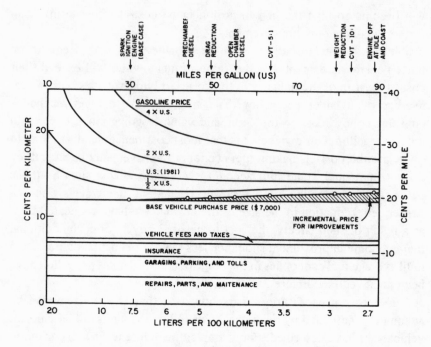

COST OF DRIVING (1981 U.S. CENTS)

FIG. 2. *The weakness of the economic incentive for improved fuel economy. Shown is the cost, in 1981 cents per mile, of driving a 1981 VW Rabbit with the estimated costs of various assumed energy-efficiency improvements amortized over its assumed 100,000-mile lifetime. It appears that a tripling of automotive fuel economy could be accomplished without significantly increasing the cost of driving. However, the economic incentive to the automobile owner is virtually nonexistent—even with a doubling of 1981 gasoline prices (about $1.85 per gallon in 1990 dollars). This enormous potential for reducing oil imports will therefore only be realized if the government intervenes in the market with, for example, fuel-economy standards or gas-guzzler taxes.* [Sources of Fuel-Economy Improvements: *The base vehicle has a standard 55-horsepower (hp) gasoline engine and an EPA composite fuel economy of 30 miles per gallon. The first fuel-economy improvement, to 44 mpg, is achieved by replacing its engine with a 39-hp prechamber diesel (already available in 1981). Estimated further improvements achieved as follows: 30-percent reduced aerodynamic drag coefficient to 0.3 (47 mpg); 30 percent reduced tire rolling resistance to 0.85 percent of gravity (49 mpg); shift to a direct-injection diesel (55 mpg); shift to a continuously variable transmission (CVT) with a 5:1 ratio range (available technology, 64 mpg); 25 percent reduction in engine peak power (71 mpg); 18 percent weight reduction to 2,000 pounds test weight (79 mpg); expansion of the CVT range to 10:1 (83 mpg) and addition of an engine-off feature to save idle fuel during deceleration and stops (89 mpg). For more information, see F. von Hippel and B.G. Levi, "Automobile Fuel Efficiency: The Opportunity and the Weakness of Existing Market Incentive,"* Resources and Conservation 10 *(1983), pp. 103–124.*]

U nfortunately, it takes some 15 years to replace substantially all the cars on the road with a new fleet: five years to retool and ten years to replace the existing fleet. If it is in the national interest of the U.S. to reduce its dependence on imported oil, and if it is recognized that a drastic improvement in the fuel economy of the U.S. national automobile fleet is crucial to achieving that goal, then the task is too important to leave to unpredictable market forces alone. We believe, therefore, that it is necessary for the U.S. government to set before the industry new long-term goals for improving automobile fuel economy.

We believe the U.S. government should also assure the automobile industry that market forces will support the mandated fuel-economy improvements that are desired by committing itself to two measures. First, it should establish a corporate average "gas guzzler" tax, which would specify that, when the average fuel economy of the fleet of cars manufactured by a company falls below the established goal, the company will be obliged to pay a tax proportional to the shortfall and to the number of cars it produced. The threat of such a tax would ultimately be reflected in the form of higher prices (to cover the tax) for the least fuel-efficient models. (In other words, the company could cater to a small number of consumers with expensive tastes if it could find them.) Second, the U.S. government should impose a stiff tax on motor-vehicle fuel, following the example of virtually all other petroleum-importing nations. Given adequate notice, the average consumer could easily offset both these taxes by buying the most fuel-efficient vehicle consistent with his or her needs. We would hope that the antiregulatory mood in Washington would not be allowed to stand in the way of establishing an assured market for a new generation of highly fuel-efficient vehicles.

In order to indicate the potential savings in fuel that are at stake, consider three projections based on three different fuel-economy goals for the fleet of cars that will reach the market in 1995. In each case we assume, for the sake of simplicity, a constant population of 150 million passenger cars and light trucks that are driven an average of 10,000 miles a year, weighted so that the newer vehicles are driven more than that and the older vehicles less. We consider three possibilities: the average on-the-road fuel economy for new light vehicles stays at the 1985 level of 23 miles per gallon projected by the Department of Energy, it increases to 40 miles per gallon or it increases to 60 miles per gallon between 1985 and 1995 and then levels off.

According to the first scenario, the consumption of fuel by the 150 million cars and light trucks continues to decline beyond 1985 as older, less efficient vehicles are retired, finally leveling off at 85 percent of the

1985 demand, or about 4.4 million barrels per day. According to the second scenario, the consumption of fuel by the year 2005 falls to half of the 1985 demand, or to about 2.5 million barrels per day. And according to the third projection, the consumption in 2005 falls to about 1.7 million barrels per day. The difference between the first scenario and the second would be equivalent to more than the capacity of the Alaska pipeline. Unlike the flow of oil from Alaska or anywhere else, however, the "flow" of saved fuel could continue indefinitely. If the U.S. light-vehicle population increases much beyond 150 million or if the average number of miles driven per vehicle year increases significantly, the projected savings would increase proportionately.

Given the prospect that the U.S. supply of domestic petroleum will probably shrink considerably below the present level of 10 million barrels per day in the 1980s and that supplementing the declining supply with synthetics will be extremely costly, we believe the first scenario, which projects an ultimate reduction in light-vehicle fuel consumption of only 1.5 million barrels per day below the current level, makes for a dangerous national policy. We argue that it is essential to set much more ambitious fuel-economy goals than those currently mandated (27.5 miles per gallon by the EPA's composite fuel-economy test). As part and parcel of the higher goals, it would be in the U.S. national interest to make certain that the domestic automobile industry is not prevented from achieving the desired targets by lack of capital. Over at least the next two decades, the flow of saved oil that could be "produced" by the automobile industry is no less great than the flow of liquid fuel that is likely to be produced by the still unborn U.S. synthetic-fuels industry. Not only the capital costs would be less; so too would be the environmental costs. Finally, taking leadership in the international fuel-economy race may be just the prescription needed to revitalize the U.S. automobile industry.

Automobiles and the West's "Umbilical Cord"

WITH WILLIAM U. CHANDLER

"**T**he umbilical cord of the West runs through the Strait of Hormuz into the Arabian Gulf and the nations which surround it." These are the words used by Defense Secretary Weinberger in 1981 to underline his request to Congress for tens of billions to build up the capabilities of our "Rapid Deployment Force."[1]

It is arguable whether a military intervention in the chaotic affairs of the nations surrounding the Persian Gulf would do more to protect or sever the West's "umbilical cord." Most would probably agree, however, that the current level of international tension would be considerably reduced if the industrialized democracies were less dependent upon Persian Gulf oil. That reductions in U.S. oil consumption could do much to bring this about can be made clear with two facts: 1) the U.S. consumes about as much oil as is produced in the Persian Gulf, and 2) the 15 percent reduction in U.S. oil consumption between 1979 and 1981 was one of the principal causes of the ensuing world oil "glut."

The U.S. light vehicle fleet accounts for about 40 percent of U.S. oil consumption—more, in 1989, than all the oil consumed by France, West Germany and Great Britain[2]—and still represents our largest single opportunity for oil savings. U.S. light vehicle fuel consumption stabilized during the 1980s as the average fuel economy of new U.S. passenger cars rose from about 14 miles per gallon in 1975 to about 25 miles per gallon on the road in 1988, offsetting the effects of the increasing size of the U.S. light-vehicle fleet. U.S. gasoline consumption has begun to grow again, however, and will continue to grow unless the average fuel economy of new U.S. passenger cars and light trucks (vans, pickups, etc.) continues to rise in the 1990s. Fuel economy improvements to 50 miles per gallon are cost-effective even at today's fuel prices, and are lower than the 60 miles per gallon that has been demonstrated by Volkswagen with a four-passenger prototype. The oil savings would be enormous and the U.S. would be equipped with automotive technology which would allow us to make a successful transition into the postpetroleum era of limited and expensive liquid fuels.

Continued steady progress toward higher automotive fuel economy will not happen by itself, however. The world oil "glut" of the mid 1980s took the pressure off Detroit to retool to produce still more efficient cars. The automakers postponed investments in fuel economy improvements in order to ameliorate their financial condition. General Motors, for example, postponed introducing its "supereconomy" S-car.

Even more serious for the long term are the implications of the Reagan administration's decision to suspend consideration of post-1985 fuel economy standards for U.S. built cars. In keeping with its general philosophy, the administration decided to leave the future fuel economy of U.S. automobiles to the working of the "free market."

Car owners do not have to pay at the gas pump, however, for the international tensions, military expenditures, and risks which have grown with the West's dependence upon Persian Gulf oil. For that reason and others, the investments of the free market in fuel economy will not be either as timely or as great as would be in the national interest. At a gasoline price of $1.25 per gallon, automobile owners can reduce their fuel costs from nine cents to five cents a mile by trading in a 15-miles-per-gallon car for a 25-miles-per-gallon car, and many did so in the early 1980s. But beyond 25 miles-per-gallon the "invisible hand" of the market for automotive fuel economy gets pretty weak. Five cents a mile is a small fraction of the average total cost of owning and driving a new car today—about 30 cents a mile in the late 1980s[3]—and the lure of additional savings in fuel costs will probably not be large enough to induce most new car buyers to spend the extra money "up front" required to buy the more efficient car—even if no loss in performance, safety or comfort were involved. Consumers generally avoid paying higher first costs when there are only modest net savings over the life of the item purchased. This may explain why cars in Europe average only about 25 miles per gallon on the road, despite gasoline prices which, in the first half of the 1970s, were already at the equivalent of $2 to $3 per gallon.

The market can, therefore, be expected to be relatively indifferent to levels of fuel economy above 25 to 30 miles per gallon (on the road). And, if both the market and the government are indifferent, the automobile manufacturers will be happy to keep on selling the 20 to 30 miles-per-gallon cars that they have tooled up to produce rather than spending tens of billions for another cycle of retooling to produce 40 to 80 miles-per-gallon vehicles.

When the marketplace produces a result which is not in the national interest, government must intervene. Detroit has already lost the opportunity to produce more than 40 miles-per-gallon cars in large numbers before about 1995, and only about one-sixth of the production facilities can undergo major retooling each year thereafter. Congress must not let pass the opportunity to increase dramatically the efficiency of the automobiles which we will be buying in the year 2000 without increasing total consumer costs.

The task of working out an automotive fuel economy policy can be divided into three parts: Congress must set a goal for fuel economy that reflects the national interest in decreased oil consumption and takes full advantage of the improvements in technology which would be cost-effective to the consumer; it must help assure the industry that consumers will want to buy the cars that will be produced as a result of this policy; and it must assure that the auto manufacturers have the capital required for retooling.

Setting the goal will be the easiest task, since the costs and benefits of improved automotive technology can be relatively easily understood. The current program of minimum corporate average fuel economy standards—with any necessary modifications to reflect the changing character of the automobile industry—could use this goal to set new higher fuel economy targets. We would suggest a target of an average of 60 miles per gallon for cars and 40 miles per gallon for light trucks.

The seriousness of the nation's interest in higher automotive fuel economy should be communicated to the new automobile buyer as well, however, with price signals such as the gas guzzler taxes and gasoline taxes which exist in all the other major oil importing nations. These taxes may become more acceptable politically if any net revenues to the government are unambiguously dedicated to the reduction of less socially desirable taxes. The government might also offer substantial financial incentives to the purchasers of new fuel-efficient cars. Finally, a strategy must be devised which will ensure the availability of the necessary capital to Detroit but will preserve an arms-length relationship between government and industry. One possibility would be incentive payments to automobile manufacturers with the payments proportional to the fuel savings achieved for the nation by their year-to-year fleet fuel-economy improvements. Adequate payments could be funded with a small percent-age of the revenues from a European-scale gasoline tax.

None of this will be easy, but it may reduce the perceived need to send our children to war in the Persian Gulf. For some reason it is easy for us to focus on trying to influence events at the far end of our umbilical cord. Our real opportunities, however, exist at our own end.

Global Risks from Energy Consumption

G lobal risks are among the most uncertain risks associated with energy technologies but are also, perhaps, the most important, since they affect relationships between the nations and hence, in a relatively direct way, affect the possibility of war.

The dangers involved are all quite serious and relatively near term. They include war over Persian Gulf oil, climate change caused by the buildup of atmospheric carbon dioxide, accelerated proliferation of nuclear weapons, and competition between food and energy for land and water.

Petroleum

There can be little disagreement that the current level of dependence on petroleum for energy in the United States is dangerous and must be transitory. It is only because the per capita use of petroleum in the rest of the world is so much less than it is in the United States that we have the possibility of shifting to other energy sources in an orderly way.

The remaining resource of recoverable conventional oil is about 35 metric tons for each of the five billion people in the world.[1] In the United States, we may have up to twice the world average per capita oil resource, but we consume about four metric tons per capita per year. At this rate, we will consume the equivalent of our entire remaining endowment of oil resources in the next 10 to 30 years. We have found that we can only sustain a rate of oil consumption anywhere near our current level by persuading other nations, one way or another, to give us a share of *their* oil. In 1989 about 45 percent of U.S. petroleum consumption was

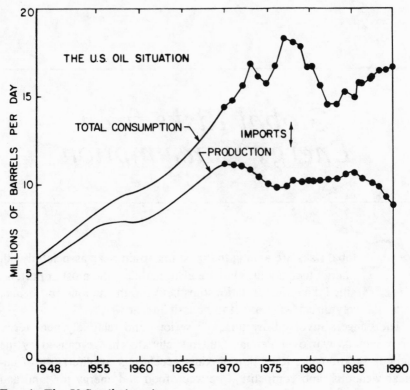

FIG. 1. *The U.S. oil situation.*

sustained by imports (see Figure 1) and, according to most governmental and industrial projections, domestic production will continue to fall.

Worldwide distribution of oil production and consumption is not stable—even at an average world per capita consumption rate of about 0.6 metric tons per year. Very few regions, other than the Persian Gulf, will be able to maintain their oil production at these levels for long, and the concentration of approximately one-half of the world's oil resources in a region populated by less than 2 percent of the world's people (see Figure 2) is a source of increasing world tension. The oil-importing nations, in particular, have found their economies vulnerable to political developments in this very unstable region.

This vulnerability will not be easy to overcome since total fossil-fuel consumption of the noncommunist world tripled between 1947 and 1978, with oil replacing coal as the dominant fossil fuel during this post-World War II period.[2] During this same time, the Persian Gulf became a major locus of world oil production. In 1947, the United States and the Middle

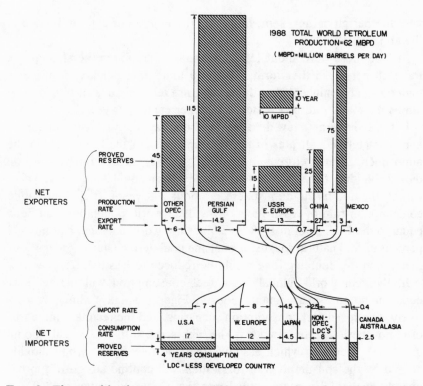

FIG. 2. *The world oil situation in 1988. Reserve data from* Oil and Gas Journal, *December 26, 1988, production data from the 1989* BP Statistical Review of the World Oil Industry, *and consumption data from U.S. Energy Information Administration,* International Energy Outlook, 1989 *and, for OPEC and other less-developed countries, by extrapolation from 1986 data in Energy Information Administration,* International Energy Annual, 1987.

East accounted for 60 and 10 percent, respectively, of world oil production. In 1978, the corresponding percentages were 16 and 34 percent.

The levels of tension resulting from the dependence of non-communist industrialized nations on oil imports from the Persian Gulf are, of course, dangerous for world peace. It is certainly a principal cause of the U.S. interest in building up its war-fighting capability during the 1980s—both conventional (the Rapid Deployment Force) and nuclear (the MX missile).

Other Fossil Fuels

To many, the answer to the petroleum problem is to shift back to the more abundant, albeit less convenient, fossils fuels, notably coal. Here we run into another global problem, however: the buildup of carbon dioxide in the atmosphere.

In 1988 there were about 150 metric tons of carbon in the atmosphere for each person in the world. About 10 times that much carbon exists underground in mineable fossil fuels. We are releasing this carbon into the atmosphere at a rate of 1.4 metric tons per capita per year.[3]

In the short term (a few decades), carbon is apparently accumulating at approximately equal rates in the surface layers of the ocean and in the atmosphere. It therefore appears that, at the current rate of carbon dioxide buildup, fossil-fuel consumption by itself could double the level of carbon dioxide in the atmosphere in about 200 years. If the per capita consumption rate of fossil fuels of the 1988 world population had been equal to the U.S. level in 1988 (five times the world average) and mix (72 percent oil and natural gas) using coal and coal-derived liquid and gaseous fuels, then the doubling time would be reduced to less than 25 years.[4]

In the real world, global fossil fuel consumption will neither stay constant nor increase instantaneously. Figures 3 and 4 show, respectively, two fossil fuel consumption scenarios, and the resultant increases of atmospheric carbon dioxide.[5] The high scenario is a classical "boom and bust" scenario, which assumes that the release of carbon dioxide caused by the consumption of fossil fuels will continue to grow approximately at the 4.3 percent annual rate that prevailed between 1860 and 1975 (with brief interruptions during the World Wars and the 1929–1933 crash). The growth only stops when the limits on the world's resources of economically mineable fossil fuels are approached around the year 2060; then a period of relatively rapid decline begins. The peak rate of fossil-fuel consumption projected for 2060 is extraordinary—corresponding to a rate of carbon dioxide release 15 times higher than the 1975 level. In absolute terms, 80 billion metric tons of carbon would be released per year or 15 metric tons per capita for a world population of eight billion. From another perspective, however, this peak rate of fossil fuel consumption is not extraordinary at all: it corresponds to a world per capita rate of consumption of energy in the form of coal and coal-derived synthetic liquid and gaseous fuels approximately equivalent only to current U.S. per capita fossil fuel energy consumption.

In the low scenario of Figure 3, the carbon dioxide emission rate peaks in 2025 at about twice the current level, followed by a symmetrical decline in emissions after 2025, as nonfossil energy sources take over. The pre-2025 low growth scenario corresponds to an approximately constant global per capita level of fossil-fuel energy consumption, if the world's population increases from 5 to 8 billion and there is a shift to coal

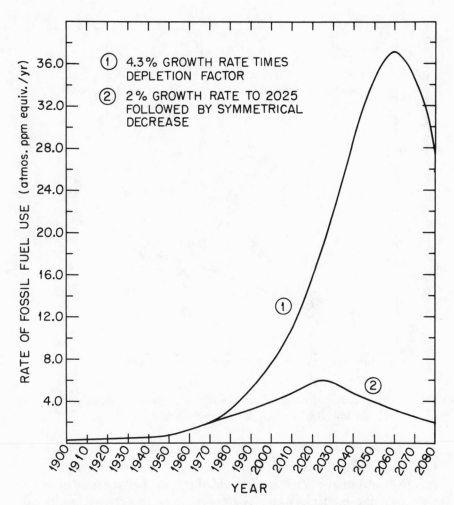

FIG. 3. *Possible limiting scenarios for the use of fossil fuels.*

during that same period. (About 1.3 times as much carbon dioxide would be released per unit energy consumed in 2025 if 100 percent of the fossil fuel consumed were coal instead of the 1988 mix of 43-23-34 percent petroleum, natural gas, and coal.) The low scenario predicts somewhat less than a doubling and the high scenario predicts somewhat more than a quadrupling of preindustrial carbon dioxide levels.

Most calculations suggest that a quadrupling of the carbon dioxide content of the atmosphere would cause a warming of global climate by an average of several degrees centigrade. This would probably be accompanied by local climate changes that would affect world agriculture, as well

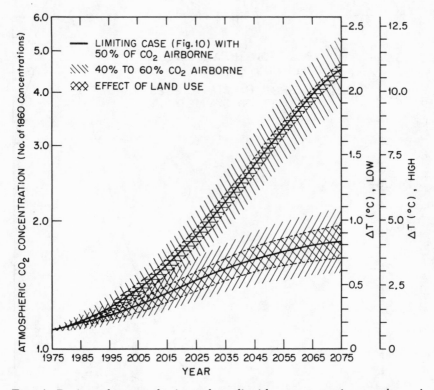

FIG. 4. *Projected atmospheric carbon dioxide concentrations and possible changes in the average surface temperature.*

as many natural systems, in currently unpredictable, but almost certainly significant, ways. A decision to continue to consume fossil fuels, subject only to their resource limitations, would, therefore, be a decision to set no weight on the probable major consequences of the changes in global climate that would result.

Fission

The environmental impacts of nuclear energy are reduced because the waste products created by the energy release are about one million times more concentrated than the waste products from fossil-fuel combustion. About 30 megawatt-days of thermal energy are released per kilogram of uranium loaded into one of today's light-water reactors. The corresponding number for the combustion of coal is about 3×10^{-4} megawatt-days per kilogram of fuel or 3×10^{-5} megawatt-days per kilogram of combustion products, including the entrained nitrogen.[6] The very concentration of the energy stored in fissionable materials creates, however, its own set of problems, particularly the problem of nuclear weapons.

Surely, the greatest threat to the future of civilization lies in the enormous stockpile of nuclear weapons built up by the United States and the Soviet Union in their mindless nuclear arms race. They each possess strategic forces containing about 10,000 warheads with a total explosive power of about five billion tons of TNT. In addition, each side possesses 10,000 to 20,000 tactical or "theater" nuclear warheads. For comparison, the total tonnage of bombs dropped in World War II is estimated at three million tons.

The danger posed by the nuclear arms race is being increased by the continuing spread of nuclear weapons and weapons manufacturing capabilities to many other nations. Although the addition to the total destructive potential already in the arsenals of the world's megadeath "superpowers" will be relatively small for many years, it takes only a few nuclear weapons to kill millions of people.

Unfortunately, despite the protestations of the nuclear industry to the contrary, the spread of nuclear weapons technologies has been closely linked to the spread of civilian nuclear technologies in the past and is likely to continue to be so in the future. The French nuclear program was so ambiguous in the early years, for example, that many of the scientists involved believed it had only civilian purposes.[7] China developed its nuclear weapons on a technological foundation that was established with the assistance of the Soviet Union under an agreement made in 1957 and dissolved a few years later—possibly because of Chinese interest in nuclear weapons.

Apparently, India produced its 1974 nuclear explosion with plutonium created in a research reactor provided by Canada. Israel is widely believed to have, at least, the ability to construct nuclear weapons rapidly with plutonium produced from a French-supplied research reactor that is not under international safeguards. South Africa is also commonly believed to have nuclear-weapons capability based on highly enriched uranium produced, with technology developed with assistance of West Germany.[8] Pakistan is known to have obtained nuclear weapons capability using equipment and knowledge procured clandestinely from the nuclear industry in Europe. Iraq used her "oil weapon" to force France to keep a commitment to supply Iraq with research-reactor fuel containing weapons grade uranium.[9] Iraq insisted on this; despite the fact that France had shown that an identical research reactor would operate satisfactorily on low enriched uranium. Israel bombed Iraq's reactor in

1981, before it became operational but the fuel, containing enough highly-enriched uranium to make a single nuclear explosive, remains in Iraq.

Of course, banning nuclear power would not put the nuclear weapons genie back into the bottle, but history suggests that civilian nuclear energy programs provide a convenient cover, as well as the training, technology, and nuclear material necessary for the construction of nuclear weapons. Furthermore, if the Japanese and West European nuclear energy establishments are successful in commercializing recycled plutonium as a nuclear fuel, separated nuclear weapons material will be circulating in such large amounts that it is likely we will soon be facing the threat of nuclear-armed terrorist groups who won't be susceptible to deterrence by the threat of nuclear retaliation.

Fission energy will only be able to supply a large fraction of the world's energy if current types of reactors, which are able to release efficiently only the energy in the rare uranium isotope, U-235, are succeeded by breeder reactors which can release the energy in the much more abundant U-238 (99.3 percent of natural uranium) or thorium-232 isotopes.

A 1-million kilowatt breeder reactor, breeding plutonium out of U-238, would discharge about 1,000 kilograms of plutonium each year. If plutonium breeders were used to supply the world with primary energy at the same rate that fossil fuel does today, 5 million kilograms of plutonium would be discharged each year or enough to make almost a million Nagasaki bombs. The diversion of even one ten-thousandth of this plutonium by terrorists would make possible the devastation of about 100 cities a year. It is sobering to note, therefore, that the U.S. government has been able to keep track of the plutonium in its weapons program to an accuracy of only about one part in a hundred.[10]

Fortunately, it is easy to demonstrate that a commitment to a plutonium economy can be postponed for decades, until the level of our long-term commitment to nuclear power can be settled. There is sufficient uranium in the Earth's deposits of high-grade uranium ore to sustain our current generation of nuclear reactors (which do not involve commerce in separated plutonium) in any number that electricity demand growth can justify well into the next century.[11]

Fusion

Fusion is another way of releasing nuclear energy and is likely to share with fission many of the same problems of maintaining the separation between military and civilian technologies. Indeed, the easiest fusion reaction to ignite, the deuterium-tritium reaction, releases approximately five times as many neutrons per unit of energy released as nuclear fission and has, therefore, been discussed as a possible basis for a fissile-fuel production facility that could "breed" plutonium or other chain-reacting material to fuel fission reactors.[12]

Solar Energy

The problems associated with our currently dominant commercial energy technologies have helped stimulate renewed interest in solar energy technologies. Other stimuli are the relatively uniform distribution of the solar resource, the possibility of exploiting it with relatively small scale facilities, and the increased costs of "conventional" energy supplies.

The most abundant form of solar energy is, of course, direct sunlight. The average rate at which energy in sunlight falls on U.S. buildings, alone, is equal to about one-half of the current rate of U.S. fossil fuel consumption.[13] Direct solar energy could be captured and redistributed in amounts equal to tens of times current human fossil energy use without serious global effects. Some indirect forms of solar energy such as wind power could also be exploited on a considerably smaller but still significant scale.[14]

Large-scale exploitation of other forms of indirect solar energy would not necessarily have such benign results, however. Consider, for example, the potential implications of a very large increase in the use of biomass (wood, grass, etc.) as fuel. Today, biomass provides approximately one-sixth as much fuel energy worldwide as do fossil fuels. It would take the energy content of almost 10 percent of the Earth's gross annual biomass production—twice as much as is harvested today to provide humans with food and fiber[15]—to equal the current level of world fossil fuel consumption. Sustaining a population of eight billion, at the level of today's U.S. per capita fossil fuel energy use, would take approximately the Earth's entire annual biomass production. Biomass productivity could be increased greatly in certain areas, but it is obvious that exploitation of biomass energy at even the current level of fossil fuel use would have global implications. "Energy plantations" could, for example, compete for land and water with food or fiber producing activities. Since more carbon is stored in living plants than in the atmosphere, the harvesting of standing biomass could also significantly increase the carbon dioxide in the atmosphere.[16]

Energy Efficiency

Our examination of the global problems associated with energy supply technologies raises the question: Why do we use so much energy anyway? This question is always fruitful because it seems that, whenever one studies in some detail a particular energy end-use, one always finds that at least one-half of the energy is wasted by inefficiencies that would cost much less to rectify than the value of the wasted energy at current prices.

In an energy-efficiency analysis of the entire U.S. economy, M. Ross and R.H. Williams concluded that an economy with twice the 1980 U.S. per capita income could be supported at a per capita level of energy consumption lower by one-quarter if investments were made in energy efficiency only up to the point where the cost of saved energy became equal to that of new energy supply.[17] A U.S. National Academy of Science study came to a similar conclusion.[18]

Opportunities for energy efficiency improvements are not limited to the United States. One of the reasons why the forests in many areas of the Third World are being depleted, for example, is because the efficiencies of Third World cooking stoves are so low.[19]

It would appear that many of the very serious global risks associated with current and projected levels of energy consumption are being undertaken to support energy waste rather than energy needs. A direct way to reduce these risks would be to increase the efficiency of energy use. U.S. security might be increased, for example, if we trained, reequipped, and redeployed the Rapid Deployment Force into our homes with the mission of reducing U.S. residential energy waste. Similarly, funds that are proposed for the construction of the B-2 bomber might be used much more effectively to improve our security if they were spent to retool our automobile factories for the production of 60-miles-per-gallon automobiles.

NUCLEAR
REACTOR
ACCIDENTS

Thyroid Protection in Nuclear Accidents

On March 1, 1954, the United States fired off a large nuclear weapon over Bikini in the South Pacific. Five hours later, coral blown miles high by the blast filtered down like snow over the inhabited atoll of Rongelap, some 100 miles downwind. This fallout was radioactive. The population was evacuated before anyone received a lethal dose of radiation, but years later, the children began, one after another, to develop thyroid tumors. By the time these children reached the age of twenty-one, almost all had undergone thyroid surgery and had been placed on thyroid medication for the rest of their lives.[1]

The cause of the damage to the children's thyroids was the radioactive iodine in the fallout, which had contaminated their drinking water. Because the thyroid gland, necessary to normal growth and metabolism, concentrates any iodine in the body, the children's small and rapidly developing thyroids had received a greatly magnified dose of radiation.

Since the story of the Rongelap children was reported in the medical literature, there have been periodic proposals to have a thyroid protection strategy available in case of a large release of contaminated steam containing radioiodine during a nuclear reactor accident.[2] Particular attention has been focused on thyroid protection because, measured in terms of the numbers of people who could be affected, thyroid damage is potentially the largest single hazard from an accident.

The number of damaged thyroids that would have resulted from a meltdown accident with failure of containment at Three Mile Island could have ranged, depending upon the wind direction, from thousands to hundreds of thousands of cases.[3]

Fortunately, medicines exist that could protect the thyroid from radioiodine. In 1978, one of these, potassium iodide, an inexpensive chemical found in small amounts in "iodized" table salts, was certified "safe and effective" for use in a radiation emergency by the Food and Drug Administration.[4] If taken in the recommended dosage just before exposure, nonradioactive iodine in potassium iodide will saturate the thyroid and block the uptake of radioiodine inhaled or swallowed during the next 24 hours.

In order to be able to protect thyroids in an emergency, however, it would be necessary to have large quantities of potassium iodide available in proper dosages. For this reason, a study group set up by the American Physical Society (APS) of which I was a member, made a recommendation to the Nuclear Regulatory Commission (NRC) in 1975 that "a national policy of stockpiling thyroid-blocking chemicals for possible emergency distribution should be established."[5]

The Commission did not follow up on our recommendation—perhaps because its regulations required that nuclear power plants be designed so that the risks from major releases of radioactivity would be "negligible."[6]

In March 1979, however, the events at Three Mile Island made the probability of a major release seem not so negligible after all; indeed, at some moments, a large release appeared likely. Therefore, three days after the prolonged emergency situation began, in a frantic effort initiated at 3:00 a.m., the Food and Drug Administration (FDA) asked first one drug company and then others to begin production of potassium iodide solution. Air Force and commercial jets and Army trucks brought 250,000 one-ounce bottles of the thyroid-blocking chemical, and 250,000 eye droppers together for assembly and then shipment to Harrisburg.[7] The government moved with impressive speed, once it had made its decision. But, if there had been a major radioactive release at Three Mile Island, the drug probably would have arrived too late.

One might have expected that after this experience, the U.S. government would immediately have taken steps to make sure that it would not be caught again without either thyroid-blocking chemicals or a distribution system. However, the Nuclear Regulatory Commission's staff has given one reason after another for not acting.

The first reason was concern about the possible side effects of potassium iodide. When asked, however, for the basis of the NRC staff's disagreement with the FDA's conclusions that "the risks from the short-term use of relatively low doses of potassium iodide in a radiation emergency are outweighed by the risks involved from exposure to radioiodine," Harold Denton (Director of the NRC's Office of Nuclear Reactor Regulation) responded in July 1979 that there was none. But

Denton offered another reason for opposing thyroid protection: "For higher doses of radiation to the thyroid (greater than one rem), it may be better to evacuate the population."[8]

If the staff's previous concern about possible side effects from potassium iodide was surprising, the implications of this new proposal were mind boggling. Thyroid doses of tens to hundreds of rem are possible more than 100 miles downwind from a reactor accident. Had there been a major release at Three Mile Island, Washington (at 90 miles) and New York (at 160 miles) would have been well within the range of thyroid-damaging doses of radioiodine. And there are many other nuclear power plants much closer to both cities. Did Denton really prefer the possibility of facing a decision to evacuate Washington or New York within a matter of hours to the alternative of having thyroid protection available?[9]

Such questions apparently had some impact because there were no more assertions from the Nuclear Regulatory Commission that evacuation was an adequate alternative to thyroid protection medicine. Early in 1980, however, a new argument against potassium iodide was discovered. The NRC staff had done a cost-benefit analysis that concluded that stockpiling "potassium iodide appears only marginally cost-effective at best."[10] The "proof" assumes, among other things, that given a population of approximately 100 power reactors, such as the United States has today, a large release of radioactive iodine from a reactor accident will occur only once in a thousand years.

Stockpiling potassium iodide against such an unlikely event would obviously be a waste of money. But can we be confident that a serious reactor accident is that improbable? Where did the staff get the one-in-a-thousand reactor years release probability anyway?

The probability estimate came from the NRC's 1975 Reactor Safety Study (also known as WASH-1400 or the Rasmussen report). The calculations made in this report became so controversial, however, that in 1977 the NRC was forced to set up a special outside committee to review them. As a result of this review,[11] the Commission announced in early 1979 that:[12]

> In the light of the Review Group conclusions on accident probabilities, the Commission does not regard as reliable The Reactor Safety Study's numerical estimate of the overall risk of reactor accident.

The staff's cost-benefit calculation was therefore based on an estimate of the likelihood of an accident that the Commission had been officially dropped as unreliable more than a year earlier.

It is now many years since the APS group recommended a thyroid protection strategy, and the NRC staff is apparently still unwilling even to *think* seriously about the subject. Why? Perhaps the answer lies in the history of the Commission.

Until 1975, the Nuclear Regulatory Commission was part of the old Atomic Energy Commission (AEC), an agency whose primary civilian mission was to promote nuclear power. Because of its promotional orientation, the AEC tended to play down serious hazards associated with nuclear power. Indeed, this tendency is what ultimately caused Congress to break up the AEC in 1974 and split off the Nuclear Regulatory Commission as a separate agency. Most of the NRC's senior staff came from the AEC, however, and these old-timers brought along with them some of the AEC's reluctance to face "sensitive" regulatory issues.[13]

The question of stockpiling potassium iodide is sensitive because, if the Commission visibly prepares for the possibility of a large release of radioactivity, the public may become convinced that such an accident is not only possibly, but probable.

It is no longer part of the NRC's job description, however, to make the political environment safe for nuclear energy. And even if it were, the agency should have learned from the history of the Atomic Energy Commission, whose overprotectiveness ultimately backfired and became the nuclear industry's biggest liability. As the public has seen the NRC continuing to avoid making some of the hard decisions on reactor safety that the Atomic Energy Commission had refused to make, it has become a majority view that the only safe nuclear power plant is the one that has not been completed. All U.S. nuclear power plants ordered after 1974 have been cancelled before completion. This might seem irrational in view of the fact that the public has quietly accepted much greater hazards, such as nuclear weapons, in its midst—but it is an understandable reaction to the NRC's failure to establish itself as a credible guardian of the public safety.

Containment of a
Reactor Meltdown

WITH JAN BEYEA

A ny good scientist or engineer believes implicitly in Murphy's law: "If something can go wrong, sooner or later it will go wrong." The U.S. Atomic Energy Commission, which until 1975 had the responsibility for ensuring the safety of U.S. civilian power reactors, had many good scientists and engineers involved in its work. And during its history, it repeatedly considered the consequences of all the safety systems in a nuclear reactor failing, the fuel melting and the volatile radioactive isotopes in the fuel being released to the atmosphere.

The answer which came back from major studies in 1957,[1] 1965[2] and 1975[3] was always that the consequences could be very serious indeed. This finding underlined the importance of preventing nuclear reactor meltdown accidents. As a result, the Atomic Energy Commission and the Nuclear Regulatory Commission (NRC), its successor in the area of nuclear safety regulation since 1975, required so many redundant safety systems on nuclear power plants that both nuclear regulators and the nuclear industry became convinced that the likelihood of a reactor meltdown accident had been reduced to a negligible level.

The massive failure of safety systems and the associated confusion which has occurred repeatedly at nuclear power plants since 1975—with serious damage resulting at Brown's Ferry in 1975[4] and Three Mile Island in 1979[5]—have, however, thrown this confidence into question. Greater public attention is required to the possibilities for increasing the public protection offered by the last barrier between radioactivity released from a molten core and the outside world: the reactor containment building.

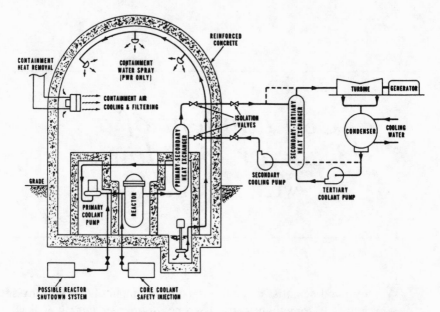

FIG. 1. *Large volume pressurized water containment. Because of its large volume (about 60,000 cubic meters), this containment can hold all of the steam released in the first minutes of a loss of coolant accident. Subsequently steam pressure must be reduced by the containment water sprays. Source: T.J. Thompson and J.G. Beckerly,* The Technology of Nuclear Reactor Safety, *Vol. 2 (Cambridge, MA: MIT Press, 1973), p. 763.*

The Containment

Reactor containment buildings are massive and well-equipped (Figures 1 and 2). Most are designed to withstand internal pressures of three to four atmospheres and may maintain their integrity at more than six atmospheres internal pressure. They also have water sprays, water pools or compartments full of ice—whose purpose is to reduce internal pressures by removing steam from the containment atmosphere.

Reactor containment buildings today are not designed to contain a reactor core meltdown accident, however. Their "design basis accident" is a loss-of-coolant accident in which large amounts of volatile radioisotopes are released from a temporarily overheated core, but in which the uncontrolled release of energy from the core into the containment atmosphere is terminated by a flood of emergency core cooling water before an actual meltdown occurs. This is essentially what happened

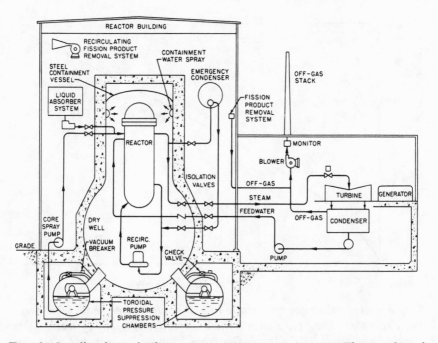

FIG. 2. *Small-volume boiling water reactor containment. The combined volume of the dry well and the connected free space over the pressure suppression pool is only one-eighth that of the containment shown in Figure 1. Steam from the dry well bubbles through the water in the pressure suppression chamber and is condensed. This could prevent overpressurization by steam but not by other noncondensable gases such as hydrogen and carbon dioxide. Source: T.J. Thompson and J.G. Beckerly,* The Technology of Nuclear Reactor Safety, *Vol. 2 (Cambridge, MA: MIT Press, 1973), p. 766.*

during the accident at Three Mile Island although, because of various errors, the core remained only partially cooled for a period of hours.

Threat of Overpressurization

If, for any reason, the emergency core cooling system were not effective and a core meltdown occurred, the buildup of internal pressure in a sealed reactor containment building could rupture it within a matter of hours. The threat would come from steam, hydrogen and other gases.

For an extended period of time after a reactor shutdown, the radioactive fission products in a reactor core generate heat at a rate great enough

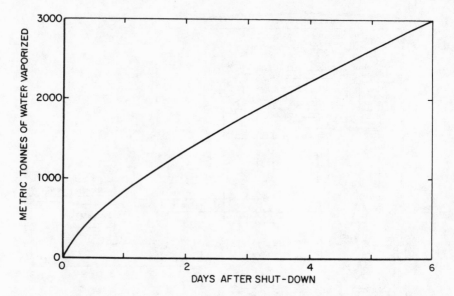

FIG. 3. *Potential steam production by radioactive after-heat (1,000 mega-watt reactor). The figure shows the cumulative amount of water which would be evaporated by the radioactive after-heat generated after shut-down by the core of a typical modern 1,000-megawatt light water reactor. In the absence of heat removal from the containment, the steam pressure so generated would threaten the containment integrity within hours.*

to turn hundreds of metric tons of water into steam per day (Figure 3). It would take only about 300 metric tons of steam to increase the pressure inside even a large (60,000 cubic meter volume) Three Mile Island type of containment building by about 10 atmospheres. It is apparent, therefore, that unless the containment cooling system operates reliably and effectively to keep steam pressure from building up, the containment will quickly be overpressured by steam alone.[6]

Hydrogen is another potential contributor to the pressurization of the containment. It is produced when water or stream comes into contact with a metal which binds oxygen so strongly that the metal can take oxygen away from water molecules. Because it absorbs relatively few neutrons, one such metal, zirconium, is the structural material of choice in the cores of water-cooled reactors. Zirconium starts reacting rapidly with steam at temperatures above 1,100°C. About one-half the zirconium in the core of Three Mile Island Unit No. 1 was oxidized during the accident there.[7]

For a small-volume (boiling-water reactor type) containment, the pressure developed by the amount of hydrogen generated at Three Mile Island would have been enough to raise the containment pressure by one to three atmospheres.

For a large-volume containment, the principal hazard associated with hydrogen would be fire or explosion, and in fact hydrogen did burn at Three Mile Island. Fortunately, however, the initial pressure in the containment building was such that the containment was able to withstand the resulting pressure increase of about two atmospheres. Some existing reactor containments would not have withstood the pressure rise associated with burning this much hydrogen—even given an initially low pressure.

In small boiling-water reactor containments, the probability of a hydrogen fire is eliminated by "inerting" the containment with an atmosphere of pure nitrogen. This is not done, however, in ice-condenser containments, designed to withstand much lower internal pressures than most other containments. On September 8, 1980, during a final review of the design of Sequoyah Nuclear Power Plants, Units 1 and 2 (which are equipped with ice-condenser containments) the NRC's watchdog Advisory Committee on Reactor Safeguards, pointed out in a letter to the Commission that: "For events involving more than 30 percent oxidation of the zirconium, hydrogen control measures may be necessary to avoid containment failure."

The remaining threat to containment integrity from overpressurization during a core meltdown accident would arise from carbon dioxide and carbon monoxide liberated as the molten core melted its way down through the concrete basement of the reactor building.[8,9]

These possibilities are sufficient to suggest why one of today's small-volume reactor containment buildings would probably rupture during a core meltdown accident and why there is a significant, although less certain, probability of failure for a large-volume pressurized-water-reactor type containment.[3]

Regulatory Response

The situation just described was first explored by an Atomic Energy Commission (AEC) advisory committee in 1966, when the AEC was just beginning to license the construction of large commercial power reactors. The advisory committee recommended in its report, however, that the Commission undertake only "a small-scale, tempered effort on [the] problems . . . associated with systems whose objective is to cope with the consequences of core meltdown. . . ." The committee did not recommend a crash program to develop better containments because it felt that "to produce effective designs, if indeed feasible, might require both considerable fundamental research and practical engineering application." Instead, the committee advised the Commission that "for the time being, assurance can be placed on existing types of reactor safeguards, principally emergency core-cooling."[10]

The Commission accepted the advice and went ahead with licensing containment buildings whose integrity depended upon the successful functioning of emergency core cooling systems. A small amount of research was conducted for a time into the possibility of improved containment concepts. As the Commission certified, time after time, that existing containment designs were adequately safe, however, the research was phased out.

Periodically, the issue of improved containment designs was brought up by outsiders. For example, in 1975, the American Physical Society Study Group on Light Water Reactor Safety recommended that "more emphasis should be placed on seeking improvement in containment methods and technology."[11] By that time, however, so many tens of billions of dollars had been invested in nuclear power plants which were already operating, or in advanced stages of construction, that nuclear-safety authorities were unwilling to question such basic safety design features.

This attitude was expressed in a memorandum written on September 25, 1972 by Joseph Hendrie, then Deputy Director for Technical Review of the Atomic Energy Commission. Hendrie was responding to the suggestion by a senior member of the Commission staff, Steven Hanauer, that "I recommend that the AEC adopt a policy of discouraging further use of pressure suppression containments." Hanauer was concerned about the safety disadvantages of small-volume containment buildings such as the General Electric boiling-water reactor pressure suppression containment shown in Figure 2, and the ice-condensor pressure suppression containment design being proposed at the time by Westinghouse. We reproduce here Hendrie's response in full:

> With regard to the attached, Steve's idea to ban pressure-suppression containment schemes is an attractive one in some ways. Dry containments have the notable advantage of brute simplicity in dealing with a primary blowdown, and are thereby free of the perils of bypass leakage.
>
> However, the acceptance of pressure-suppression containment concepts by all elements of the nuclear field, including Regulatory

and the ACRS [Advisory Committee on Reactor Safeguards], is firmly imbedded in the conventional wisdom. Reversal of this hallowed policy, particularly at this time, could well be the end of nuclear power. It would throw into question the operation of licensed plants, would make unlicensable the GE and Westinghouse ice-condensor plants now in review, and would generally create more turmoil than I can stand.

This memorandum became public as a result of a Freedom of Information Act suit by the Union of Concerned Scientists, reinforced by congressional pressure following Hendrie's appointment to the chairmanship of the Nuclear Regulatory Commission in 1977.

Filtered Vents

As more and more nuclear power plants went into operation, the attention of those who wished to improve reactor containment designs turned to safety systems which could be "retrofitted" onto existing plants and to one specific idea in particular. This was a "filtered vent" system which could relieve the pressures inside a dangerously pressurized containment building by releasing some of its radioactive gases to the atmosphere through a large filter system. There, the most dangerous radioactive species would be trapped before filtered containment gases were allowed to escape. It would be relatively easy to add such a system onto an already completed containment building because the filter system could be installed in a separate building outside the existing containment building and connected to it through a large valve and underground pipe (Figure 4).

The installed cost of one of these systems has been estimated to be between $1 million and $20 million per reactor, an amount which is small in comparison with the more than $1 billion total cost of a modern nuclear power plant.[13]

Despite the attractive aspects of the vented containment concept, the Nuclear Regulatory Commission investigated it extremely slowly and cautiously. While the Commission's slowness can only be deplored, its caution is appropriate: prescriptions for nuclear safety, like those for drugs, should be both safe and effective and the staff had concerns in both areas.

In the area of effectiveness, the staff's concerns focused on the possibility that, in certain accident sequences, the pressure buildup inside the containment might be so rapid that no exhaust system of realistic size

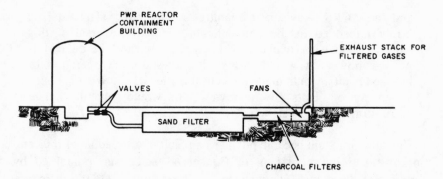

FIG. 4. *General arrangement of a pressurized water reactor (PWR) filtered vent system. If the pressure inside the containment climbed to a dangerous level, the isolation valves could be opened and some of the containment gas released through sand and activated charcoal filters.*[12]

could filter and release the gases inside fast enough to save it. The pressure rise associated with a hydrogen fire could, for example, be very rapid. Rapid increases in steam pressure could also occur within the containment of a pressurized water reactor as a result of sudden contacts between large amounts of molten core and large amounts of water.

According to current ideas, a melting reactor core would not drip away. Instead, it is believed more likely that a large fraction of the core would suddenly collapse and fall into the water remaining at the bottom of the reactor pressure vessel. In the past, there has been concern in the reactor safety community about the possibility such an event resulting in a "steam explosion" violent enough to propel the top of the reactor vessel through the shell of the containment building. This concern has been downgraded in more recent studies, but inside even a large containment building, a rapid increase in pressure of about one atmosphere could occur.

In some scenarios, where the primary pressure system around the reactor core and its attached piping remain intact until the core actually melts through the pressure vessel, the melt-through would relieve the steam pressure in the primary system, with the result that some water in the system could be mobilized and pour into the pressure vessel on top of the molten core. This could cause a rapid pressure rise of one to three atmospheres. And finally, after melting through the pressure vessel, the molten core could, once again, fall into a pool of water collected in the cavity below the vessel. Another rapid increase in pressure could then result.[9]

There appear to be strategies that can reduce the threat of containment failures resulting from such pressure increases if, in fact, further analysis should establish this threat as a serious one: For example, the Nuclear Regulatory Commission is already beginning to require hydrogen "igniters," capable of burning any accumulating hydrogen in stages before concentrations can build to levels where a single burn will be intense enough to endanger containment. The magnitude of some steam pressure rises associated with core meltdowns in pressurized water reactors could be reduced by relieving the pressure in the primary system and flooding the containment building with water to a level which covers the pressure vessel when a meltdown appears inevitable. And, as we have seen, a filtered vent would make possible still another strategy: early venting to reduce the pressure base on which any subsequent sudden pressure increases would build.

The possibility of early venting is two-edged, however, because it requires a judgment that nothing else can be done to prevent a major release of radioactivity. That judgment might be wrong or the filtered venting system might even operate accidentally. The resulting releases would be dominated by the nonfilterable radioactive noble gases which would contribute about one-thousandth of the cumulative radiation dose from an uncontained meltdown accident. The Commission's safety concern about filtered venting, therefore, focused on the fact that a filtered vent system, while offering some protection against large releases of radioactivity to the atmosphere, would also increase, by an uncertain amount, the frequency of public exposure to very much smaller releases.

This concern is akin to the one about automobile seat belts—that by slowing a passenger's escape from a vehicle in some accidents, a seat belt could contribute to, rather than prevent, a death. Seat belts, as we know from statistics, save vastly more lives than they endanger. In the case of reactor core meltdown accidents (fortunately) we have no statistics yet. If the Commission made a careful judgment, however, it seems likely that the final conclusion would be that, for a well-designed system, the reduction in the risks from large releases would greatly exceed the increased risks from small releases.

The Industry Response

In response to the Three Mile Island accident, the U.S. nuclear industry could have put its own resources into investigating the possibilities for the reduction of radioactive releases following core-melt accidents. Unfortunately, it did not. Instead, the industry mounted a concerted campaign to convince the public and government that, even in case of containment failure, the resulting release of radioactivity to the atmosphere would be much less than had been thought. In particular, the electrical utilities' Electric Power Research Institute (EPRI) published a study which concluded, in effect, that improved containments are not necessary.[14]

The EPRI report claimed that, even in the event of a core meltdown accident and a containment failure, "due to the solubility of the volatile fission product compounds and the aerosol behavior mechanisms, the off-site dispersion of radioactive materials (other than gases) following a major LWR [light-water reactor] accident will be small." The electric utilities' public relations departments and the nuclear industry press sprang into action and advertised these claims with great fanfare, noting that, "If findings like these are verified . . . it would go far toward deflating the doomsday predictions of anti-nuclear groups."[15] The industry was probably concerned that the adoption of accident mitigation techniques, such as off-site preparations for emergencies and retrofitting containment buildings with filtered venting systems, could be interpreted by the public as tacit admissions that serious accidents can happen.

The Nuclear Regulatory Commission, aside from a few staff comments in the trade press, expressed no public reservations concerning the significance of these claims, which tended to give them further credibility.

The Commission did, however, authorize an effort to examine the Institute's claims as a collaborative enterprise between Commission staff members and technical experts at three major national laboratories. In March 1981 this team stated in a draft report:[16]

> The results of this study do not support the contention that the predicted consequences of the risk dominant accidents have been overpredicted by orders of magnitude in past studies. For example, the analysis in this report indicates that . . . 10 to 50 percent of the core inventory of iodine could be released to the environment.

Under pressure from the industry, the Commission subsequently rewrote the summary language so that it no longer appeared to be a rebuttal to the Electrical Power Research Institute report. Nevertheless, the technical conclusions remained the same.*

* In 1985, the American Physical Society's Study Group on Radionuclide Release from Severe Accidents at Nuclear Power Plants concluded that, under some circumstances, delayed failure of the containment building might reduce radioactive releases relative to those estimated in the N.R.C.'s 1975 *Reactor Safety Study* but that, under other circumstances, the releases might not be reduced at all. [*Reviews of Modern Physics* 57 (1985), supplement.]

Role of Public Pressure

There are by now many examples of public pressure being required to offset the paralyzing effect of industry opposition to nuclear safety initiatives—especially when the purpose of the initiatives is to mitigate the consequences of nuclear reactor accidents.

It was only after congressional pressure developed for improved emergency planning in the aftermath of Three Mile Island, for example, that the Commission converted the recommendations of a Nuclear Regulatory Commission/Environmental Protection Agency task force report into Commission policy and extended the emergency planning zone for accidents out to 10 miles (16 kilometers) from reactors.

In Sweden, it appears that the political pressure from that country's debate over nuclear power forced a decision in favor of filtered venting. Prior to that country's March 1980 referendum on the future of nuclear power, the pro-nuclear side was eager to support every safety measure proposed by a special Swedish government committee of enquiry, created after the Three Mile Island accident. Filtered venting was one measure recommended by the committee. After the referendum, the Swedish government, noting that subsequent studies had failed to uncover any basis for a reconsideration of the decision, indicated in a parliamentary bill that it would move forward to implement filtered venting starting with the Barsebäck reactor located just 20 kilometers across the sound from Copenhagen.[17]

Without the pressure of a political referendum, it is doubtful that progress on filtered venting would have been any faster in Sweden than it has been in the United States.

Unfortunately, there are no comparable political events on the horizon in the United States. It is possible, therefore, that it will take an accident more serious than Three Mile Island to overcome the inertia holding back further development of containment improvements in the U.S. If a large release of radioactivity occurs in such an accident, the U.S. nuclear industry may well follow the example of its Swedish counterpart and endorse containment improvements in an attempt to salvage a future for nuclear power in the United States.

The prognosis for our society will be bleak, however, if we protect ourselves, only after experiencing every variety of disaster. It is, therefore, to be hoped that the Commission and its watchdogs will press ahead with work on accident consequence mitigation strategies.

The Commission received exactly this recommendation from its Three Mile Island "Lessons Learned Task Force" in October 1979:[18]

The Task Force recommends . . . that a notice of intent to conduct rulemaking be issued to solicit comments on the issues and specific facts relating to the consideration of controlled, filtered venting for core-melt accidents in nuclear power plant design and that a decision on whether and how to proceed with this specific requirement be made within one year of the notice.

The Commission, however, did not commit the necessary resources.

The Commission could also be pressured into adopting the recommendation made to it in a September 10, 1980 letter from its Advisory Committee on Reactor Safeguards: that it proceed without further delay to require utilities to do design and risk-reduction studies with regard to the installation of filtered vent systems on their nuclear power plants.[19]

Of course, the filtered-vent strategy should not be pursued to the exclusion of other containment-improvement strategies which may also prove useful. We have focused on vented containment here because it is specific evidence for our more general contention that there is a great potential for enhancing the capabilities of reactor containment buildings to retain radioactivity from accidents which might otherwise contaminate an area "the size of Connecticut."

Appendix: An Area the Size of Connecticut

Among nuclear power opponents in the late 1970s, one of the most widely used characterizations of the hazard from reactor accidents was based on a quote from the files of the long-suppressed 1965 Atomic Energy Commission study on reactor accident consequences: "The possible size of such a disaster might be equal to that of the state of Pennsylvania."[2]

What exactly would happen over this area?

The study found—as have many studies since[3,11,20]—that the most widespread danger from a reactor accident would be thyroid damage from the ingestion of radioactive iodine. It found that milk might be contaminated with radioiodine above the protective action limits specified by the Federal Radiation Council over "areas which would range from 10,000 to 100,000 square kilometers."[2] The area of Pennsylvania is 115,000 square kilometers; hence the comparison.

The problem of milk contamination by radioiodines is, in principal, a relatively manageable one.[21] We therefore focus instead on two potential consequences of reactor core meltdown accidents which are less manageable and could also affect huge areas. They are the hazards of

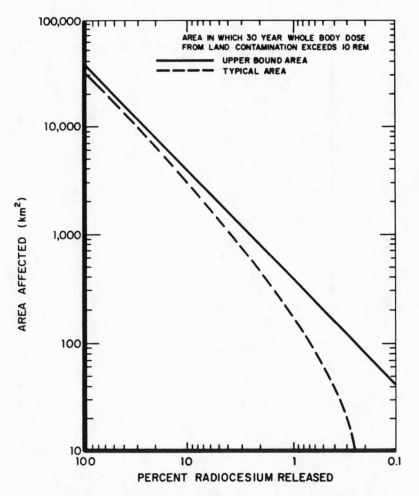

FIG. 5. *Land-contamination area. The curves show, as a function of the percentage release of radioactive cesium from a 1,000-megawatt nuclear power reactor that has operated for at least two years, the area over which the resulting 30-year gamma-ray whole-body dose to a resident population would exceed 10 rem. The solid curve represents our estimate, using the simplified atmospheric-dispersion "wedge" model, of a plausible upper bound to the contamination area. The dashed curve, calculated using a standard Gaussian-plume model, represents what might occur under typical conditions.*[27]

long-term contamination of land and property by radioactive cesium; and thyroid damage resulting from the inhalation of radioactive iodine-131.

For land contamination, we have set the threshold at a standard level corresponding, in the absence of decontamination, to a cumulative

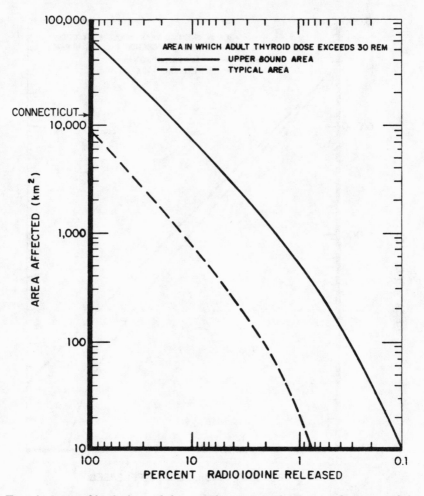

FIG. 6. *Area of high thyroid doses. The curves show, as a function of the percentage release of the radioiodines from a 1,000-megawatt nuclear power reactor that has operated for at least a few weeks, the area over which the thyroid of an adult could receive a radiation dose of greater than 30 rem from inhaled radioactive iodine. As in Figure 5, the solid and dashed curve represent respectively estimated upper bound and typical areas.*[27]

whole-body dose from penetrating external gamma radiation of 10 rem to any resident population over the first 30 years following the accident. (The duration of land contamination will be dominated by 30-year half-life cesium-137.) This 10-rem dose would be approximately twice higher than the average equivalent whole-body dose from natural background radiation over the same period and might cause a few extra cancer deaths among every 1,000 people exposed at that level.[22]

In the case of thyroid irradiation, we have chosen a threshold dose from inhalation of 30 rem for the thyroids of adults. The dose to the thyroids of exposed children in the same area might exceed 150 rem.[23] The Environmental Protection Agency's guideline threshold dose to the thyroid for mandatory evacuation is 25 rem.[24] For an *x-ray* dose of 150 rem to a child's thyroid, the probability of subsequent thyroid surgery has been found to be a few percent.[25] There has been less follow-up on the consequences per rem to the thyroid of internal beta-radiation emitted by iodine-131 but the U.S. Food and Drug Administration assumes that iodine-131 irradiation is as damaging to the thyroid per rem as x-ray radiation.[26]

Figures 5 and 6 show, as a function of the percentage release into the atmosphere of the inventories of radioactive cesium and iodine from the core of a modern commercial power reactor, "typical" and realistic upper bound areas over which the long-term doses from ground contamination and the thyroid inhalation doses would exceed thesholds specified above.[27] The upper bound curves in the figures are about the highest which can be obtained for reasonable choices of parameters using the standard simplified "wedge" model for atmospheric dispersion. We show no lower limit for the area which could be affected because it could be essentially zero. A heavy rain could, for example, scrub the radioactive aerosols from the air soon after they were released from the containment.

For an uncontained meltdown, most studies predict a release of 10 to 90 percent of the radioactive iodines and cesiums in the core.[3,16] It is apparent from Figures 5 and 6 that the area affected by such releases with doses above the specified thresholds could be on the order of 10,000 square kilometers. Even if this is closer to the area of the state of Connecticut than Pennsylvania, it is still a very substantial area. It is also apparent that if reactor containment systems could be made effective enough to reduce any releases to less than 1 percent of the core inventories the areas at risk could be decreased by about 100-fold.[28]

Chernobyl: Estimating the Long-Term Health Effects*

WITH THOMAS B. COCHRAN

The accident that occurred at Unit 4 of the Chernobyl Nuclear Power Station in April 1986, resulted in a near-worst-case release of fission products. But it is important to remember that comparable consequences from industrial accidents are not unique to nuclear power plants—nor is the Soviet Union the only country in which massive releases of highly toxic materials have occurred. For example, the accident at Union Carbide's chemical plant in Bhopal, India, is reported to have killed more than 2,000 people and injured more than 100,000 others. The principal difference is that most of the health effects of the Chernobyl episode will be statistically undetectable because they will be spread anonymously through a population of hundreds of millions over decades.

About 300 people—mostly firefighters and others on site during the Chernobyl accident—are reported to have received radiation doses large enough to be hospitalized. Twenty-six of these died within weeks.[1] Long-term health effects can be expected to be relatively invisible, but much more numerous, because much of Europe was exposed to low radiation doses from the fission products that were released to the atmosphere by the accident. The associated individual risks are very small for all but those populations within a few tens of kilometers of the accident. However, these small risks, added up over hundreds of millions of individuals, could total thousands, to tens of thousands, of cancer deaths and similar numbers of generally nonfatal thyroid tumors. These

* These estimates were originally made in response to a request from the *New York Times*.

potential long-term health effects have been for years the principal concern of those arguing for design improvements in the containments around U.S. nuclear reactors.[2]

About 3 percent of all fissions produce an atom of iodine-131, which has an eight-day half-life. (After eight days, half of any particular collection of iodine-131 atoms will have undergone radioactive decay and, after eighty days—or 10 half-lives—only one in a thousand will remain.) Most of the radiation doses caused by iodine-131 were therefore incurred during the first few weeks after the Chernobyl accident.

Another consequence of iodine-131's short half-life is that the amount of the isotope in a reactor core at any time depends primarily upon the reactor's average power level during the previous few weeks. If Chernobyl Unit 4 had been operating at its full power of 3.2 million kilowatts heat output for several weeks (something about which there continues to be considerable uncertainty), the core would have contained about 80 million curies of iodine-131 in relatively volatile chemical combinations.[3] The initial overheating and the subsequent destruction of the reactor containment and burning of the core would have released a large fraction of this iodine-131 into the atmosphere.

Iodine-131 is of special concern as an internal hazard because it concentrates in the thyroid which would, as a result, be irradiated much more intensely than the rest of the body. The adult thyroid inhalation radiation doses from a Chernobyl-scale release could be more than 100 rads out to a distance of 100 miles (160 kilometers) downwind from the accident.[4] The doses to the smaller thyroids of children would be higher still. A 100-rad dose to the thyroid would be associated with an extra 1 to 6 percent chance of developing thyroid tumors during the next 30 years.[5]

The hazard from radioactive iodines to children's thyroids has been of special concern to public health authorities since the 1954 U.S. nuclear test "Bravo" blanketed Rongelap, an inhabited South Pacific atoll, with radioactive fallout. Before the Rongelap natives were evacuated, they drank water contaminated with radioactive iodines. Nineteen children under age ten received an estimated average thyroid dose of about a thousand rads.

All but one of these 19 subsequently suffered serious thyroid problems by age 21. Fifteen developed thyroid tumors, which were treated surgically, followed by a lifetime prescription for medication with thyroxine hormone to prevent recurrence. Two other children lost their thyroid function entirely—something that was only discovered when they failed to grow normally. Two of the three children who were in utero at the time their mothers were exposed to radioactive iodines also developed thyroid tumors in their twenties.[6]

Because of the Polish public health authorities' concern about the possibility of such consequences from Chernobyl, when they became aware of the high concentrations of iodine-131 in the air coming into Poland from the Soviet Union, they made the dramatic decision to give a thyroid protection chemical to all Polish children under age 17. The medication, a compound containing normal nonradioactive iodine, acts by raising the level of iodide in the bloodstream to the point that the thyroid cannot take more in. Then, radioactive iodine that is absorbed into the body by-passes the thyroid and is excreted in the urine.[7,8] Since the thyroid-blocking medication does not reduce the radiation dose from radioactive iodines ingested or inhaled more than a few hours earlier, distribution by the Polish authorities was probably not rapid enough to greatly reduce thyroid doses of iodine-131 due to inhalation, but it may have reduced doses due to contamination of food.

Many other European governments acted to protect their populations from food contaminated by iodine-131 and other fission products from the Chernobyl accident by monitoring levels of contamination and by forbidding the distribution of foods contaminated above a certain level. Perhaps the greatest concern was milk contamination, because cows feeding on pasture would ingest relatively large amounts of iodine-131 and pass on much of it in their milk. Public-health authorities therefore ordered that milk cows be confined to barns and fed relatively uncontaminated stored feed. Milk found to be contaminated above permissible levels was diverted to the making of cheese and other products that could be stored until the iodine-131 had decayed to safe levels.

Despite all the countermeasures, it is likely that there will be tens of thousands of cases of thyroid tumors as a result of the iodine-131 released from Chernobyl. However, only about one-quarter of these thyroid tumor cases will involve malignancies, and thyroid malignancies have a fatality rate of only about 10 percent—that is, only a few percent of the total number of tumor cases will be fatal.

About 5 percent of all fissions in a nuclear reactor result in the production of a cesium-137 atom. Cesium-137, like iodine-131, would have been in relatively volatile chemical form in the core of

Chernobyl Unit 4 and therefore also would have been released in large quantities by the explosion and fire. Cesium-137 atoms have a 30-year half-life, and they are therefore much less intensely radioactive than iodine-131, but they represent a much longer-lived hazard. The radiation level above land contaminated by cesium-137 will remain elevated for decades.

Contamination by cesium-137 is therefore the primary determinant of which areas around the Chernobyl reactor will have to remain evacuated for years or be decontaminated at great cost before they are suitable again for long-term human habitation. Cesium-137 contamination will also slightly increase the cancer rate in areas where the contamination level is deemed too low to warrant such drastic actions. The hazard will be both from external radiation and from food grown in contaminated areas.

The accumulation of cesium-137 in Unit 4 would have depended upon the length of time the average fuel bundle had been in the reactor before the accident. Because of its long lifetime, cesium-137 builds up steadily until the fuel is replaced. The mixture of isotopes released by the Chernobyl accident indicates that the average lifetime of the fuel in the reactor had been about the equivalent of 400 full-power days—or about two years.[9] After 400 days of full-power operation, the Chernobyl reactor would contain about three million curies of cesium-137. If spread uniformly over an area of 30,000 square kilometers (12,000 square miles), one-tenth of this amount could contaminate the land to a level of 10 curies per square kilometer. This would increase the average indoor radiation level for decades by about 0.075 rads per year, i.e. by approximately one-third the effective background radiation level from cosmic rays and naturally-occurring radioactive isotopes.*[10] The contamination level is probably considerably higher in the 30-kilometer-radius zone around the Chernobyl reactor that was evacuated initially—an area of about 3,000 square kilometers (1,200 square miles). Subsequently a still larger area has been evacuated.[11] The extra radiation dose over a lifetime in an area contaminated with 10 curies of cesium-137 per square kilometer—about 2.5 rads—would result in an extra lifetime cancer risk of 0.1 to 0.4 percent with the extra risk of death by cancer about half as large.[12] Risks further downwind would be much less. We assume that the doses will be increased by roughly 50 percent as a result of cesium-137 contamination of food.[13]

* This allows for a two-thirds reduction of the radiation level during the first few years due to leaching of the cesium-137 into the soil—as observed for the cesium-137 from atmospheric nuclear tests—and a further 70 percent reduction of the resulting average dose (a combined reduction of 90 percent) due to the shielding provided by buildings.

Although the level of radioactive contamination downwind from Chernobyl inside the Soviet Union would be much greater than outside, at the time of this writing little information had been reported on radiation exposures to the Soviet population. Most of the direct evidence as to the scale of the release was based on radiation levels reported from other countries in Europe. Even there, however, there were great uncertainties. For example, one Swedish group found that the standard procedure of filtering air to measure its concentration of radioactivity was yielding values for iodine-131 concentrations that were only 20 to 25 percent of the actual values. Apparently, most of the iodine-131 was not being trapped on the filters because it was in vapor form.[14]

In Stockholm, the concentration of iodine-131 in the air from Chernobyl averaged about 10 becquerels per cubic meter of air during April 28 and 29, then declined gradually and fell below one becquerel per cubic meter two days later before rising to another one-day peak of about one on May 8.* The adult thyroid inhalation doses associated with breathing air contaminated at a level of 10 becquerels per cubic meter for two days would be about 0.014 rads. The dose averaged over all ages would be 0.015–0.025 rads.[15] The measured concentration of cesium-137 averaged about one becquerel per cubic meter on April 28 and was proportional to the iodine-131 concentration on subsequent days.[16] In most other Swedish locations, the measured concentrations of iodine-131 and cesium-137 in the air were lower than in Stockholm, but in Simpevarp, on the coast 200 kilometers south of Stockholm, a value of 190 becquerels per cubic meter was reported.

The Swedish government also made many measurements of the level of iodine-131 deposited on large grass fields and recommended that cows not be allowed into pastures contaminated to levels above about 10,000 becquerels per square meter. Near Stockholm, the contamination level was found to be slightly lower than this, but on Gotland, a large island in the Baltic halfway between Sweden and Latvia, levels of 40,000 becquerels per square meter were measured. Studies by a United Nations (UN) scientific committee and by the U.S. Food and Drug Administration have estimated respectively that cows pastured on land with a peak iodine-131 contamination of 10,000 becquerels per square meter would produce milk contaminated at peak levels of 200 and 1,100 becquerels per liter with resulting adult thyroid doses of 0.03 and 0.22 rads respectively. Taking into account the higher thyroid doses received by infants and children

---

* Radioactivity is measured in terms of disintegrations per unit of time. One becquerel is one disintegration per second. One curie is the rate of disintegrations in one gram of radium: 37 billion per second.

would raise the UN and Food and Drug Administration contamination-dose factors for iodine-131 contamination to 0.08 and 0.35 rads per 10,000 becquerels per square meter respectively (using in both cases the UN numbers for the milk consumption of children and their thyroid dose per unit of iodine-131 intake).[17]

The most detailed maps that we have seen of cesium-137 contamination come from Sweden and show a very large variability in contamination levels. Two areas along the coast north of Stockholm are contaminated to levels more than 10 times higher than the rest of the country. Apparently, these "hot spots" were due to rainstorms that passed over these areas at the time and "dumped" the radioactivity out of the air. Similar hot spots were created by rainfall all over Europe.

Contaminated air from Chernobyl arrived in the United Kingdom on May 2, four days later than in Sweden, but the concentrations of fission products were similar to those in the air that had passed over Stockholm. The average air concentration of iodine-131 was measured at about two becquerels per cubic meter for about a day, but was probably considerably higher because of the presence of undetected gaseous iodine-131. The concentration of cesium-137 was about one becquerel per cubic meter. Measured concentrations of iodine-131 on grass were typically about 500 becquerels per square meter in the south of the country and about 8,000 becquerels per square meter in the north, where rain greatly increased deposition levels.[18]

Two groups attempted to use computer models to quickly obtain a more complete understanding of the dispersion of the radioactivity released from Chernobyl: in the United States, at the Department of Energy's Lawrence Livermore National Laboratory and, in Europe, at Imperial College, London. Both groups used atmospheric dispersion models specifically developed to project radiation doses from reactor accidents.[19,20]

The results of these calculations were not so much predictions as attempts to explain and interpolate between the early measurements that were being reported. Both groups used barometric pressure maps to derive the winds, and the Imperial College group also took into account the effect of rainfall. The amounts and timing of the releases of radioactivity, its initial height distribution, and the rates at which airborne iodine-131 and cesium-137 deposit on the ground were all adjustable parameters. Some of the assumptions used had to be changed as harder

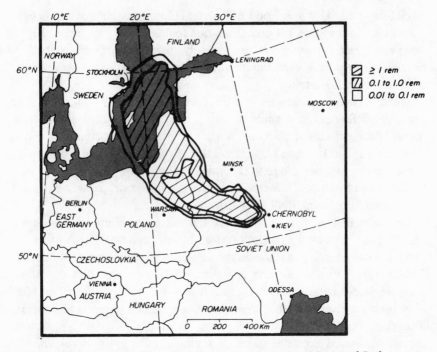

FIG. 1. *This map, based on the Lawrence Livermore National Laboratory calculations, shows cumulative thyroid inhalation doses through April 27, 1986, one day after the accident at the Chernobyl reactor.*

data became available, but the maps produced by the first round of calculations were illuminating.

Figure 1, for example, shows the Livermore calculated map of thyroid inhalation doses due to exposures during the weekend of the accident, April 26 and 27. The contours shown are for doses of 0.01, 0.1 and 1.0 rads. The shape of the contours reflects the fact that the Livermore group assumed that most of the release occurred during Saturday, April 26, when the low-level air passing over Chernobyl was on a trajectory that carried it across Belorussia and the Soviet Baltic republics toward Sweden. Figure 2 shows the calculated results of two more days of exposure (through April 29). Because of a shift of the low-altitude winds, a lobe of elevated iodine-131 levels had developed over Poland.

The Imperial College projections were in qualitative agreement with the Livermore maps in Eastern Europe but extended over Western Europe as well and were reported by the lead author to be in "reasonable agreement with the measurements in Central Europe as far as we can tell with the large scatter in the data." Because of the greater coverage of the Imperial

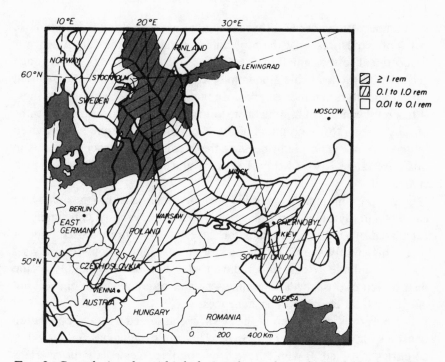

FIG. 2. *Cumulative thyroid inhalation doses through April 29, three days after the accident.*

College maps and their inclusion of deposition by rain, we have used them for making our consequence estimates. The Imperial College group estimated a release of 10 to 15 million curies of iodine-131 and one to two million curies of cesium-137 to the atmosphere from the accident—mostly on the weekend of April 26 and 27 but tailing off through the following Monday and Tuesday.* The deposition, which was calculated through 9:00 a.m. May 8, accounted for 70 percent of the releases. The remainder was presumably still airborne and much of it had by then probably drifted over the regions surrounding Europe. About one-third of the radioactivity was estimated to have been deposited in the Soviet Union—mostly in Belorussia.

I n calculating the consequences of the radiation exposure to the population in Europe, we made the usual assumption used in estimat-

* Subsequent release estimates by the Soviet (ref. 21) and U.S. (ref. 22) governments were respectively 1 and about 4 million curies of cesium-137 and 17 and about 40 million curies of iodine-131.

ing numbers of cancer and thyroid tumor cases resulting from low-dose radiation exposures: that the probability of incurring the consequence is proportional to the radiation dose. This "linear hypothesis" is in rough accord with the available epidemiological data on most radiation-caused cancer and thyroid tumors in the dose range of tens and hundreds of rads. It has not been possible, however, to test it at the lower doses of tenths of rads to rads to which much of the population of Europe was exposed by the Chernobyl accident, because the predicted incidence of effects in this dose range is well below 1 percent and is therefore hard to detect statistically.

One important implication of the linear hypothesis is that the number of cancers and thyroid tumor cases resulting from Chernobyl can simply be calculated by summing the radiation doses of the entire exposed population. This greatly simplifies the task of calculating the long-term consequences of large releases of radioactivity, because the details of the distribution of doses will determine who was at greatest risk but will not effect the total estimated consequences.

For purposes of estimating the risks, we assumed average population densities for the regions of the Soviet Union, Scandinavia, and the other countries involved. It would have been possible to calculate the overlaps of the computer-generated radiation exposure distributions with the real nonuniform population distribution, but because the computer maps do not accurately capture the great local variations in exposure, we left this task to a time when the thousands of measurements of actual exposures would be collected in one place and analyzed.

We calculated the individual doses in a given area from the computer-estimated level of land contamination or the level and duration of air contamination in that area multiplied by the appropriate exposure-dose coefficient. The population dose was then estimated by adding up the individual doses, using the regional average population density. Finally, the consequence numbers were calculated by multiplying the population doses by the appropriate dose-consequence coefficients. Ranges of values for all the exposure-dose and dose-consequence coefficients have already been quoted above. In estimating the uncertainties of the final estimates, we assumed an uncertainty of a factor of four in the total population doses because of uncertainties in the Imperial College maps and the use of averaged population densities. The errors in local population doses will be much larger, but these errors will tend to average out.

We estimated:

· 2,000–40,000 thyroid tumor cases from iodine-131 inhalation, of which a few percent might be fatal. The average dose associated with these thyroid tumor cases is only about one rad, corresponding to an individual risk of less than one in one-thousand.

· 10,000–250,000 potential thyroid tumor cases from iodine-131 absorbed through the grass-cow-milk route in the absence of actions by the public health authorities to block this exposure route. These actions would have greatly reduced the actual numbers of thyroid tumor cases, but our estimates explain their importance.*

· 3,500–70,000 cancer cases from whole-body doses of cesium-137 (external and internal), of which approximately half might be fatal.[†] This number would be very little reduced by evacuation and decontamination efforts because most of the extra cancer deaths would be caused by relatively low radiation doses hundreds of miles downwind from Chernobyl where costly mitigation measures will not be considered.[‡] If, before the accident, the lifetime risk of cancer death in such an area were 20 percent, then after the accident, it might be increased by only 0.1 percent, that is to 20.1 percent. Nevertheless, it is the addition of such small extra risks over many millions of individuals that results in our estimate of thousands to tens of thousands of extra cancer deaths.

As a result of all the compounding uncertainties in the factors involved, our estimates of the long-term health consequences of the Chernobyl accident are uncertain even as to order of magnitude. They serve to indicate, however, that the short-term health consequences may be only the visible tip of a very large iceberg. Because of the radioactive pollution of Europe by the Chernobyl accident, thousands to tens of thousands of people may develop cancer or thyroid tumors over the next few decades.

* Reports of 150,000 thyroid illnesses, 60,000 among children and 13,000 requiring on-going treatments in the Ukraine and Belorussia alone suggest that the Soviet public health authorities did not take effective action to protect the thyroids of the population downwind. Clines, F.X., *New York Times*, December 30, 1990, p. 1.
[†] The U.S. Department of Energy subsequently estimated 28,000 fatal cancers—virtually all in the USSR and Eastern Europe (Ref. 22).
[‡] The average dose to the 200 million most exposed people would be the equivalent to that from about one year's extra background radiation or approximately the dose absorbed one generation earlier from the cesium-137 deposited by the global fallout from atmospheric nuclear tests (0.1 rad).

FINAL
THOUGHTS

Blessed Are The
Troublemakers*

W e have come a long way in our understanding of nuclear weapons since the fifties. We had a conservative president, then—Dwight D. Eisenhower. He seemed a little ridiculous to many of us who were in high school and college at that time. He couldn't talk straight, took long naps, and spent a lot of time on the golf course.

In retrospect, Eisenhower looks much better now than he did to us then. But some of the things he said about nuclear weapons, look very foolish now. Eisenhower said about nuclear weapons, "I see no reason why they shouldn't be used just exactly as you would use a bullet or anything else."[1] He liked them because, as was commonly said during his administration, they provided "more bang for the buck." He also threatened a number of countries with nuclear weapons—often for trivial reasons.

In 1958, for example, defeated Chinese leader Chiang Kai-shek moved much of his army from Taiwan to a small island, Quemoy, three miles off the Chinese mainland—presumably because he still hoped somehow to restore his regime on the mainland. Understandably, the mainland Chinese bombarded the island with artillery. There was concern in the U.S. government that the bombardment was in preparation for an attempt to capture the island. This concern is also understandable but what is hardly understandable, from our current perspective, is that Eisenhower was prepared to use nuclear weapons, if necessary to defend the island.[2]

That kind of thinking made a lot of sense to the American people in the

* Based on a Commencement address given at the Cambridge School of Weston, June 13, 1987. I graduated from this school in 1955.

1950s; but not any more. We have sobered up significantly about employing nuclear weapons, in part because the U.S. no longer has a monopoly or near-monopoly of nuclear arms. In part, too, because we have learned from the prolonged debate that has been going on ever since nuclear weapons were used for the first and only time against Japan.

Curiously, it is difficult to reject nuclear weapons altogether because, if we do, we must reject war completely. For thousands of years, war conquest, heroes, monuments, and loot have been central to our culture. It's hard to let all that go.

Those who have advised the Soviet leader, Gorbachev, in his foreign policy decisions that have ended the Cold War, believe that the present debate is between the "new thinking" and the "old thinking." New thinking says that nuclear weapons have made war between industrialized countries obsolete. We cannot fight each other because nuclear weapons have made us each others' hostage. Old thinking says that nuclear weapons have not changed things that much and that the Roman saying, "If you want peace, you must prepare for war," is still true today. In particular the old thinkers believe that we must show that we are prepared to use nuclear weapons, if necessary.

The debate is going on, not only between us, but inside us, too. For example, I have never feared a Soviet invasion of Western Europe because I knew that the Soviet leadership must realize that such an invasion could lead to a nuclear war. Oddly, therefore, I depend on nuclear weapons, to some degree too, making it difficult for me to figure out how to get rid of them.

We saw the same confusion in President Reagan's thoughts. He was certainly, in great part, an old thinker. For example, he named the MX missile the "Peacekeeper," apparently because he thought of the U.S. much as a sheriff in an old western movie, who had a six-shooter called the "peacekeeper." The mythic sheriff could do amazing things with his gun. He was even able to shoot a gun out of an outlaw's hand, without seriously hurting him. The nuclear Peacekeeper is supposed to be able to do the same thing: its warheads are so accurate that, in theory, they could destroy Soviet missiles in their reinforced-concrete underground shelters.

The sheriff's gun was supposed to keep outlaws out of town. Similarly, those around President Reagan told him that the MX would keep the Soviets from getting out of line. The Soviets would know that we could use the MX to destroy their missiles.

The analogy with an Old West shootout is good in one respect: the Soviets have similar missiles, so we are in a fast-draw world. But this hair-trigger situation makes it easy to make a mistake. Too bad Reagan didn't make a film in which one of the townspeople is bitten on his rear end by a horsefly and the sheriff, thinking that the man was going for his gun, shoots him dead!

There are also other problems with the analogy. First, each of the 10 nuclear warheads on an MX missile is so powerful it would kill everyone in an area of about 100 square miles around its target. And the radioactive fallout from a group of these warheads, exploding over a Soviet missile field, would kill people hundreds of miles downwind. Perhaps 10 million people would be killed in a U.S. attack on Soviet missile silos—a little different from shooting a gun out of Gorbachev's hand. It means that a president who undertook such an attack would be remembered as one of history's great killers.

Another difference between a gun duel and a missile duel is that, while a bullet at a distance of 100 feet takes a few hundredths of a second to reach its target, an intercontinental ballistic missile takes tens of minutes to reach its target on the other side of the world. So, by the time an MX warhead reached its target, the Soviet missile it was on its way to destroy might already be on its way to the U.S. Even if we destroyed all Soviet intercontinental missiles, before they could attack us, the Soviets would still have enough nuclear weapons on submarines and at other sites to destroy us many times over. And the 10 million deaths caused by our attack would give them sufficient motivation for revenge. In short, this approach is definitely a hard way to get rid of nuclear missiles.

President Reagan was in part a new thinker, too. He joined Mikhail Gorbachev repeatedly in statements that included the sentence, "Nuclear war cannot be won and must not be fought." That is certainly progress since Eisenhower's time.

Congress, under public pressure, has also learned about nuclear war since the fifties. Congress provided President Reagan with only half of the Peacekeeper missiles he requested.

Meanwhile, in Europe, the story has been similar. Things have changed a lot there since the fifties, too. Back then, when the U.S. placed intermediate-range missiles in Western Europe, Europeans felt safer. We took those missiles out in the early sixties, when we obtained long-range missiles and bombers that could reach the Soviet Union from the U.S.

In the late seventies, however, some U.S. nuclear strategists worried that, since the Soviet Union had achieved parity with the U.S. in nuclear weaponry, the U.S. threat to defend Western Europe with nuclear weapons, if necessary, might no longer be credible. It was therefore decided to reintroduce missiles into Western Europe that could reach Moscow.

It turned out to be much more difficult to reintroduce intermediate-range missiles into Western Europe in the 1980s, however, than it had been to introduce them originally in the 1950s. Even though most Western Europeans still believed that their security depended upon the nuclear threat, they now saw accidental nuclear war as a threat comparable to if not greater than that of a Soviet invasion. The West European governments could only persuade their people to go along by arguing that new U.S. missiles were needed to balance the nuclear threat to Europe from Soviet intermediate-range missiles. So when Gorbachev accepted President Reagan's proposal that both sides get rid of the missiles, NATO was forced to agree.

It will not be easy to further fully denuclearize Europe, however. Tens of millions of people were killed in European wars, long before nuclear weapons were invented. No one wants to make Europe safe for that kind of war again. Tanks and fighter bombers, which could reenact World War II, are already in place, ready to move at short notice. So we have to defuse the huge non-nuclear military confrontation in Europe at the same time that we defuse nuclear confrontation.

Some of the lessons we learned from the nuclear debate have been applicable to conventional disarmament, however. Although nuclear weapons were originally justified as a way to destroy non-nuclear forces, their primary targets became each other. Similarly, the principal task of tanks on each side of the dividing line in Central Europe became that of destroying each other. The same is true of the fighter-bombers. We have had to learn to see arms control as a way to get rid of these devices as well as nuclear weapons. Thanks to the invention of nuclear weapons, we are beginning to understand that war itself is now absurd.

Governments have not taught us about the absurdity of war in the nuclear age, however. Outsiders have taught us that lesson. For example, when President Truman announced the bombing of Hiroshima, he identified the target as an army base.[3] He neglected to say that the army base was located in the middle of a populated city. We later learned from private citizens, such as journalist John Hersey, what had happened.[4] Most of us now remember Hiroshima with horror, not pride.

Similarly, our government didn't tell us about the dangers of radioactive fallout. It was independent citizens who opened up the subject. For example, physicist Ralph Lapp wrote about what happened to the men on the Japanese fishing vessel, *The Lucky Dragon*, accidently dusted with fallout from one of our nuclear tests in 1954.[5] Subsequently, independent scientists showed that the much lower levels of radioactive fallout that were being caused worldwide by atmospheric testing might ultimately cause millions of cancers and genetic defects.[6] What the scientists discovered and told the public helped drive bomb tests underground.

A Reagan administration official, T. K. Jones, informed us that anyone could survive a nuclear war: "Dig a hole, cover it with a couple of doors and then throw three feet of dirt on top . . . if there are enough shovels to go around, everybody is going to make it. It's the dirt that does it."[7] But independent physicians later explained that things weren't quite that simple.[8]

We are becoming slowly wiser about the folly of nuclear war—and war more generally—through the efforts of individuals—not our governments.

As another example of an individual making a difference, recall that an independent biologist, with not very impressive credentials, sparked the environmental movement. Rachel Carson uncovered what she could about the effects of pesticides in the environment and then published in 1962, *Silent Spring*, a book which communicated her alarm. Her book resonated with an unease people were feeling about the mindless poisoning of air, water, and food and so they began to organize. As a result, we have environmental protection laws, the Environmental Protection Agency, and environmental groups with hundreds of thousands of members. The movement is now so politically powerful that its anger was able to drive the head of the EPA and the secretary of the Interior out of office during the Reagan administration.

Similarly, a young lawyer, Ralph Nader, researched auto safety in the U.S. and launched the consumer-protection movement. And ordinary people—mostly young—stopped the Vietnam War.

These movements did not happen by themselves. Indeed, if it weren't for activists and troublemakers, we might have already experienced a catastrophe by now—perhaps even the ultimate catastrophe.

Therefore, I conclude with the invocation, "blessed are the troublemakers."

References

Scientists as Citizens

1. Testimony before the Senate Appropriations Subcommittee on Transportation, p. 1336. August 27, 1970.

2. Report by the Panel on Environmental and Sociological Impact of the President's SST *ad hoc* review committee, March 1969. The report and other material generated by panels and members of the review committee were introduced by Representative Sidney Yates into the *Congressional Record* October 31, 1969: H10432–46. Some of this material is also reproduced as an appendix to Shurcliff's book (Ref. 3). Congressman Reuss tells how he used the Freedom of Information Act to force the release of the reports in the *Congressional Record* November 18, 1969: E9733.

3. Shurcliff, W. A. *SST and Sonic Boom Handbook*. New York: Ballantine, 1970.

4. We have presented a case study of the involvement of scientists as insiders and outsiders in the SST debate in Primack, J., and von Hippel, F. *Advice and Dissent: Scientists in the Political Arena*. Chaps. 2 and 4. New York: Basic Books, 1974; New American Library, 1975.

5. We discuss further examples in *Advice and Dissent* (Ref. 4).

6. Report of L. L. Beranek, chairman, SST Community Noise Advisory Committee to W. M. Magruder, director of SST Development, Department of Transportation, February 5, 1971.

7. Lydon, C. *New York Times* March 1, 1971, p. 15.

8. Subcommittee on Physical Effects of the Committee on SST-Sonic Boom, *Report on Physical Effects of the Sonic Boom*. Washington, D.C.: National Academy of Sciences, National Research Council, 1968.

9. *New York Times* March 5, 1968.

10. Results of government tests over a number of cities with military jets, compiled by Shurcliff (Ref. 3), give an average of about $600 damage awards per million "man-booms" even for booms considerably less intense than those that would have accompanied the SST. If we then assume that each of 400 SST's flies 10,000 miles (1 mile = 1.6 km) daily at supersonic speeds, creating a boom path 50 miles wide, populated with an average density in the

United States of about 60 people per square mile, we obtain a rough estimate of $2.5 billion annual damage. Although this estimate could doubtless be made more exact, it certainly indicates that sonic boom damage is not a negligible problem.

11. Hearings before the Subcommittee on Energy, National Resources, and the Environment of the Committee on Commerce, United States Senate, *Effects of 2,4,5-T on Man and the Environment*. 91st Cong., 2d sess., April 7 and 15, 1970. This history is summarized in the testimony of Surgeon General Jesse Steinfeld on pp. 178–180.

12. Whiteside, T. *Defoliation*. New York: Ballantine, 1970, pp. 21 and 85.

13. Galston, A. in *Patient Earth*. Edited by J. Harte and R. Socolow. New York: Holt, Rinehart, & Winston, 1971.

14. Carson, R. *Silent Spring*. Boston: Houghton Mifflin, 1962.

15. *Cyclamate Sweeteners*, and *The Safety and Effectiveness of New Drugs (Market Withdrawal of Drugs Containing Cyclamates)*. Hearings before a Subcommittee of the Committee on Government Operations, House of Representatives, June 10, 1970 and May 3, 1971, respectively.

16. *Regulation of Cyclamate Sweeteners*. Thirty-Sixth Report by the House Committee on Government Operations, October 8, 1970, p. 13.

17. Turner, J. S. *The Chemical Feast*. Chap. 1. New York: Grossman, 1970.

18. Sutton, H. *Saturday Review* interview, August 15, 1970.

19. The summary of the panel report is reproduced in the Hearing before the Senate Committee on Foreign Relations, *Underground Weapons Testing*. 91st Cong., 1st sess., September 29, 1969. The panel report was released that same morning: *Underground Nuclear Testing*, AEC Report TID 25810, September 1969, pp. 51ff.

20. Pitzer's address, "Affecting National Priorities for Science," before the American Chemical Society, April 14, 1969 (*Chem. Eng. News* 21: 72–74) was partly devoted to the underground testing issue. Pitzer had just received permission from the president's science adviser to make public his personal views on the issue. For his congressional testimony, see Ref. 19, p. 33.

21. Hearings before the Subcommittee on Arms Control, International Law, and Organization of the Senate Committee on Foreign Relations, 91st Cong., 2d Sess., March–June, 1970. *ABM, MIRV, SALT, and the Nuclear Arms Race*. Foster's citation of the committee report appears on pp. 442–444; rebuttals by Drell and Goldberger appear on pp. 525–580. Senator Fulbright was finally able to obtain a declassified version of the report and inserted it in the *Congressional Record* along with his comments on pp. S12901ff., August 6, 1970.

22. Madison, James. Letter to W. T. Barry, 4 August, 1822. We thank Paul Fisher, director of the Freedom of Information Center, University of Missouri, for providing us with this reference.

23. The functions of the advisory system have been widely discussed; see, for example, *The Presidential Advisory System*. Edited by T. E. Cronin and

S. D. Greenberg. New York: Harper and Row, 1969. The essay by H. Brooks, reprinted in that volume, is especially useful.

24. A short case study of the effectiveness of the Colorado Committee in this and two other cases may be found in chapter 12 of *Advice and Dissent* (Ref. 4).

25. Boffey, P. *Science* 171, 1971: p. 43.

26. Cahn, A. H. *Eggheads and Warheads: Scientists and the ABM*. thesis. Massachusetts Institute of Technology, 1971.

27. A well-publicized example of such an attack was the Operations Research Society of America report criticizing congressional testimony of several scientists against the Safeguard ABM System. (ORSA *Ad Hoc* Committee on Professional Standards, *Operations Res.* 19, 1971: p. 1123). The first part of the ORSA report purports to be a statement of ethics for operations analysts, but it provides little ethical guidance beyond urging loyalty to one's employer under almost all circumstances. The report's attack on the anti-ABM scientists focuses upon a very narrow technical issue, from the analysis of which the report then draws a broad and unjustifiable condemnation of the ABM critics. (For detailed criticism of the ORSA report, see statements of numerous technical experts collected and reprinted in the *Congressional Record* February 17 and 29, 1972; March 7, 1972; pp. S1921–51, S2612–13, and S3521–23.

28. Gillette, R. *Science* 176, 1972: p. 492.

29. The Federation of American Scientists, 307 Massachusetts Avenue, NE, Washington, D.C., is the only registered lobby of scientists. The FAS has been traditionally interested in issues associated with nuclear weapons, but has provided testimony before Congress on many other technological issues.

30. A good example of such a university-based program is the Stanford Workshops on Political and Social Issues (SWOPSI). More than a hundred "workshop" courses for academic credit at Stanford University were sponsored by SWOPSI during its first three years of existence (1969–72). These produced more than a dozen comprehensive and authoritative reports on subjects like *Air Pollution in the San Francisco Bay Area, Balanced Transportation Planning for Suburban and Academic Communities, Logging in Urban Counties,* and *DOD-sponsored Research at Stanford.* Several of these reports had considerable political impact.

31. For a discussion of the manner in which such groups can be organized, see Nader, R., and Ross, D. *Action for a Change—A Student's Manual for Public Interest Organizing.* New York: Grossman, 1971.

Peer Review of Public Policy

1. U.S. Atomic Energy Commission, *Reactor Safety Study: An Assessment of Accident Risks in US Commercial Nuclear Power Plants.* WASH-1400, 1974 (draft); U.S. Nuclear Regulatory Commission, *Reactor Safety Study . . .,* NUREG 75/104, 1975 (final version).

2. *Health Effects of Exposure to Low Levels of Ionizing Radiation.* National

Academy Press, Washington, D.C. (1990), gives the current status of the debate over this proportionality.

3. Lewis, H. W.; Budnitz, R. J.; Castleman, A. W.; Dorfan, D. E.; Finlaysen, F. C.; Garwin, R. L.; Hebel, L. C.; Keeny, Jr., S. M.; Muller, R. A.; Taylor, T. B.; Smoot, G. F.; and von Hippel, F. *Rev. Mod. Phys.* 47, 1975: Suppl. 1.

4. Oversight hearing before the Subcommittee on Energy and Environment of the U.S. House of Representatives Committee on Interior and Insular Affairs, January 1977; the subcommittee's report, *Observations on the Reactor Safety Study* was published January 1977. See also von Hippel, F. *Bull. At. Sci.* February 1977: p. 42.

5. Lewis, H. W.; Budnitz, R. J.; Kouts, H. J. C.; Lowenstein, W. B.; Rowe, W. D.; von Hippel, F.; and Zachariasen, F. *Risk Assessment Review Group Report to the US Nuclear Regulatory Commission.* NRC Report NUREG/CR-0400, 1978.

6. U.S. Atomic Energy Commission, *Proposed Environmental Statement on the Liquid Metal Fast Breeder Receptor Program.* WASH-1535, 1974.

7. Feiveson, H. A.; Taylor, T. B.; von Hippel, F.; and Williams, R. H. *Bull. At. Sci.* December 1976: 10; Feiveson, H. A., and Taylor, T. B. *ibid.*, 14; von Hippel, F., and Williams, R. H. *ibid.*, 20; Feiveson, H. A.; von Hippel, F.; and Williams, R. H. *Science* 203, 1979: p. 330.

8. Cochran, T. B. *The Liquid Metal Fast Breeder Reactor, An Environmental and Economic Critique.* Baltimore: Johns Hopkins University Press, 1974.

9. Edison Electric Institute, *Economic Growth in the Future, the Growth Debate in National and Global Perspective.* New York: McGraw-Hill, 1976.

10. Data for Fig. 3 were obtained from the following sources: *EEI Pocketbook of Electric Utility Industry Statistics.* New York: Edison Electric Institute, 1974; *Monthly Energy Review.* U.S. Department of Energy, DOE/EIA-0035; *Historical Statistics of the United States: Colonial Times to 1970*, U.S. Department of Commerce, 1975; *Statistical Abstract of the U.S.*, U.S. Department of Commerce (annual); *Economic Indicators.* U.S. Government Printing Office (monthly).

11. U.S. Department of Energy, Energy Information Administration, *Annual Report to Congress.* 1978, Vol. 3 (DOE/EIA-0173/3); U.S. Department of Commerce, Bureau of Economic Analysis, *Survey of Current Business*, October 1980.

12. See, for example, *Electrical World*, September 15, 1976: p. 52.

13. Ayers, T. G.; Benedict, M. T.; Culler, Jr., F. L.; Everett III, J. T.; Laney, R. V.; Starr, C.; and Walske, C. *LMFBR Program Review.* U.S. Energy Resources Development Administration, 1977; Cochran, T. B.; Train, R. E.; von Hippel, F.; and Williams, R. H. *Proliferation Resistant Nuclear Power Technologies.* U.S. Energy Resources Development Administration, 1977.

14. "Annual Electric Industry Forecast." *Electrical World*, September 1977, 1980, 1989.

15. "Annual Electric Industry Forecast." 1986.

16. U.S. Department of Energy, *An Assessment Report on Uranium in the United States of America*. Report #GJO-111(80), 1980.

17. *Electrical World*, January 1981: 29. See also Ref. 7.

18. p. 19. Hearing before the Subcommittee on Arms Control, International Law, and Organization of the Senate Foreign Relations Committee, *U.S.–USSR Strategic Policies*. (sanitized transcript of a top secret hearing) March 4, 1974.

19. p. 13. Hearing before the Subcommittee on Arms Control, International Law and Organization of the Senate Committee On Foreign Relations, *Briefing on Counterforce Attacks*. (sanitized transcript of a top secreting hearing) September 11, 1974.

20. Drell, S., and von Hippel, F. *Scientific American* November 1976: p. 27.

21. Wiesner, J.; Brown, H.; Drell, S.; Garwin, R.; Keeny, S.; MacDonald, G.; Miller, G.; Neel, J.; and Wood, A. "Response of The *Ad Hoc* Panel on Nuclear Effects" to the Office of Technology Assessment, February 25, 1975; reprinted in *Analyses of Effects of Limited Nuclear Warfare*. Committee Print prepared for the Subcommittee on Arms Control, International Organizations and Security Agreements of the Senate Foreign Relations Committee, September 1975.

22. Department of Defense, "Sensitivity of Collateral Damage Calculations to Limited Nuclear War Scenarios." July 11, 1975; reprinted in *Analyses of Effects of Limited Nuclear Warfare* (Ref. 21). See also von Hippel, F.; Levi, B. G.; Postol, T. A.; and Daugherty, W. H. *Scientific American* September 1988: p. 36, reprinted as "Civilian Casualties from Counterforce Attacks" in this volume.

The Advisor's Dilemma

1. Quoted in Terkel, S. *Harpers* February 1972: p. 52.

2. The socialization of the science advisor is discussed along with many other problems of the executive science advisory system by Perl, M. L. *Science* 173, 1971: p. 1211.

3. Jason Division, Institute for Defense Analysis, "The Effects of U.S. Bombing on North Vietnam's Ability to Support Military Operations in South Vietnam: Retrospect and Prospect." August 29, 1966, reprinted in part in Sheehan, N., *et al.*, *The Pentagon Papers*. pp. 502–509. New York: Bantam Books, 1971. A follow-up Jason study in December 1967 again concluded Vietnam was militarily ineffective; see *The Pentagon Papers*. Vol. 4, pp. 222–225, 231. Boston: Beacon Press, 1971.

4. McNamara, R. S., memorandum for President Johnson, "Actions Recommended for Vietnam." October 14, 1966, reprinted in Sheehan, N. *The Pentagon Papers*, pp. 542–551.

5. Sheehan, N. *The Pentagon Papers*, pp. 483–485. A more complete discussion of the organization of the Jason study is given by Shapley, D. *Science* 179: 459. Also illuminating is Langer, E. *Science* 174, 1971: pp. 923–928.

6. See, for example, Dickson, P., and Rothschild, J. *Washington Monthly* May 1971: p. 6.

7. After a year's delay the report was forced out into public view by the Senate Foreign Relations Committee. For a fascinating glimpse into how the advisory system was used and abused in this case see the hearing: U.S. Senate, Committee on Foreign Relations, *Underground Nuclear Weapons Testing*. 91st Cong., 1st sess., September 29, 1969.

8. *Oper. Res.: Jo. Oper. Res. Soc. Am.* 19, 1971: p. 1123.

9. Reference 8, p. 1134.

10. U.S. Congress, *House Concurrent Resolution 175*. 85th Cong., 2d sess., 1958.

11. Garwin, R. L., and Bethe, H. *Sci. Am.* March 1968: p. 21.

12. The article was partly based upon a talk by Bethe and Garwin at the annual meeting of the American Association for the Advancement of Science in December 1967. Cahn, A., in *Eggheads and Warheads: Scientists and the ABM*. p. 91. Ph.D. dissertation, MIT, Department of Political Science, Science and Public Policy Program, 1971, states that "Bethe claims he spent the last ten days before his scheduled talk on the phone, urging Defense officials to clear it [and that director of Defense Research and Engineering] John Foster gave up a Saturday golf date on December 23 to clear the article personally." Cahn quotes Garwin as saying that he submitted his talk to John Foster only "for comment, not clearance, and received guidance on questions of classification regarding thermonuclear weapons."

13. *New York Times* March 16, 1969, p. 1.

Due Process for Dissent

1. Engineers Joint Council, *Guidelines to Professional Employment for Engineers and Scientists*. New York: E. J. C., August 1, 1978.

2. Olson, J. *Prof. Eng.* August 1972: p. 30.

3. Subcommittee on Economy in Government (Joint Economic Committee), *Air Force A7D Brake Problem* (record of hearings on August 13, 1969). Washington, D.C.: U.S. GPO, 1969.

4. Review Panel on New Drug Regulation, *Investigation of Allegations Relating to the Bureau of Drugs, Food and Drug Administration*. Washington, D.C.: Department of Health, Education, and Welfare, 1977. Senate Committee on Governmental Affairs, *The Whistleblowers*, Washington, D.C., GPO, 1978.

5. Nixon, A. C. in *Legal Rights of Chemists and Engineers*. Washington, D.C.: American Chemical Society, 1977 (Advances in Chemistry Series No. 161).

6. Committee on Social Implications of Technology, IEEE, *Newsletter on Technology and Society* (June 1978). No. 22. New York: Institute of Electrical and Electronics Engineers.

7. Ewing, D. W. *Freedom Inside the Organization: Bringing Civil Liberties to the Workplace*. New York: Dutton, 1977.

8. Nader, R.; Petkas, P.; and Blackwell, K. eds. *Whistle-Blowing*. New York: Grossman, 1972, p. 4.

9. For an overview of federal and state whistleblower protections, see Kohn, S. M. and Kohn, M. D., *Antioch Law Journal* 4, Summer 1986: pp. 99–152.

10. *The Dismissal of A. Ernest Fitzgerald by the Department of Defense* (record of hearings on November 17 and 18, 1969). Washington, D.C.: U.S. GPO, 1969.

11. Devine, T. M. and Aplin, D. G., "Abuse of Authority: The Office of the Special Counsel and Whistleblower Protection," *Antioch Law Journal* 4, Summer 1986: pp. 5–71.

The Importance of Defending Andrei Sakharov

1. Sakharov, A. D. "Peace Progress, and Human Rights." The Nobel Peace Prize Lecture, 1975 (reprinted in Sakharov, A. *Alarm, and Hope*. New York: Vintage, 1978.

2. Sakharov, A. D. *Progress, Coexistance and Intellectual Freedom*. New York: Norton, 1968.

3. *The New York Times* February 21, 1980, p. A2.

4. Medvedev, A. *The Rise and Fall of T. D. Lysenko*. p. 216. New York: Columbia, 1969.

5. *FAS Public Interest Report*, March 1976.

The Freeze and the Counterforce Race

1. U.S. Senate Committee on Foreign Relations and House Committee on Foreign Affairs (1980), *Fiscal Year 1981 Arms Control Impact Statements*. pp. 46, 50, 56, and 338.

2. Forsberg, R. *Call to Halt the Nuclear Arms Race*. American Friends Service Committee, Clergy and Laity Concerned, Fellowship of Reconciliation, Institute for Defense and Disarmament Studies, 1980.

3. *New York Times* May 18, 1982, p. A1.

4. *The Military Balance, 1981–1982*. p. 104. London: International Institute for Strategic Studies, 1981.

5. *U.S. Department of Defense, Annual Report, Fiscal Year 1980*. p. 117. January 1979.

6. U.S. Senate Armed Services Committee, *Department of Defense Authorization for Appropriations for Fiscal Year 1982: Part 7, Strategic and Theater Nuclear Forces,. Civil Defense*. Feb.–March 1981. pp. 3802, 3880, and 3924.

7. DeLauer, R. *Astronautics Aeronautics* May 1982: p. 39.

8. *The New York Times* May 29, 1982, p. A1.

9. Steinbruner, J. D. *Foreign Policy* Winter 1981–82: p. 16.

10. Glasstone, S. and Dolan, P. J. *The Effects of Nuclear Weapons*. 3rd ed. pp. 111 and 115. Washington, D.C.: U.S. Departments of Defense and Energy, 1977.

11. See, for example, *Analyses of Effects of Limited Nuclear War*. p. 51. Senate Committee on Foreign Relations, Subcommittee on Arms Control, International Organizations and Security Agreements, Committee Print, 1975; and Drell, S. D., and von Hippel, F., *Sci. Am.* November 1976: p. 27.

12. U.S. Office of Technology Assessment, *MX Missile Basing*. p. 106. 1981; and U.S. Office of Technology Assessment, *The Effects of Nuclear War*. p. 91. 1979.

13. Tinajero, A. A. *U.S./USSR Strategic Offensive Weapons: Projected Inventories Based on Carter Policies*. U.S. Congressional Research Service, Report No. 81-238F, 1981.

14. U.S. Senate Armed Services Committee, Subcommittee on Strategic and Theatre Nuclear Forces, *Hearings on Strategic Force Modernization Programs*. Oct.–Nov. 1981. pp. 43, 168, 179, 187, 203, 254, and 405.

15. Bennet, B., and Foster, J. in *Cruise Missiles: Technology, Strategy, Politics*. Edited by R. K. Betts. p. 152. Washington, D.C.: The Brookings Institution, 1981.

16. *World Armaments and Disarmament*. Stockholm International Peace Research Institute, 1980, pp. XLII, XLIII, and 182.

17. Nitze, P. H. in the *Congressional Record*, July 20, 1979: S10077.

18. Ustinov, D. F. in *Pravda*, July 12, 1982; quoted in *The New York Times*. July 13, 1982, p. A3.

19. York, H. *Race to Oblivion*. p. 232. New York: Simon and Schuster, 1970.

20. See, for example, Perle, R. Assistant Secretary of Defense for International Security Policy, *The New York Times* September 7, 1982, p. A23.

21. Bundy, McG. *Foreign Affairs* October 1969: p. 1.

22. Smith, G. L. *Double Talk: The Story of the First Strategic Arms Limitation Talks*. Garden City, NY: Doubleday, 1980.

23. See, for example, Primack, J., and von Hippel, F. *Advice and Dissent, Scientists in the Political Arena*. New York: Basic Books, 1974. New York: New American Library, 1975.

24. *March 4, Scientists and Society*. Edited by J. Allen. p. 142. Cambridge, MA: MIT, 1970.

Debating Edward Teller

1. Scheer, R. *With Enough Shovels: Reagan, Bush and Nuclear War*. New York: Random House, 1982.

2. Tinajero, A. A. *U.S./USSR Strategic Offensive Weapons: Projected Inventories Based on Carter Policies*. U.S. Congressional Reference Service Report #81-238 F, 1981; Forsberg, R. *Sci. Am.* Nov. 1982: 52; Nitze, P. H. Annex II to statement in *Military Implications of the Treaty on the Limitation of Strategic Offensive Arms and Protocol Thereto (SALT II Treaty)*. Hearings before the U.S. Senate Committee on Armed Services, part 3, Oct. 1979, pp. 891–914.

3. McNamara, R. S. *Fiscal Year 1969–73 Defense Program and the 1969 Defense Budget*. Statement to Senate Armed Services Committee, 1968, p. 57.

4. Arkin, W. M.; Cochran, T. B.; and Hoenig, M. M. *Arms Control Today* April 1982: p. 1.

5. Paine, C. *Bulletin of the Atomic Scientists* Nov. 1982: pp. 5–12.

6. Glasstone, S., and Dolan, P. J. *The Effects of Nuclear Weapons*. 3rd ed. Washington, D.C.: U.S. Departments of Defense and Energy, 1977.

7. Abrams, H. L. in *The Final Epidemic: Physicians and Scientists on Nuclear War*. Edited by Ruth Adams and Susan Cullen, pp. 192–218. Chicago: Educational Foundation for Nuclear Science, 1981.

8. Haaland, C. M.; Chester, C. V.; and Wigner, E. P. *Survival of the Relocated Population of the U.S. after a Nuclear Attack*. pp. 23 and 41. Oak Ridge National Laboratory, Report #ORNL-5041, 1976.

9. Oughterson, A. W., and Warren, S. *Medical Effects of the Atomic Bomb in Japan*. p. 30. New York: McGraw-Hill, 1956.

10. U.S. Arms Control and Disarmament Agency, *An Analysis of Civil Defense in Nuclear War*. Washington, D.C.: ACDA, 1978. Quoted in Katz, A. M. *Life After Nuclear War*. Chap. 10. Cambridge, MA: Ballinger, 1981.

11. See, for example, "A Method for Dealing with Certain Fallout Questions." attachment to prepared statement of Paul H. Nitze for presentation before the Senate Committee on Foreign Relations, July 12, 1979, reprinted in the *Congressional Record*, July 20, 1979, pp. S1080–81.

12. Winter, S. *Economic Viability after Thermonuclear War: The Limits of Feasible Production*. Santa Monica, CA: RAND, RM-3436-PR, 1963; Katz, A. M. *Life After Nuclear War*.

13. Boffey, P. M. *New York Times* Oct. 18, 1982, p. A1.

14. U.S. Congress, Office of Technology Assessment, *MX Missile Basing*, "Ballistic Missile Defense." Chap. 3. Washington, D.C.: U.S. GPO, 1981.

15. Feiveson, H., and von Hippel, F. *Physics Today* Jan. 1983: pp. 36–49.

16. Knox, J. B., and others, *Program Report for FY 1981*. "Atmospheric and Geophysical Sciences Division of the Physics Department," UCRL-51444-81.

17. Knox, J. B., and others, *Program Report for FY 1980*. "Atmospheric and Geophysical Sciences Division of the Physics Department," UCRL-51444-80.

18. Knox, J. B., and others, *Program Report for FY 1979*. "Atmospheric and Geophysical Sciences Division of the Physics Department," UCRL-51444-79.

19. Duewer, W. H.; Wuebbles, B. J.; and Chang, J. S. *Effects of a Massive Pulse Injection of NO_x into the Stratosphere*. UCRL-80397, April 1978.

20. Luther, F. M. "The Ozone Layer: Assessing Manmade Perturbations." *Energy and Technology Review*, UCRL-5200-78-1, Jan. 1978.

21. Luther, F. M. *Annual Report of the Lawrence Livermore Lab to the High Altitude Pollution Program—1977*. AD-AO 57-139, May 1978.

22. McCracken, M. C., and Chang, J. S. *Preliminary Study of the Potential Chemical and Climatic Effects of Atmospheric Nuclear Explosions.* UCRL-51653, April 1975.

23. Chang, J. S., and Duewer, W. H. *Possible Effects of NO$_x$ Injection in the Stratosphere Due to Atmospheric Nuclear Weapons Tests.* UCRL-74480, May 1973.

24. Chang, J. S. *Comments on the Possible Effect of NO$_x$ Injection in the Stratosphere Due to Atmospheric Nuclear Weapons Tests.* UCRL-74425, Jan. 1973.

25. Kearny, C. *Nuclear War Survival Skills.* ORNL-5037, Oak Ridge National Laboratory, Sept. 1979.

26. Lynch, F. X. *Science* 142, 1963: pp. 665–667.

27. Alabin, N. I., and others, *Civil Defense.* Moscow: 1970. ORNL/TR-2793 (Oak Ridge National Laboratory translation), Dec. 1973.

28. Akimov, N. I., and others, *Civil Defense.* Moscow: 1969. ORNL/TR-2306 (Oak Ridge National Laboratory translation), April 1971.

29. Harvey, T. F. *Influence of Civil Defense on Strategic Countervalue Fatalities.* UCID-19370. Lawrence Livermore National Laboratory, April 28, 1982.

30. Weiseltier, L. *New Republic* Jan. 10 and 17, 1983: pp. 7–38.

Non-governmental Arms Control Research: The New Soviet Connection

1. Garthoff, R. L. in *Ballistic Missile Defense*, Edited by A. B. Carter and D. N. Schwartz. p. 298n. Washington D.C.: Brookings Institution, 1984.

2. Aleksandrov, V., and Stenchikov, G. in *Proc. on Applied Mathematics*, Computing Center, USSR, Moscow: Academy of Sciences, 1983. Golitsyn, G. S., and Ginsburg, A. S. *Possible Climatic Consequences of Nuclear War and Some Natural Analogues: A Scientific Investigation*, Committee of Soviet Scientists for Peace and Against the Nuclear Threat, Moscow, 1984.

3. Talbot, S. *Master of the Game.* pp. 347–348. New York: Norton, 1988.

4. *FAS Public Interest Report* February 1988, p. 14.

5. Primack, J. R., *et al.*, *Science* 244, 1989: p. 407.

6. Schrag, P. G. *Listening for the Bomb: A Study in Nuclear Arms Control Verification Policy.* p. 84. Boulder, CO: Westview, 1989.

Attacks on Star War Critics

1. *The Fallacy of Star Wars.* Edited by J. Tirman. New York: Vintage Books, 1984, based on studies conducted by a group co-chaired by R. L. Garwin, K. Gottfried, and H. W. Kendall. See also the article-length version, Bethe, H. A.; Garwin, R. L.; Gottfried, K.; and Kendall, H. W. *Sci. Am.* Oct. 1984. Carter, A. *Directed Energy Missile Defense in Space.* Washington, D.C.: Office of Technology Assessment, 1984.

2. Garwin, R. L., and Bethe, H. A. *Sci. Am.* March 1968.

3. *Space-Based Missile Defense*. Cambridge, MA: Union of Concerned Scientists, March 1984.

4. Garwin, R. L. "How Many Orbiting Lasers for Boost-Phase Intercept?" *Nature* 315, May 23, 1985: p. 286.

5. Bundy, McG.; Kennan, G. F.; McNamara, R. S.; and Smith, G. *Foreign Affairs* Winter 1984: p. 264.

6. Brzezinski, Z.; Jastrow, R.; and Kampelman, M. M. "Search for Security: The Case for the Strategic Defense Initiative." *New York Times Magazine* Jan. 27, 1985.

7. Quoted in Drell, S. D.; Farley, P. J.; and Holloway, D. *The Reagan Strategic Defense Initiative: A Technical, Political, and Arms Control Assessment.* 1984. Stanford, CA: Center for International Security and Arms Control, p. 105.

Fissile Weapons Materials

1. von Hippel, F.; Albright, D. H.; and Levi, B. G. *Quantities of Fissile Materials in U.S. and Soviet Nuclear Weapons Arsenals.* PU/CEES Report No. 168. Center for Energy and Environmental Studies, Princeton University, July 1986.

2. von Hippel, F., and Levi, B. G. "Controlling Nuclear Weapons at the Source: Verification of a Cutoff in the Production of Plutonium and Highly Enriched Uranium for Nuclear Weapons." in *Arms Control Verification: The Technologies That Make it Possible*. Edited by K. Tsipis, D. Hafemeister, and P. Janeway. Pergamon-Brassey's International Defense Publishers, 1986.

3. Taylor, T. B. *Sci. Global Security* 1, 1989: p. 1.

A Low-Threshold Nuclear Test Ban

1. *The New York Times* February 27, 1987, p. A3.

2. *Congressional Record* August 8, 1986, p. H5754.

3. A low-threshold test ban has also been discussed in several articles and reports that focus primarily on questions of verifiability. See Kidder, R. *On the Degree of Verification Needed to Support a Comprehensive Test Ban*. Report #UCRL 95155 Rev. 1. Livermore, CA: Lawrence Livermore National Laboratory, December 1986: Everden, J.; Archambeau, C.; and Cranswick, E. *Rev. Geophys.* 24, 1986: pp. 143–215; and Richards, P., and Lindh, A. *Issues in Sci. and Technol.* March 1987: pp. 101–108.

4. This history is reviewed in Seaborg, G. T. *Kennedy, Khrushchev, and the Test Ban.* pp. 18 and 19. Los Angeles: University of California Press, 1981.

5. See, for example, Everden, J.; Archambeau, C.; and Cranswick, E. Ref. 3, p. 147.

6. U.S. Congress, Office of Technology Assessment, *Seismic Verification of*

Nuclear Testing Treaties. Washington, D.C.: U.S. Government Printing Office, 1988.

7. Everden, J.; Archambeau, C.; and Cranswick, E. Ref. 3, p. 149.

8. Robinson, C. P. in *Review of Arms Control and Disarmament Activities*. pp. 140–142. Hearings of the House Armed Services Committee, 1985.

9. *Congressional Budget Request: Atomic Energy Defense Activities*, Vol. 1, FY 1988. Washington D.C.: U.S. Department of Energy, 1987; and hearings before the House Committee on Appropriations. Washington D.C.: U.S. GPO, 1987, part 6, pp. 643, 736.

10. Wagner, R. L. in *Department of Energy National Security and Military Applications of Nuclear Energy Authorization Act of 1984*, p. 33. Hearings before the U.S. House Committee on Armed Services. Washington, D.C.: U.S. GPO, 1983.

11. *National Security Strategy of the United States*. p. 21. Washington, D.C.: The White House, 1987.

12. Cochran, T. B.; Arkin, W. M.; and Hoenig, M. M. *U.S. Nuclear Forces and Capabilities*. pp. 116, 121, 137 and 145. Cambridge, MA: Ballinger, 1984.

13. In seven generations of fission, the total energy release can increase 1000-fold. See, for example, Glasstone, S., and Dolan, P. J., *The Effects of Nuclear Weapons*, 3rd ed. p. 17. Washington, D.C.: U.S. GPO, 1977. The length of time between fissions is roughly the average time of travel of the fission neutrons within the fissile material. After compression, the fissile material in the core of a nuclear explosive has a radius of only 2–3 cm. The time required for a typical fission neutron, with a kinetic energy of one million electron volts, to travel 4 cm is about one 1000th of a microsecond.

14. For a mole of D–T gas (4 grams) in a volume of 0.6 cc and at an ion temperature of 100 million °K, the reaction time constant is about 0.01 ms. At temperatures one-tenth and five times as great, the reaction time constants are 10,000 and 0.1 times as long, respectively. Reducing the volume (i.e., increasing the gas density) tenfold would reduce the reaction time constant by the same factor. See, for example, Post, R. F. *Annu. Rev. Nucl. Sci.* 20, 1970: p. 518. We use the usual conversion from energy to temperature scales: 1 eV = 11,600 °K. The Kelvin and Centigrade temperature scales are the same except that 0 °K is at absolute-zero temperature (-273 °C).

15. A fission releases approximately 200 MeV (million electron volts) of energy, and the fissioning atoms contain almost 100 electrons each. Therefore, if the core material were fully ionized and in thermal equilibrium, the fission of 1 percent of the atoms would give each particle an energy of about 20,000 eV (electron volts). Our assumption of complete ionization and our neglect of the energy absorbed in the ionization process make this a very rough result, since the initial average binding energy of the electrons is on the order of 10,000 eV.

16. The critical mass of weapon-grade plutonium at normal density and inside a thick neutron reflector is about 6 kg; see Paxton, H. C. *Los Alamos Critical-Mass Data*. Report #LA-3067-MS, Rev. p. 40. Los Alamos, NM: Los Alamos Laboratory, 1975. This was the amount of plutonium in the core of the Nagasaki bomb. (Groves, L. R. "Memorandum for the Secretary of

War." July 18, 1945, reprinted as Appendix P in Sherwin, M. J. *A World Destroyed*. New York: Alfred A. Knopf, 1975.) Subsequent design improvements resulted in dramatic reductions in the amount of fissile material required to make a fission explosive to a fraction of a critical mass ("frac crit"). See, for example, Bethe, H. A. *Los Alamos Sci*. Fall 1982: pp. 44–45.

17. Taylor, T. B. *Public Interest Report* (Federation of American Scientists) December 1986: 4.

18. For a review of the available public information on this mechanism, see deVolpi, A.; Marsh, G. E.; Postol, T. A.; and Stanford, G. S., *Born Secret: The H-Bomb, the Progressive Case and National Security*. New York: Pergamon Press, 1981. The physics, as applied to inertial-confinement fusion, is reviewed in Johnson, T. H. *Proc. IEEE* 72, 1984: pp. 548–594.

19. The energy density in a blackbody radiation field increases with temperature as $1.37 \times 10^{13} \times T^4$ joules/m^3. (T in keV, 1 keV = 11.6×10^6 K.) The kinetic portion of the energy density ($k_b \times T/2$ per degree of freedom) of the completely ionized gas produced by the fissioning of the primary may be approximated by $7.2 \times 10^{10} \times T$ joules/kg, assuming an average of one gram-mole of (i.e., 6.0×10^{23}) electrons per two grams of mass for the mixture of core, reflector, and chemical explosive. We adopt a warhead density of 2,500 kg/m^3, which is the approximate density of both the old W-33 kiloton-range tactical warhead and the modern W-79 kiloton-range enhanced-radiation warhead in the U.S. arsenal. (Cochran, T. B. *et al. U.S. Nuclear Forces and Capabilities*. pp. 47 and 77.) Given this warhead density, the calculated energy densities are approximately equal when T = 2.3 keV and the total energy density is approximately 3×10^{11} joules/kg (0.08 kt/kg).

20. Cochran, T., *et al. U.S. Nuclear Forces and Capabilities*. p. 36.

21. Kidder, R. E. Lawrence Livermore National Laboratory, "Militarily Significant Nuclear Explosive Yields." in *Proceedings of the Department of Energy Sponsored Cavity Decoupling Workshop, Pajaro Dunes, California, 29–31 July 1985*. Report # CONF-850779, p. V-25. Washington, D.C.: Department of Energy.

22. Cochran, T., *et al., U.S. Nuclear Forces and Capabilities*. p. 28.

23. Westervelt, D. R. Los Alamos National Laboratory, "The Role of Laboratory Tests." in *Nuclear Weapon Tests: Prohibition or Limitation?*, Josef Goldblat and David Cox, editors, Oxford University Press, 1988, p. 56.

24. Carter, J. *Keeping Faith*, p. 229. New York: Bantam Books, 1982.

25. Bradbury, N.; Garwin, R.; and Mark, C. Letter to President Carter; reprinted in *Effects of a Comprehensive Test Ban Treaty on United States National Security Interests*. Hearings before the Panel on SALT and the CTB, House Committee on Armed Services. p. 181. Washington, D.C.: U.S. GPO, 1978.

26. Brown, P. Lawrence Livermore National Laboratory. *Energy and Technology Review* September 1986: 13.

27. Rosengren, J. W. *Some Little-Publicized Difficulties with a Nuclear Freeze*. Report #RDA-TR-122116-001. Marina Del Rey, CA: R&D Associates, 1983.

28. Kidder, R. E. *Evaluation of the 1983 Rosengren Report from the Standpoint*

of a Comprehensive Test Ban. Lawrence Livermore National Laboratory, June 17, 1986, Report #UCID-20804. Emphasis in original.

29. Rosengren, J. W. *Stockpile Reliability and Nuclear Test Bans: A Reply to a Critic's Comments.* Report #RDA-TR-138522-001. Arlington, VA: R&D Associates, 1986. Kidder, R. E. *Stockpile Reliability and Nuclear Test Bans: Response to J.W. Rosengren's Defense of His 1983 Report.* Lawrence Livermore National Laboratory, 1987, Report #UCID-20990.

30. Ray E. Kidder, *Maintaining the U.S. Stockpile of Nuclear Weapons During a Low-Threshold or Comprehensive Test Ban,* Lawrence Livermore National Laboratory (LLNL) Report UCRL-53820, 1987. George H. Miller, Paul S. Brown, and Carol T. Alonso, *Report to Congress on Stockpile Reliability, Weapon Remanufacture, and the Role of Nuclear Testing* LLNL Report UCRL-53822, 1987.

31. Department of Defense/Arms Control and Disarmament Agency/Department of Energy, joint answer to a question for the record in *Nuclear Testing Issues.* p. 46. Hearing before the Senate Armed Services Committee, April 29, 1986.

32. Brown, H. in *Implications of Abandoning SALT.* Hearing before the House Foreign Affairs Committee, April 15, 1986. p. 13. Washington, D.C.: U.S. GPO, 1986.

33. Agnew, H. Letter to Representative Jack F. Kemp, April 19, 1977, reprinted in *Effects of a Comprehensive Test Ban Treaty.* p. 193.

34. Harold Brown has stated that "I can support an agreement to limit nuclear tests to a few a year at 10–15 kt and all others to 1–2 kt" (private communication to Paine, C.E. May 5, 1987).

35. In a policy paper on "Nuclear Weapons Testing." Policy Paper #5, January 1987, p. 29, the U.S. Department of Energy opposed a test ban on just these grounds: "The U.S. and the Soviets have different target sets: the Soviets have invested heavily in hardening their targets while we have not. To hold those important Soviet assets at risk without unacceptably high levels of collateral damage, we must optimize the yield-to-weight ratio of our warheads. Because of this, nuclear testing appears to be more important to the U.S. than to the Soviet Union. Based on available evidence, we think that we rely more on high technology and on optimized warhead characteristics in our nuclear warhead design than do the Soviets. In a no-test environment, Soviet missile throw-weight and volume advantages could permit the Soviets to fall back on previously tested, heavier, and relatively simpler warhead designs which generally should be more reliable and rugged."

36. Brown, P. *Energy and Technology Review.*

37. Cochran, T., *et al., U.S. Nuclear Forces and Capabilities.* pp. 65, 79, 126, 133, 182, 200, and 297.

38. We would like to acknowledge useful discussions with Steve Fetter of the Center for International Security Studies of the University of Maryland on questions relating to IHE. For a discussion of the potential consequences of a plutonium-dispersal accident, see Steve Fetter and Frank von Hippel "The

Hazard from Plutonium Dispersal by Nuclear Warhead Accidents," *Science and Global Security* 2, 1990: p. 21.

39. Thorn, R. N., and Westervelt, D. R. *Hydronuclear Experiments*. Laboratory Report #LA-10902-MS. Los Alamos, NM: Los Alamos National Laboratory, 1987.

40. See Fetter, S. *Toward a Comprehensive Test Ban:* p. 38. Cambridge, MA: Ballinger, 1988.

41. Norris, R. S.; Cochran, T. B.; and Arkin, W. M. *Known U.S. Nuclear Tests, July 1945 to 16 October 1986*. Natural Resources Defense Council Report #86-2 (Rev. 1). Washington, D.C.: National Resources Defense Council, 1986.

42. Mark, J. C. in *Public Interest Report*. p. 12. Washington, D.C.: Federation of American Scientists, December 1986. Dan Fenstermacher, "The Effects of Nuclear Test-Ban Regimes on Third-generation-weapon Innovation," *Science and Global Security* 1, 1990: p. 187.

43. Mark, C. in *Public Interest Report* December 1986: p. 12.

44. Garwin, R. Ref. 39, p. 13.

Civilian Casualties from Counterforce Attacks

1. Subcommittee on Arms Control, International Organizations and Security Agreements of the U.S. Senate Committee on Foreign Relations. *Analyses of Effects of Limited Nuclear Warfare*. Washington, D.C.: U.S. GPO, 1975. See also Sidney Drell and Frank von Hippel, "Limited Nuclear War," *Scientific American* November 1976: pp. 27–37.

2. For more details, see Daugherty, W.; Levi, B.; and von Hippel, F. in *International Security* 10, Spring 1986: 3–45. Also see Levi, B. G.; von Hippel, F. N.; and Daugherty, W. H. *International Security* 12, Winter 1987/88: pp. 168–189.

3. Postol, T. A. in *The Medical Implications of Nuclear War. Possible Fatalities from Superfires Following Nuclear Attacks in or near Urban Areas*. Compiled for the Institute of Medicine, National Academy of Sciences. National Academy Press, 1986.

4. See Scott D. Sagan, "SIOP-62: The Nuclear War Briefing to President Kennedy," *International Security* 12, Summer 1987: pp. 22–51, at 50–51.

Beyond START

1. See Daugherty, W. H.; Levi, B. G.; and von Hippel, F. in *International Security* 10, Spring 1986: 3; and Levi, B. G.; von Hippel, F.; and Daugherty, W. H. *International Security* 12, Winter 1987/88: p. 168.

2. *A Comprehensive Concept of Arms Control and Disarmament, Adopted by Heads of State and Government at the Meeting of the North Atlantic Council in Brussels on 29th and 30th May 1989*. p. 6. Brussels: NATO Information Service, 1989.

3. To our knowledge, the term "finite deterrence" was first used in the late 1950s by U.S. Navy advocates of a strategic force of 720 single-warhead ballistic missiles based on 45 submarines. See, e.g., Rosenberg, D. A. *International Security* 7, Spring 1983: p. 3.

4. For a discussion of the U.S. dependence on launch-under-attack capabilities, see Blair, B. *Strategic Command and Control: Redefining the Nuclear Threat*. pp. 234–238. Washington, D.C.: Brookings, 1985. In September 1985, General Robert T. Herres, commander of the North American Aerospace Defense Command, testified before Congress that: "We in the military would like to provide the National Command Authority with the flexibility to be able to ride out at least some portion of a nuclear attack if that should be necessary . . . . We have been able to keep up with the capability to launch on warning, but to go beyond that takes quite a lot of investment." In "Our Nation's Nuclear Warning System: Will It Work If We Need It?" Hearings before a Subcommittee of the U.S. House Committee on Government Operations, September 26, 1985, p. 72. See also Marsh, G. E. *Bull. At. Sci.* May 1989: p. 3.

5. General John Chain, Hearing before the Committee on Armed Services, United States Senate, *Testing and Operational Requirements for the B-2 Bomber*, July 21, 1989. Washington, D.C.: U.S. GPO, 1989.

6. General Chain was arguing in particular for the B-2 bomber, which would be counted under START as carrying one warhead, although it could carry 16: "I can tell you, as the person who has to target, that 1,000 weapons is critically important to me. We are talking 15 percent of the total weapons that I would have available to me to be able to flesh out the SIOP [Single Integrated Operational Plan]." Reference 5, p. 59.

7. This statement was included in the Joint Summit Statements issued at Geneva, November 21, 1985; Washington, December 10, 1987; and Moscow, June 1, 1988.

8. See Refs. 1.

9. See, e.g., Harwell, M. A., *et al. Environmental Consequences of Nuclear War*, Vol. II: *Ecological and Agricultural Effects*. New York: Wiley, 1985.

10. See, e.g., Senator William S. Cohen, *Arms Control Today* 19, October 1989: pp. 3–8.

11. Kaufmann, W. *Glasnost, Perestroika, and U.S. Defense Spending*. Table 12. Washington, D.C.: Brookings, 1990. Kaufmann assumes a U.S. strategic nuclear force with 4,100 warheads in 1999; our finite-deterrence force has 2,000. Both Kaufmann's hypothetical force and our finite-deterrence force would allow cancellation of the B-2 bomber, the MX missile, and the Trident II missile. However, Kaufmann's force does not include deployment of the new single-warhead Midgetman ICBM that we have included in the U.S. finite-deterrence force.

12. Quoted in Ball, D. *Politics and Force Levels*. p. 85. Berkeley: University of California Press, 1980.

13. As of 1989, France had half-completed the conversion of its six 16-launcher ballistic-missile submarines (SSBNs) from single-warhead missiles to

MIRVed missiles carrying six warheads each. France also had 18 single-warhead intermediate-range ballistic missiles (IRBMs) and 33 Mirage-4 nuclear bombers, each equipped with a single short-range attack missile (SRAM). Britain was modernizing its ballistic-missile submarine force with four 16-launcher Trident submarines, to be equipped with Trident II (D-5) missiles carrying up to 12 warheads each. Britain also had 220 Tornado and 25 Buccaneer nuclear-capable fighter-bombers that can carry 1–2 nuclear bombs each. China had a force of 100–200 single-warhead intermediate-range and 10–20 intercontinental-range land-based ballistic missiles, and a force of 100 intermediate-range bombers, and was in the early stages of deploying a force of submarine-launched ballistic missiles. Stockholm International Peace Research Institute (SIPRI), *SIPRI Yearbook 1989: Armaments and Disarmament.* pp. 18–20, 28, 30–31, and 34. Oxford: Oxford University Press: 1989.

14. Garwin, R. L. *Bull. At. Sci.* March 1988: pp. 10–13.

15. In July 1989, Victor Karpov, Soviet Deputy Foreign Minister for Arms Control and Disarmament, suggested that the Soviet government would be willing to dismantle the Moscow ABM system as part of a deal which guaranteed the long-term survival of the ABM Treaty. Quoted in Smith, R. J. and Remmick, D. *Washington Post* July 11, 1989, pp. A1 and A19.

16. The START agreement sets a 6,000-warhead ceiling on the total number of *counted* warheads on strategic ballistic missiles and long-range bombers in each country's arsenal, and a 4,900-warhead subceiling on the total number of ballistic-missile warheads. The agreement limits to 1,600 the number of strategic delivery vehicles and to 1,540 the number of warheads permitted on 154 Soviet "heavy missiles" (the SS-18). Strategic bombers not armed with long-range air-launched cruise missiles (ALCMs) will be counted as carrying only one nuclear warhead each. *Joint Summit Statement*, The White House, December 10, 1987.

17. *Report to the Congress on the Analysis of Alternative Strategic Nuclear Force Postures for the United States Under a Potential START Treaty,* submitted by President Bush on July 25, 1989. The United States has also proposed that 72 SLBM launchers not be counted in the START limits, because three of the Trident submarines would be in overhaul at any one time. See IDDS, *Arms Control Reporter.* p. 611.B.556. Brookline, MA: Institute for Defense and Disarmament Studies [IDDS], 1989.

18. The Soviet submarine which currently carries the SS-N-23 is the 16-launcher Delta IV, of which five had been deployed as of 1989; U.S. Department of Defense (DoD), *Soviet Military Power*, 1989. p. 46. Washington, D.C.: U.S. DoD, 1989. The other modern Soviet ballistic-missile submarine, the 20-launcher Typhoon (of which five had been deployed in 1989) carries the 10-warhead SS-N-20. Dependence on the SS-N-20 would therefore require only 40 percent as many launchers for a given number of warheads. There is no obvious reason why the SS-N-23 could not be retrofitted into the Typhoon. It has also been suggested that the SS-N-23 could be retrofitted into the Soviets' fourteen 16-launcher Soviet Delta III submarines. *Hearings on the Fiscal Year 1988–89 DoD Budget* before the Subcommittee on Seapower

and Strategic and Critical Materials, House Armed Services Committee, February 24, 1987, p. 9.

19. Gordon, M. R. *New York Times* November 13, 1989.

20. Cochran, T. B.; Arkin, W.; and Hoenig, M. M. *Nuclear Weapons Databook*, Vol. 1: *U.S. Nuclear Forces and Capabilities*. pp. 121 and 145. Cambridge, MA: Ballinger, 1984; Cochran, T. B.; Arkin, W. M.; Norris, R. S.; and Sands, J. I. *Nuclear Weapons Databook*, Vol. 4: *Soviet Nuclear Weapons*. pp. 150 and 151. New York: Ballinger, 1989.

21. Of course, such a campaign would be exceedingly dangerous because it would put the attacked side under great pressure to "use or lose" its SLBMs. See Posen, B. R. in *International Security* 7, Fall 1982: p. 332.

22. A group of Soviet scientists has proposed a finite-deterrence force that would contain 600 single-warhead ICBMs. They argue that such a force could be kept under tight central control and would not be subject to uncertainties about the effectiveness of the other side's air defenses or antisubmarine warfare. In the first edition of the Soviet scientists' report, it was proposed that the ICBM force be mobile based to protect it against highly accurate counterforce warheads. In the second edition, it was suggested that some of the missiles might be based in silos which could be well-shielded against the powerful electromagnetic pulses that might in the future be produced by nuclear-powered microwave generators. Committee of Soviet Scientists for Peace and Against the Nuclear Threat, *Strategic Stability Under the Conditions of Radical Nuclear Arms Reductions*. 2nd ed. Moscow: Committee of Soviet Scientists for Peace and Against the Nuclear Threat, November 1987.

23. Chain, Ref. 5, p. 16.

24. For a warhead with a yield, Y, measured in megatons (Mt), the maximum area affected by blast exceeding a specific overpressure is proportional to $Y^{2/3}$. This number is called the "equivalent megatonnage" of the warhead (EMt) because it expresses the blast area of the warhead as a fraction of the blast area of a 1-Mt warhead. The Hiroshima bomb, for example, had $Y = 0.015$ Mt and $Y^{2/3} = 0.06$ EMt. The equivalent megatonnage of a nuclear stockpile is obtained by adding up the EMt of the constituent warheads. We have calculated EMt for the START and finite-deterrence arsenals from the yields shown in footnote *a* of Table 1. The U.S. and Soviet START arsenals shown in Table 1 would contain about 4,000 EMt.

25. Marshal Sergei Akhromeyev, former head of the Soviet General Staff and a military adviser to President Gorbachev, suggested in 1989 that the Soviet Union might agree to eliminate the rail-based version of the SS-24 if the United States did not pursue its plan for rail-basing the MX. Smith, R. J. *Washington Post* July 24, 1989, p. A18. So far, nothing has come of this suggestion.

26. This modernization program is reported in U.S. DoD, *Soviet Military Power, 1989*, p. 45, which also claims that the accuracy and the yields of the warheads of the SS-18 Mod-5 version are greater than those of the Mod-4.

27. The proposed basing scheme for the U.S. Midgetman that we have chosen to analyze in our barrage calculations below is that in which alert missile

carriers are stationed by twos inside the fences around Minuteman missile silos. A second proposed mobile-basing scheme would have the missile carriers in random motion on government reserves. See Hobson, A. in *The Future of Land-Based Strategic Missiles*. New York: American Institute of Physics, 1989, p. 191.

28. See R. L. Garwin, *International Security* 8, Fall 1983: pp. 52–67.

29. For ballistic-missile reentry vehicle flight times, see Feiveson, H. and von Hippel, F. *Physics Today*, January 1983: 36.

30. For a 50 percent alert rate, this corresponds to 10 bombers on a base, or 13 bases for the assumed 125 bombers in a finite-deterrence force. For comparison, in 1988 the United States deployed its strategic bombers at 17 bases. *Air Force Magazine*, May 1988: 194–202.

31. The assumptions made in our barrage-attack calculations include the following: (i) *Launcher Hardness and Scatter Areas*: The bombers would scatter in all directions from the air base and would reach a constant radial airspeed of 12.5 km/minute three minutes after brake release. We assume that a peak blast overpressure of 0.2 atmospheres would be required to destroy the bombers. (We would like to thank David Ochmanek of RAND for discussions of these assumptions. See also Quanbeck, A. H. and Wood, A. L. *Modernizing the Strategic Bomber Force: Why and How*. Washington, D.C.: Brookings, 1976.) Because of various constraints imposed by the terrain and the existing road system, we assume that the average truck-carried mobile missile could only scatter into an area equivalent to a semicircle around its base point. Its average radial speed could be as high as 1 km/minute. The hardened mobile launchers would have a blast resistance of 2.0 atmospheres. See Ref. 27, p. 51. (ii) *Nuclear-Explosion Lethal Radii*. It is assumed that the weapons attacking the aircraft flyout routes are exploded at an altitude of three kilometers. Because of reflection of the blast wave from the ground, the lethal volume corresponding to a given blast overpressure has the approximate shape of a cylinder with a hemisphere of equal radius on top, with the radii being approximately the horizontal radii that would be calculated for a free-air expression (2.2 [3.8] km for 0.2-atmosphere peak blast overpressure from a 100-kt [500-kt] explosion). (See Glasstone, S. and Dolan, P. J. *Effects of Nuclear Explosions*, 3rd ed. Washington, D.C.: U.S. Departments of Defense and Energy, 1977, Figure 3.72 and associated altitude corrections.) We make the approximation that any aircraft within the horizontal destruction radius of an explosion is destroyed, no matter what its altitude. For the barrage attack against mobile-missile launchers, we assume that the explosion occurs at a height that maximizes the area covered by overpressures exceeding the hardness of the launcher. (See *ibid.*, Figure 3.73b, and associated scaling factors.) (iii) *Warhead Exchange Ratios*. The lethal areas of destruction of a 100-kt (500-kt) weapon against bombers and hardened mobile-missile carriers would be about 15 (44) and 2.5 (7.3) km^2, respectively. The approximate number of 100-kt warheads required to blanket the scatter area as a function of time (t in minutes) after detection of the attacking missiles can then be expressed as follows. For bombers: $0.9(t-8)^4$, $8 < t < 11$;

$32(t-9.5)^2$, for $t > 11$. For mobile missiles: $0.6(t-8)^2$. For 500-kt warheads, these numbers would be divided by 2.9.

32. See Feiveson and von Hippel, Ref. 29, p. 36.

33. Adams, P. *Defense News* July 31, 1989, p. 3.

34. It would take 70,000 equivalent megatons, for example, to barrage a Soviet ballistic-missile submarine deployment area equal to one-half of the area of the Arctic Ocean (seven million square kilometers). A single one-megaton underwater explosion could destroy a submarine within an area of approximately 100 square kilometers (5.6-kilometer radius). See Ref. 28, p. 58.

35. We have assumed that, after breakout, six Typhoon submarines are each equipped with 20 SS-N-20s carrying 10 warheads each, and 14 Delta IV submarines are each equipped with 16 SS-N-23s carrying 4 warheads each. The SS-N-23 has been tested with 10 warheads, but these were presumably lighter and had lower yield so that switching to them would not significantly increase the barrage threat.

36. See, e.g., Bunn, M. *Technology Review* January 1988: 28.

37. See, e.g., Fenstermacher, D. *Science and Global Security*, Spring 1990: pp. 187–223.

38. *Joint Summit Statement*, Washington, D.C., December 10, 1987.

39. Mozley, R. *Science and Global Security* Spring 1990: pp. 303–321.

40. See, e.g., Garwin, T. *Tagging Systems for Arms Control Verification*, No. AAC-TC-10401 (Marina del Rey, Calif.: Analytical Assessments Corporation, 1980). This report also discusses the idea of "virtual tagging." In this scheme, a country would maintain for the other side records of the locations of all its treaty-limited items, with the time that these reports were actually recorded being confirmed by some device as simple as placing a sealed dated envelope in a safe that could only be opened by the cooperation of both sides (a "dual-key" system). Short-notice spot checks could be made of deployment areas and the results for the sites visited checked against the records.

41. Current U.S. plans are to deploy 758 nuclear-armed SLCMs and about 3,000 non-nuclear SLCMs that are outwardly indistinguishable from the nuclear versions. Thomas, V. *Science and Global Security* 1, Fall 1989: p. 27.

42. Thomas, Ref. 41.

43. Lewis, G. N.; Ride, S. K.; and Townsend, J. S. *Science* November 10, 1989: 765.

44. Report of the Defense Policy Panel of the Committee on Armed Forces of the U.S. House of Representatives, *Breakout, Verification and Force Structure: Dealing with the Full Implications of START*, Committee Print No. 21, May 24, 1988, p. 4.

45. Letter from Secretary of Defense Frank Carlucci to Representative Les Aspin, Chairman of the House Armed Services Committee, September 20, 1988.

46. See Fetter, S.; Frolov, V. A.; Mozley, R.; Prilutsky, O. F.; Rodionov, S. N.; Sagdeev, R. Z.; and Miller, M. *Science and Global Security* 1, Spring 1990:

225–302, for a discussion of the techniques that might be used to check for the presence of warheads.

47. Schuricht, V. and Lattimore, J. *IAEA Bulletin* January 1988, p. 8.

48. For a detailed treatment of the problems of verifying a fissile-material cutoff agreement, see von Hippel, F. and Levi, B. G. in *Arms Control Verification*. Edited by Kosta Tsipis, David W. Hafemeister, and Penny Janeway. Washington, D.C.: Pergamon-Brassey's, 1986.

49. *The INF Treaty*, Hearings before the U.S. Senate Committee on Foreign Relations; see, e.g.: Part I, January 25, 1988, Secretary of State George Shultz, p. 59; January 26, 1988, U.S. INF Negotiator Maynard W. Glitman, pp. 121–122; Part II, February 1, 1989, Secretary of Defense Carlucci, p. 8; and Report of the Committee, April 14, 1988, pp. 58–59.

50. Taylor, T. B. *Science and Global Security* 1, Fall 1989: p. 1.

51. Today, in Western Europe and Japan, plutonium is being recycled in the fuel of standard power reactors. However, the economic rationale for this activity is weak or nonexistent and the associated circulation of plutonium exposes it to diversion risks. See Albright, D. and Feiveson, H. *Science* March 27, 1987: pp. 1555–1556.

52. For a more detailed discussion, see von Hippel, F. "Verifying Warhead and Fissile-Material Declarations" in *Reversing the Arms Race: How to Achieve and Verify Deep Reductions in the Nuclear Arsenals*. Edited by F. von Hippel and R. Sagdeev. New York: Gordon and Breach Science Publishers, 1990, pp. 61–82.

53. President Gorbachev proposed a phaseout of tactical naval nuclear weapons at the 1989 Malta U.S.–Soviet summit conference; Gordon, M. R. *New York Times* December 6, 1989, p. A16. Paul Nitze made the same suggestion in 1988 while he was the State Department's arms control adviser; Talbott, S. *Master of the Game*. p. 380. New York: Norton, 1988. Both suggestions were made as parts of efforts to overcome the U.S.–Soviet impasse over limitations on nuclear-armed SLCMs. The United States is, in any case, phasing out all nonstrategic naval nuclear weapons other than SLCMs and bombs; Gordon, M. *New York Times* April 30, 1989, p. A-1.

54. Although we have focused in this paper on the deep reductions of strategic forces, similar arrangements could and should be worked out to make deep cuts in the tactical nuclear arsenals.

Automobiles and the West's "Umbilical Cord"

1. U.S. Secretary of Defense, Casper W. Weinberger, testifying before the U.S. Senate Armed Services Committee, March 4, 1981, as reported in the *New York Times* of March 5, 1981, p. B11.

2. The U.S. consumed an average of 6.7 million barrels of gasoline in 1989—more than 90 percent in light vehicles. West Germany, France and the United Kingdom consumed a combined total of 5.9 million barrels of petroleum for all uses. *BP Statistical Review of World Energy*. London, British Petroleum: 1990, pp. 8, 10.

3. *Statistical Abstract of the United States, 1989*. Washington, D.C.: U.S. Government Printing Office, 1989, Table 1030.

Global Risks from Energy Consumption

1. One barrel (bbl.) of crude petroleum weighs about 0.136 metric tons. Most estimates of ultimately recoverable world crude oil resources fall in the range of 1,600 to 2,300 billion bbl. As of 1975, an estimated 336 billion bbl had been produced (U.S. Congress, Office of Technology Assessment, *World Petroleum Availability, 1980–2000*. Washington, D.C.: U.S. GPO, 1980.) The annual rate of production since then has been about 22 billion bbl per year which would bring the total production through 1990 to about 670 billion bbl.

2. In 1947, total world consumption of coal, oil, and natural gas outside of the Communist nations was the energy equivalent of 1.3 billion metric tons (MT) of oil, with coal accounting for 60 percent. In 1978, the corresponding level of energy consumption was the energy equivalent of 4.2 billion MT of oil, with oil accounting for 60 percent and coal only 20 percent (British Petroleum, *BP Statistical Review of the World Oil Industry*. London, 1979). It has been assumed here that coal has two-thirds the heating value of oil per ton.

3. In 1988, the world consumed the fossil-fuel energy equivalent of 7.1×10^9 metric tonnes of oil (43 percent oil, 34 percent coal, and 23 percent natural gas). This is about 1.3 metric tonnes of oil equivalent per capita per year for a 1988 global population of about 5.3 billion. Oil is about 87 percent carbon by weight and natural gas and coal contain, respectively, 0.8 and 1.4 times as much carbon per unit of stored energy as oil. On average, therefore, the combustion of the energy equivalent of one metric ton of petroleum in 1988 released 1.03 metric tons of carbon in carbon dioxide to the atmosphere.

4. The factor of 5 between U.S. and world average per capita energy consumption would result in a factor of 9 increase in carbon dioxide production because coal contains 1.2 times as much carbon per unit energy as the 1988 world fossil-fuel mix and because the conversion of coal to liquid and gaseous synthetic fuels would have an energy efficiency of about 0.6.

5. Baes, Jr., C. F.; Goeller, H. E.; Olsen, J. S.; and Rotty, R. M. *The Global Carbon Dioxide Problem*. ORNL-5194. Oak Ridge, TN: Oak Ridge National Laboratory, 1976.

6. The ratio of waste stream masses is reduced to a factor of 250 if the wastes associated with uranium mining and enrichment are included. In 1977, the average uranium ore being mined was only about 0.15 percent uranium. In the isotopic enrichment process that precedes the manufacture of fuel for today's chemical light-water power reactors (enrichment from 0.7 to about 3 percent ^{235}U), approximately five-sixths of the uranium ends up in the depleted (0.2 percent ^{235}U) uranium "tails" stream at the enrichment plant.

7. Scheinman, L, *Atomic Energy Policy in France Under the Fourth Republic*. Princeton, NJ: Princeton University Press, 1965.

8. Rogers, B., and Carvenka, Z. *The Nuclear Axis*. New York: Times Books, 1978.

9. Wade, N. *Science* 209, 1980: p. 1001.

10. In 1977, the U.S. Energy Research and Development Administration (ERDA) reported that "ERDA plants dating from the establishment of the Atomic Energy Commission in 1946 showed a cumulative Inventory Difference through September 30, 1976, of 1,490 kilograms of plutonium." (ERDA Press Release, "ERDA Issues Report on Inventory Differences for Strategic Nuclear Materials." August 4, 1977.) The U.S. inventory of weapons plutonium is about 100,000 kilograms (see chapter on "Fissile Weapons Materials").

11. Feiveson, H. A.; von Hippel, F. N.; and Williams, R. H. *Science* 203, 1979: pp. 330–337.

12. Bethe, H. A. *Physics Today* 32, 1979: pp. 44–51.

13. U.S. buildings cover a ground area of about 10 billion m^2, and the annual average level of "insolation" in the United States is about 170 W/m^2. The total annual insolation on the U.S. building area is, therefore, about 5×10^{19} joules, which is more than one-half of the U.S. annual use of commercial energy. Of course, only a small fraction of this energy could be collected and used to displace fossil fuels.

14. Wind turbines spaced about 20 rotor diameters apart over that one-sixth of the North American land area which has an average wind power density exceeding 400 W/m^2 could produce 3.5 times as much electric power on average as the U.S. consumed in 1990. Thompson, G. *The Prospects for Wind and Wave Power in North America*. Report No. 117. Princeton, NJ: Princeton University Center for Energy and Environmental Studies, 1981.

15. In 1978, the world produced an estimated 1.5 billion MT of grain (29 percent wheat, 24 percent corn, 24 percent rice, 13 percent barley, 5 percent soybeans, and 3 percent oats). (United Nations, *World Statistics in Brief*. New York: United Nations, 1979.) Associated with this grain production was about 2.4 billion tons (dry weight) of crop residue. (Burwell, C. C. *Science* 199, 1978: pp. 1041–1048.) The world also supported about 2.8 billion domesticated food-producing grazing animals (45 percent cattle, 39 percent sheep, and 16 percent goats) (U.N., *op cit.*) which consumed about three billion metric tons of dry biomass, including much of the grain and crop residues. Assuming that one-half of the food for these animals was derived from forage, the total of grain, grain crop residues, and forage would come to about six billion metric tons dry biomass. In 1977, an estimated 2.5 billion m^3 (1.3 billion metric tons) of wood were harvested for fiber (lumber, paper, etc.) (U.N., *op cit.*) A comparable amount of logging residue was left in the forest. (The OTA estimates that U.S. logging residues, not including stumps, currently have a dry weight equal to approximately 55 percent of the harvest. U.S. Congress, Office of Technology Assessment, *Energy from Biological Processes*. Washington, D.C.: U.S. GPO, 1980.) The total dry weight of plant materials harvested and left annually as residues in human agriculture and forestry activities, therefore, comes to about eight billion metric tons or about five percent of the estimated annual primary production of the Earth's land plants. (The global annual primary production of land biomass is estimated to be 1.72×10^{11} metric tons of dry organic matter and to have an energy

content equal to about 70 billion metric tons of petroleum. Rodin, L. E.; Bozilevich, N. I.; and Rozov, N. N. in *Productivity of World Ecosystems.* Washington, D.C.: U.S. National Academy of Sciences, 1975.

16. There were about 700 billion metric tons of carbon stored in the atmosphere in 1990. According to Rodin, Bazilevich, and Rozov (Ref. 15), "the total phytomass of the land is estimated to be 2.4×10^{12} metric tons dry weight." About one-half of this phytomass would be carbon, and 56 percent is located in the tropical zone. Pimental estimates that the carbon in the world's soil humus is 1.34 billion metric tons, of which 16 percent is in the tropic zone. Pimental, D. "Increased CO_2 Effects on the Environment and in Turn on Agriculture and Forestry" in *Report of the Workshop on Environmental and Societal Consequences of a Possible CO_2 Induced Climate Change.* Springfield, VA: U.S. Department of Energy, National Technical Information Service, 1980. Other estimates of total organic carbon stored in tropical plants and soil were, one-third to one-half as large, however. U.S. Department of Energy, *The Role of Tropical Forests on the World Carbon Cycle.* CONF-800350. Springfield, VA: National Technical Information Service, 1980.

17. Ross, M., and Williams, R. H. *Our Energy Regaining Control.* New York: McGraw-Hill, 1981.

18. U.S. National Academy of Sciences, Committee on Nuclear and Alternative Energy Systems, Demand and Conservation Panel, *Science* 200, 1978: pp. 142–152.

19. According to a comprehensive study of energy use in an Indian village, (Reddy, A. K. N., and Subramanian, D. K. *Proceedings of the Indian Academy of Sciences C2*, part 3, 1979.) it was found that the energy content of the wood consumed for cooking purposes was 8×10^9 J per capita per year—twice the annual per capita primary energy consumption for cooking in the United States (Blue, J. L.; Lowe, K. H.; Hurlbut, B. J.; Liepins, G. E.; Rose, A. B.; Smith, M. A.; and Strohlein, M. G. *Buildings Energy Use Data Book, Edition 2*, p. xxi. ORNL-5552. Oak Ridge, TN: Oak Ridge National Laboratory, 1979.)

Thyroid Protection in Nuclear Accidents

1. Conard, R. A., and others, *A Twenty-Year Review of Medical Findings in a Marshallesic Population Accidentally Exposed to Radioactive Fallout*, BNL 50424. Upton, NY: Brookhaven National Laboratory, 1975.

2. Chester, R. O., and Chester, C. V. "Emergency Planning for Accidental Radioactivity Releases from a Licensed Nuclear Facility." in *Health Physics Division Annual Progress Report for Period Ending July 31, 1973.* ORNL-4903. p. 172. Oak Ridge, TN: Oak Ridge National Laboratory, 1973; "Report to the American Physical Society by the Study Group on Light Water Reactor Safety," *Rev. Mod. Phys.* 47, Summer 1975: p. S109; National Council on Radiation Protection and Measurements, *Protection of the Thyroid Gland in the Event of Releases of Radioiodine.* p. 55. NCRP, 1977.

3. Jan Beyea, *Some Long-Term Consequences of Hypothetical Major Releases of Radioactivity to the Atmosphere from Three Mile Island*. Report to the President's Council on Environmental Quality. Princeton NJ: Princeton University, Center for Energy and Environmental Studies, 1980. The calculated number of cancer deaths under the same assumption ranged from hundreds to tens of thousands. See also U.S. Nuclear Regulatory Commission, *Reactor Safety Study*. pp. 117–25. WASH-1400, 1975.

4. *Federal Register* Dec. 15, 1978: p. 58,798.

5. "Report to the American Physical Society" (note 2).

6. Since in early 1975 the Nuclear Regulatory Commission had just been severed from the old Atomic Energy Commission, I must refer to an AEC document for a contemporary articulation of this position. The following passage is taken from the AEC publication, *The Safety of Nuclear Power Reactors and Related Facilities*. pp. 5–19. WASH-1250, 1973: "Defense in depth through multiple physical barriers, quality assurance for design, manufacture and operation, continued surveillance and testing and conservative design are all applied to provide and maintain the required high degree of assurance that potential accidents more severe than the design basis accidents will remain of such low probability that environmental risk is negligible." In a design-basis accident, the NRC estimated that only one in 10 million radioactive iodine atoms in the reactor core would be released from the containment building of a pressurized water reactor and even less from the containment of a boiling water reactor. In contrast, for an accident involving a reactor core meltdown and a failure of the containment building (as a result of over-pressure or a steam explosion), it was estimated that 10 to 90 percent of the radioactive iodine in the core would be released to the atmosphere. See U.S. Reactor Safety Study, Table VI-2-1.

7. Reinhold, R. *New York Times* April 4, 1979, p. A16.

8. Memorandum for Commissioners Richard T. Kennedy and John Ahearne from Harold R. Denton, Director, Office of Nuclear Reactor Regulation, "Use of Thyroid Blocking Agents in an Emergency Response Program." July 13, 1979. Enclosure, "Response to Commissioner Ahearne's Questions Concerning Thyroid Blocking Agents." p. 3.

9. von Hippel, F. letter to NRC Commissioner John Ahearne, August 14, 1979. For two calculations of average thyroid doses versus downwind distance that are in close agreement with each other, given the same assumptions about the magnitude of the release, see Aldrich, D. C.; McGrath, P.; and Rasmussen, N. C. *Examination of Offsite Radiological Emergency Protective Measures for Nuclear Reactor Accidents Involving Core Melt*. Nuclear Regulatory Commission, NUREG CR-1130, 1978; or Beyea, J. "Some Long-Term Consequences" (note 3). The NRC report shows *adult* thyroid doses of 130 and 30 rems, respectively, at distances 90 and 160 miles downwind from a large release of radioactive iodines from a reactor accident. Thyroid doses to children would be 2 to 5 times higher. [The NRC value for the child/adult dose ratio is two (which is then approximated as one). The EPA value is five. (U.S. EPA, *Environmental Analysis of the Uranium Fuel Cycle, Part II: Nuclear Power Reactors*. EPA-520/9-74-003-C, pp. 113–118.)]

10. Aldrich, D. C., and Blond, R. M. *Examination of the Use of Potassium Iodide (KI) As an Emergency Protective Measure for Nuclear Reactor Accidents*. p. 31. U.S. NRC Draft NUREG/CR-1433, March 1980. Two other assumptions made in this widely distributed draft report are as follows:

  · In discussing the benefits, its "cost-benefit" analysis does not take into account the fact that the thyroid blocking medicines would protect the thyroids of a large fraction of the U.S. population from reactor accidents at more than one reactor. Within 200 miles of New York City, for example, there are 13 operating power reactors. Within about 100 miles from Washington, D.C. there are 10 operating reactors. The quantitative cost-benefit analysis assumes implicitly, however, that each person in the United States is within 200 miles from, at most, one reactor.

  · On the cost side of the analysis, the report assumes that any thyroid protection strategy would necessarily require the stockpiling of 200 million bottles, each containing a 14 days' supply of potassium iodide for an adult.

11. *Risk Assessment Review Group Report to the U.S. Nuclear Regulatory Commission*. NUREC/CR-0400. Washington, D.C.: NRC, 1978.

12. Nuclear Regulatory Commission, "NRC Statement on Risk Assessment and the Reactor Safety Study Report (WASH-1400) in Light of the Risk Assessment Review Group Report." January 18, 1979.

13. The President's Commission on the Accident at Three Mile Island (generally known as the Kemeny Commission) expressed its concern about this attitude in its report: "While some compromises between the needs of safety and the needs of an industry are inevitable, the evidence suggests that the NRC has sometimes erred on the side of the industry's convenience rather than carrying out its primary mission of assuring safety." *The Need for Change: The Legacy of TMI* (1979). p. 19.

Containment of a Reactor Meltdown

1. U.S. Atomic Energy Commission, *Theoretical Possibilities and Consequences of Major Accidents in Large Nuclear Power Plants*. WASH-740, 1975.

2. U.S. Atomic Energy Commission, *Documents Relating to the Re-examination of WASH-740*. Approximately 200 unpublished documents, dating from 1964 to 1966, were made available to the public in the Commission's public document room in 1973 as a result of suits and threats of suits under the Freedom of Information Act. See also Burnham, D. "A.E.C. Files Show Effort to Conceal Safety Perils." *New York Times* Nov. 11, 1974.

3. U.S. Nuclear Regulatory Commission, *Reactor Safety Study*. WASH-1400 or NUREG-75/014, Washington, D.C.: 1975. Initiated by the Atomic Energy Commission, this study was published in its final form by the Nuclear Regulatory Commission.

4. U.S. Congress, Joint Committee on Atomic Energy Hearings, *Brown's Ferry Nuclear Plant Fire* Sept. 16, 1975; Ford, D. F.; Kendall, H. W.; and Tye, L. S. *Brown's Ferry: The Regulatory Failure*. Cambridge, MA: Union of Concerned Scientists, 1976.

5. *Report of the President's Commission on the Accident at Three Mile Island,* 1979.

6. We have assumed containment atmosphere temperatures of about 150 °C in these calculations. The free volume in a containment typical of those used in most operating U.S. boiling water reactors is about 7,900 cubic meters. The *effective* free volume of boiling water reactor containments may be less than half of their nominal volumes, however, since the volume over the pressure suppression pool is connected to that of the "dry well" by what amounts to a one-way valve. Therefore, it would be possible, in principle, for steam to drive the "noncondensable" gases into the 40 percent of the total free volume over the pressure suppression pool, leaving the pressure in that chamber at a much higher level than in the dry well surrounding the reactor vessel after the stream condensed. (See Fig. 2 for a representation of these chambers in a boiling water containment.) The range of pressures cited in the text allows for this possibility.

7. In the Three Mile Island accident an estimated 44 to 63 percent of the 22,600 kilograms of zirconium in the core were oxidized. See *Report of the President's Commission on the Accident at Three Mile Island* (staff reports), II, p. 14.

8. For a "high-carbonate concrete" having 80 weight percent $CaCO_3$ and an initial radius of the core debris on the reactor cavity floor of 3.05 m the "WECHSL" code predicts that the core will have penetrated 80 centimeters into the concrete 10 hours after it has landed on the surface and will have thereby released 27 metric tonnes of CO_2, 13 of CO, 9 of H_2O, and 0.14 of H_2. The carbon monoxide and hydrogen result from reactions between CO_2 and H_2O and hot metals (steel and zirconium) in the melt. The oxides of carbon would add about two-thirds of an atmosphere to the pressurization of a small containment. A "medium-carbonate" concrete is characterized as having 46 weight percent $CaCO_3$ and therefore presumably would release about half as much CO_2 plus CO. Another code, "INTER," predicts about twice as much gas evolved as WECHSL. See also Murfin, W. B., I., p. 5. 18 (note 9).

9. Murfin, W. B. *Report of the Zion/Indian Pool Study.* U.S. NRC NUREG-CR-1409-1413, 1980, summary, p. 49.

10. Report of the Task Force on Power Reactor Emergency Cooling, "Emergency Core Cooling," U.S. AEC, TID-24226. p. 9. 1966.

11. *Rev. Mod. Phys.* 47, 1975: Supplement 1, p. S7.

12. Gosset, B.; Simpson, H. M.; Cave, L.; Chan, C. K.; Okrent, D.; and Catton, I. *Post-Accident Filtration as a Means of Improving Containment Effectiveness.* University of California at Los Angeles, UCLA-ENG-7775, 1977. The principal radioisotopes which would not be removed by such a filtered vent system would be the noble gases: radioactive krypton and xenon.

13. Carlson, D., and Hickman, J. *A Value-Impact Assessment of Alternate Containment Concepts.* NUREG/CR-0165. Washington, D.C.: Nuclear Regulatory Commission, 1978. The Murfin Report (note 9) estimates a $20 million price tag. More elaborate versions would cost more.

14. Levenson, M., and Rahn, F. (Electric Power Research Institute), "Realistic

Estimates of the Consequences of Nuclear Accidents.'' paper presented at the International Meeting of the American Nuclear Society, Washington, D.C., Nov. 20, 1980.

15. O'Neill, J. *Nucl. Indus.* Dec. 1980: 27.

16. U.S. Nuclear Regulatory Commission, *Technical Bases for Estimating Fission Product Behavior During LWR Accidents.* NUREG-0722, draft (March 6, 1981; final, June 1981). The basic points made in the NRC experts' review were immediately apparent to knowledgeable readers of the Institute report. For accidents in which the damage is sufficient to open large pathways from the core to the containment, there will not be sufficient water available to trap the radioactive materials of concern, nor will the pathway be so tortuous that a significant amount will stick to surfaces before reaching the containment atmosphere. Similarly, if the containment fails early enough, there will be insufficient time for aerosols to settle to the reactor building floor before the release of the containment atmosphere. See for example, von Hippel, F. an invited briefing to the NRC as recorded in the transcript, "NRC Meeting on Iodine Release from Accidents and Estimates of Consequences." pp. 38–61. Nov. 18, 1980.

17. Government bill to Swedish Parliament, 1980/81: p. 90.

18. Nuclear Regulatory Commission, *TMI-2 Lessons Learned Task Force Final Report.* NUREG-0585. pp. 3–5. Washington, D.C.: 1979.

19. Advisory Committee for Reactor Safeguards letter to the NRC on "Additional ACRS comments on Hydrogen Control and Improvement of Containment Capability." Sept. 8, 1980. The point was reiterated in a Feb. 10, 1981 ACRS letter, "ACRS Report on Requirements for Near-Term Construction Permits and Manufacturing Licenses."

20. Beyea, J. "Some Long-Term Consequences of Hypothetical Major Releases of Radioactivity to the Atmosphere from Three Mile Island," a report to the President's Council on Environmental Quality. Report #109. Princeton, NJ: Princeton University, Center for Energy and Environmental Studies, 1980.

21. The longest lived radioiodine of concern for reactor accidents is eight-day half-life iodine-131, of which only one-thousandth the original will remain after eight weeks. The area of land contamination will, therefore, have decreased after eight weeks by orders of magnitude from its original size. During the period of contamination it would be quite straightforward to arrange where necessary that dairy cattle be shifted from pasture to relatively uncontaminated stored feed, and to divert any contaminated milk to the production of powdered milk, cheese, etc., which could be stored until its radioactive contamination had decayed to negligible levels. Such actions were taken in many areas affected by the 1986 Chernobyl release.

22. U.S. National Academy of Sciences, Committee on the Biological Effects of Ionizing Radiation, *Health Effects of Exposure to Low Levels of Ionizing Radiation.* Washington, D.C.: 1990, pp. 172, 23.

23. U.S. Environmental Protection Agency, *Environmental Analysis of the Uranium Fuel Cycle II: Nuclear Power Reactors.* EPA-520/9-73-003-C. Table 40. Washington, D.C.: 1973.

24. U.S. Environmental Protection Agency, *Manual of Protection Action Guides and Protective Actions for Nuclear Incidents*. EPA-520/1-75-001. Table 5.2. Washington, D.C.: 1975.

25. Hempelmann, L.H., and others, *J. Natl. Cancer Inst.* 55, 1975: p. 519.

26. U.S. FDA, *Proposed Recommendations on Use of Potassium Iodide as a Thyroid Blocking Agent in a Radiation Emergency*. April, 1981. For an early release, the thyroid dose from the 21-hour half-life isotope iodine-133 would be approximately one-third that of iodine-131. In March 1954, 22 Marshallese children on Rongelap atoll received an estimated 700 to 1200 rem thyroid dose from drinking water contaminated with such short-lived radioiodines from the "Bravo" H-bomb test. Almost all subsequently had thyroid surgery and were put on lifetime thyroid hormone medication. (Conard, R. A., and others, *Review of the Medical Findings in a Marshallese Population Twenty-Six Years After Accidental Exposure to Radioactive Fallout*. BNL 51261. Upton, Brookhaven National Laboratory, 1980.)

27. A detailed discussion of the derivation of Figs. 5 and 6 may be found in Beyea, J., and von Hippel, F. *Nuclear Reactor Accidents: The Value of Improved Containment*. Report #94. Princeton, NJ: Princeton University, Center for Energy and Environmental Studies, 1980.

28. For a filtered vent containment, doses in excess of 10 rem would be received from the noble gases over an area which would be smaller than 100 square kilometers.

Chernobyl: Estimating the Long-Term Health Effects

1. *New York Times* June 4, 1986, p. A12. According to Dr. Robert Gale, the U.S. marrow transplant expert, an additional 200 persons were hospitalized in Kiev: *New York Times* July 3, 1986, p. A4.

2. Beyea, J., and von Hippel, F. *Bull. At. Sci.* Aug./Sept. 1982: pp. 52–59 (chapter on "Containment of a Reactor Meltdown" in this volume).

3. U.S. Nuclear Regulatory Commission, *Reactor Safety Study: An Assessment of Accident Risks in U.S. Commercial Nuclear Power Plants*. Report #WASH-1400 [NUREG-75/014]. Appendix 6, Sec. 3. 1975. This same reference is the source of all the fission yields and reactor inventories quoted in this article.

4. Aldrich, D. C.; McGrath, P.; and Rasmussen, N. C. *Examination of Offsite Radiological Emergency Protective Measures for Nuclear Reactor Accidents Involving Core Melt*. U.S. Nuclear Regulatory Commission Report #NUREG/CR-1131). Fig. 5.14. Washington, D.C., 1978.

5. Committee on the Biological Effects of Ionizing Radiation, *The Effects on Populations of Exposure to Low Levels of Ionizing Radiation: 1980*. p. 304. Washington, D.C.: National Academy Press, 1980. *Induction of Thyroid Cancer by Ionizing Radiation*. Table 11.3 Washington, D.C.: National Council on Radiation Protection and Measurement, 1985. We assume that three benign tumor cases will occur for each malignant one.

6. Conard, R. A. *et al.*, *Review of Medical Findings in a Marshallese Population*

Twenty-Six Years after Accidental Exposure to Radioactive Fallout. Report BNL-5161. Appendix 4, Table 1. Upton, NY: Brookhaven National Laboratory, 1980.

7. Food and Drug Administration, *Potassium Iodide as a Thyroid-Blocking Agent in a Radiation Emergency: Final Recommendations on Use*. Washington, D.C.: Food and Drug Administration, Bureau of Radiological Health and Bureau of Drugs, April 1982.

8. von Hippel, F. *Bulletin* Oct. 1980: 44–46 (chapter on "Thyroid Protection in Nuclear Accidents" in this volume); House Subcommittee on Oversight and Investigations, *Emergency Preparations for Radiological Accidents: The Issue of Potassium Iodide*. 97th Cong., 2d sess., March 5, 1982.

9. Devell, L., *et al.*, *Nature* 321, May 15, 1986, pp. 192–93; Hohenemser, C., *et al.*, *Environment* June 1986. This means that it is unlikely that the reactor might have been in use as a "dual-purpose" reactor, like the U.S. Department of Energy's very similar N reactor at Hanford, Washington, which has produced plutonium for nuclear weapons as well as electricity. Because it is easiest to make nuclear weapons using plutonium-239 with a low concentration of plutonium-240, which builds up as a result of neutron capture on plutonium-239, the production of weapon-grade plutonium would involve fuel staying in the reactor about one-tenth as long as appears to have been the case at Chernobyl Unit 4 before the accident.

10. U.N. Scientific Committee on the Effects of Atomic Radiation, *Ionizing Radiation: Sources and Biological Effects*. p. 102, Table 17. New York: United Nations, 1982.

11. Barringer, F. *New York Times* June 15, 1986, p. 1, quotes *Pravda* as saying that 60,000 children had been evacuated from contaminated areas of Belorussia—many from outside the 30-kilometer evacuation zone. Further evacuations were ordered three years later in areas where the contamination was such that lifetime radiation doses above 35 rems were expected. (Clines, F. X. *New York Times* September 30, 1989, p. 4.) The soil contamination level threshold set by the Soviet government for evacuation as of the end of 1990 was 15 curies per square kilometer. Ukrainian and Byelorussian scientists were apparently arguing for 5 curies/km². (Clines, F. X. *New York Times* December 30, 1990, p. 1.)

12. Committee on the Biological Effects of Ionizing Radiation, *Health Effects of Exposures to Low Levels of Ionizing Radiation*, Washington, D.C.: National Academy Press, 1990, pp. 23, 172.

13. *Ionizing Radiation*, Ref. 10, p. 241, Table 30.

14. Devell, L., *et al.*, Ref. 13, p. 193.

15. *Reactor Safety Study*, Ref. 3, Tables VI-D-2 and VI-D-5; Report to the American Physical Society of the Study Group on Light Water Reactor Safety," *Rev. Mod. Phys.* 47, 1975: p. S99, Table 36.

16. *Activities of the Swedish Authorities Following the Fallout from the Soviet Chernobyl Reactor Accident*. Fig. 2. Stockholm: Swedish Institute of Radiation Protection, 1986.

17. *Ionizing Radiation*, Ref. 10, pp. 220 and 234, Table 13; U.S. Food and Drug Administration, *Fed. Register* Oct. 22, 1982: 47,073–47,084.

18. Fry, F. A.; Clarke, R. H.; and O'Riordan, M. C. *Nature* 321, May 15, 1986: pp. 193–95.

19. Knox, J. B., and Dickerson, M. B. ("technical contacts"), "ARAC [Atmospheric Release Advisory Capability] Preliminary Dose Estimates for Chernobyl Reactor Accident." The dispersion model is described in Dickerson, M. B., *et al.*, *ARAC Status Report, 1985*. UCRL-53641. Livermore, CA: Lawrence Livermore National Laboratory.

20. ApSimon, H. M., and Wilson, J. J. N. "Preliminary Analysis of Dispersion of the Chernobyl Release, Paper Given at the [U.K.] Nuclear Inspectorate on 20th May 1986." ApSimon, H. personal communications to Frank von Hippel, June 19 and 22, 1986, July 16, 1986. See also ApSimon, H., and Wilson, J. *New Sci.* (July 17, 1986): 42–45. The atmospheric dispersion model is described in ApSimon, H. H.; Goddard, A. J. H.; and Wrigley, J. *Atmos. Environ.* 19: 99–125. A deposition velocity of 0.1 centimeter per second was assumed in calculating the inhalation thyroid doses from the iodine-131 dry deposition levels.

21. USSR State Committee on the Utilization of Atomic Energy, *The Accident at the Chernobyl Nuclear Power Plant and its Consequences*, prepared for the International Atomic Energy Agency expert's meeting in Vienna, August 25–29, 1986.

22. U.S. Department of Energy, *Health and Environmental Consequences of the Chernobyl Nuclear Power Plant Accident*. DOE/ER-0332. Springfield, VA: NTIS, 1987.

Blessed Are the Troublemakers

1. Eisenhower public statement, March 16, 1955, as quoted in McGeorge Bundy, *Danger and Survival: Choices About the Bomb in the First Fifty Years*. New York: Random House, 1988, p. 278.

2. Bundy (Ref. 1, pp. 273–287) reviews the discussion in the Eisenhower administration about nuclear-weapons use during both the 1954 and 1958 crises over the islands of Quemoy and Matsu. He concludes that Eisenhower personally regarded nuclear weapons as a very last resort.

3. This part of Truman's announcement is quoted in Gregg Herkin, *The Winning Weapon: The Atomic Bomb in the Cold War, 1945–1950*. New York: Vintage, 1982, p. 1.

4. John Hersey, *Hiroshima*. New York: Modern Library, 1946.

5. Ralph Lapp, *The Voyage of the Lucky Dragon*. New York: Harper and Brothers, 1957.

6. For a discussion of the contributions of independent scientists to the understanding of the radioactive fallout problem, see Barry Commoner, *Science & Survival*. New York: Viking Press, 1967, especially pp. 53–54. Andrei Sakharov in "Radioactive Carbon from Nuclear Explosions and Nonthresh-

old Biological Effects" (*Soviet Journal of Atomic Energy* 4, June 1958: p. 6) estimated that each megaton of testing in the atmosphere would ultimately cause 10,000 severe health effects. This estimate still appears to be valid. See Frank von Hippel, "Revisiting Sakharov's Assumptions," *Science and Global Security* 1, 1990: pp. 185–186. The estimated cumulative yield of nuclear tests in the atmosphere is 545 megatons (*Sources and Effects of Ionizing Radiation.* New York: United Nations, 1982, p. 227).

7. Robert Scheer, *With Enough Shovels: Reagan, Bush, and Nuclear War.* New York: Random House, 1982, p. 18.

8. The U.S. group, Physicians for Social Responsibility and the international group, Physicians for the Prevention of Nuclear War, worked primarily by giving thousands of talks to local and professional groups about the effects of nuclear war. For one of their written critiques of U.S. civil defense planning, see *The Counterfeit Ark: Crisis Relocation for Nuclear War*, edited by Jennifer Leaning and Langley Keyes. Cambridge, MA: Ballinger, 1984.

Acknowledgments

Grateful acknowledgment is made to the following publications for permission to reprint previously published material.

SCIENTISTS AS CITIZENS, by Frank von Hippel and Joel Primack, was adapted from an invited talk given at the annual meeting of the American Physical Society, January 1972. It was first published as "Public Interest Science" in *Science*, volume 177, September 29, 1972, pages 1166–1171. Copyright 1972 by the American Association for the Advancement of Science.

PEER REVIEW OF PUBLIC POLICY was originally published as "The Emperor's New Clothes—1981" in *Physics Today*, July 1981, pages 34–41.

THE ADVISOR'S DILEMMA was adapted from chapter 16 of *Advice and Dissent: Scientist in the Political Arena*, by Joel Primack and Frank von Hippel. Copyright 1974 by Joel Primack and Frank von Hippel. Reprinted by permission of Basic Books, Inc., Publishers, New York.

DUE PROCESS FOR DISSENT, by Frank von Hippel and Rosemary Chalk, originally appeared as "Due Process for Dissenting Whistle-blowers" in *Technology Review*, June/July 1979. Reprinted with permission from Technology Review, copyright 1979.

THE IMPORTANCE OF DEFENDING ANDREI SAKHAROV is reprinted from *Physics Today*, April 1980, pages 9–11.

THE FREEZE AND THE COUNTERFORCE RACE, by Frank von Hippel and Harold A. Feiveson, originally appeared in *Physics Today*, January 1983, pages 36–49.

DEBATING EDWARD TELLER was originally published as two articles in *Bulletin of the Atomic Scientists*. Frank von Hippel's "The Myths of Edward Teller" appeared in March 1983, pages 6–12. Edward Teller's "On Facts and Hopes" appeared with von Hippel's response April 1983, pages 42–44.

NON-GOVERNMENTAL ARMS-CONTROL RESEARCH: THE NEW SOVIET CONNECTION was originally published in the November 1989 issue of *Physics Today*, pages 39–46.

ATTACKS ON STAR WARS CRITICS originally appeared in the *Bulletin of the Atomic Scientists*, April 1985, pages 144–150.

FISSILE WEAPONS MATERIALS, by Frank von Hippel, David H. Albright, and Barbara G. Levi, was adapted from "Stopping the Production of Fissile Materials for Weapons" in *Scientific American*, September 1985, pages 40–47. Copyright 1985 by Scientific American, Inc. All rights reserved.

A LOW-THRESHOLD NUCLEAR TEST BAN, by Frank von Hippel, Harold A. Feiveson, and Christopher E. Paine, is reprinted from *International Security*, Fall 1987, pages 135–151, with added excerpts from "A Low-Threshold Test Ban is Feasible" by the same authors in *Science*, volume 23, October 1987, pages 455–459, 463, and 464.

THE NUCLEAR LABORATORIES VERSUS A TEST BAN, by Frank von Hippel and Josephine Anne Stein, originally appeared as "Laboratories vs. a Nuclear Ban" on the Op-ed page of *The New York Times*, March 28, 1986. Copyright 1986 by The New York Times Company. Reprinted by permission.

REDUCING THE CONFRONTATION was delivered as a speech to General Secretary Mikhail Gorbachev, other senior officials of the Soviet government, and the 1,500 participants in the eight International Forums on Drastic Reductions in Nuclear Weapons for a Nuclear-Free World, at the Kremlin Palace, February 16, 1987. It was first published as "A U.S. Scientist Addresses Gorbachev" in the *Bulletin of the Atomic Scientists*, May 1987, pages 12–13.

CIVILIAN CASUALTIES FROM COUNTERFORCE ATTACKS, by Frank von Hippel, Barbara G. Levi, Theodore A. Postol, and William H. Daughtery, was adapted from an essay originally published in *Scientific American*, September 1988. Copyright 1988 by Scientific American, Inc. All rights reserved.

BEYOND START by Harold A. Feiveson and Frank von Hippel first appeared in *International Security*, Summer 1990, pages 154–179.

AUTOMOBILE FUEL ECONOMY, by Frank von Hippel and Charles Gray, was adapted from "The Fuel Economy of Light Vehicles" in *Scientific American*, May 1981, pages 48–59. Copyright 1981 by Scientific American, Inc. All rights reserved.

AUTOMOBILES AND THE WEST'S "UMBILICAL CORD", by Frank von Hippel and William U. Chandler, was originally published in *Energy Conservation Bulletin*, volume 1, number 6, April/May 1982.

GLOBAL RISKS FROM ENERGY CONSUMPTION was originally published in *Health Risks of Energy Technologies*, edited by Curtis C. Travis and Elizabeth L. Etnier, Westview Press, pages 209–227. Copyright 1983 by the American Association for the Advancement of Science.

THYROID PROTECTION IN NUCLEAR ACCIDENTS was originally published as "The NRC and Thyroid Protection—One Excuse after Another" in the *Bulletin of Atomic Scientists*, October 1980, pages 44–46.

CONTAINMENT OF A REACTOR MELTDOWN, by Frank von Hippel and Jan Beyea, originally appeared in the *Bulletin of Atomic Scientists*, September 1982, pages 52–59.

CHERNOBYL: ESTIMATING THE LONG-TERM HEALTH RISKS, by Frank von Hippel and Thomas B. Cochran, originally appeared in the *Bulletin of Atomic Scientists*, August/September 1986, pages 18–24.

BLESSED ARE THE TROUBLEMAKERS was originally presented as a commencement address, Cambridge School of Weston, June 13, 1987.

The author is also grateful to the following individuals for permission to reprint material authored or coauthored by them:

David H. Albright, head of the nuclear project for Friends of the Earth.

Jan Beyea, senior staff scientist for the National Audubon Society.

Rosemary Chalk, study director for the panel on scientific responsibility and conduct of research at the National Academy of Science.

William U. Chandler, senior research scientist and director of advanced international studies unit at Battelle Pacific Northwest Laboratories.

Thomas B. Cochran, senior staff scientist for the National Resources Defense Council.

William H. Daughtery, doctoral candidate in political science at Columbia University.

Harold A. Feiveson, senior research policy analyst at the Center for Energy and Environmental Studies at Princeton University.

Charles L. Gray, Jr., director of emission control, technology division, U.S. Environmental Protection Agency.

Barbara G. Levi, senior associate editor for *Physics Today*.

Christopher E. Paine, legislative assistant for atomic energy and arms control for Senator Edward Kennedy.

Theodore A. Postol, professor of science, technology, and national security policy at the Massachusetts Institute of Technology.

Joel Primack, professor of physics at the University of California at Santa Cruz.

Josephine Anne Stein is an independent researcher.

Edward Teller, senior research fellow at the Hoover Institute at Stanford University and associate director emeritus at the Lawrence Livermore National Laboratory.

Finally, the author would like to thank the following foundations and philanthropists who supported his research during the period that these articles were written: Carnegie Corporation of New York, John A. Harris IV, W. Alton Jones Foundation, Max and Anna Levinson Foundation, John D. and Catherine T. MacArthur Foundation, New-Land Foundation, Rockefeller Brothers Fund, Rockefeller Family Fund and Rockefeller Family and Associates.

Index

About the Author

Frank von Hippel is one of the most prominent actors on the international arms-control stage. Scientist, author, activist, he has participated in some of the most pivotal technology debates of our time, often playing a central role.

In the mid-seventies, von Hippel organized the American Physical Society's Reactor Safety Study, an independent investigation that helped discredit the U.S. government's defense of the safety of civilian nuclear power reactors. He has also championed the distribution of potassium iodide to help prevent thyroid cancer in the aftermath of reactor accidents—a method introduced at Chernobyl, following von Hippel's urging.

Von Hippel coauthored a Carter Administration minority report which correctly predicted that national electricity demand would not grow sufficiently to justify plutonium breeder reactors. His pioneering studies also revealed that automobile efficiency could be increased far beyond most estimates.

A key figure in non-governmental arms control discussions, von Hippel led a team of U.S. scientists engaged in cooperative verification research with Soviet counterparts. This research has laid the technical basis for the verified dismantlement of nuclear warheads and deep nuclear reductions. Because of his expertise and consistency, his advice has been welcomed by Gorbachev's arms-control inner circle.

The author of more than 100 technical and policy articles, von Hippel received the American Physical Society's Forum Award for *Advice and Dissent: Scientists in the Public Arena*, a book he coauthored with Joel Primack. He is now U.S. chair of the editorial board of the new international periodical, *Science and Global Security*. During the early eighties, von Hippel was the elected chairman of the Federation of American Scientists. He now heads its research arm.

ABOUT THE AUTHOR

Von Hippel received his undergraduate degree at MIT and his doctorate in theoretical physics from Oxford, where he was a Rhodes Scholar. He is now on the faculty of Princeton University's Woodrow Wilson School of Public and International Affairs and is affiliated with that university's Center for Energy and Environmental Studies.